"Moving seamlessly between the intimate and the institutional, [Greenwood] remains alert to the injustices of the system while capturing the romance of her subjects' stories."

—*The New Yorker*

"An empathetic and well-characterized book that will add complexity to debates about mass incarceration."

—*Kirkus Reviews*

"A piercing look at love and marriage when a partner is behind bars."

—*San Francisco Chronicle*

"An extraordinary look at a common but unexamined phenomenon in American culture."

—*Newsweek*

"This riveting, compulsive book gives voice to a community often judged and dehumanized."

—*Shondaland*

"Prison love, Greenwood's complex and thoughtful investigative journalism reveals, is equal in a very real sense—both sides are intent upon delivering what the other needs. While burdened by a thousand obstacles, bureaucracies, and the very real physical separation of walls, barbed wire, and armed guards, they never quite lose their focus on each other. It is somewhat beguiling, this possibility of deep connection, which requires time and paper and a sort of intentionality that the free world takes for granted. It is ironic, too, that it is the kept apart, the imprisoned, who would reveal the necessity of it."

—*The Baffler*

"Journalist Greenwood (*Playing Dead*) paints a colorful portrait of the world of MWIs . . . Enriched by the author's curiosity and empathy, and shot through with memorable details (Jo and Benny 'toast[ed] each other with blue Powerade from the vending machine'), this is an intriguing look at a little-known world."

—*Publishers Weekly*

"An utterly engrossing and deeply human portrait of love behind bars, [*Love in the Time of Incarceration*] turns the caricature of the groupie 'prison wife' on its head, revealing the trials and triumphs of loving someone caught up in the prison system. This is the kind of nonfiction that reads like the best of fiction—nuanced, evocative, and ultimately, enlightening."

—Susannah Cahalan,
New York Times bestselling author of
Brain on Fire and *The Great Pretender*

"I started reading this book and couldn't stop. There's nothing quite so beguiling as impossible love affairs, but what sets this book apart is the empathy and normalcy with which Greenwood writes about her subjects. It's a clear-eyed, compassionate look at prison love stories, and I found every relationship riveting."

—Lisa Taddeo,
#1 *New York Times* bestselling author of
Three Women

"Big-hearted and insightful, funny and heartbreaking, [*Love in the Time of Incarceration*] paints a complex portrait of couples who came together during—and in spite of—incarceration. Greenwood delves deeply into these experiences, revealing paradoxes in the romantic lives of her subjects that will resonate with readers everywhere. A page-turner and a triumph."

—Ayelet Waldman, author of
A Really Good Day

"[A] tour de force of empathetic nonfiction storytelling. Elizabeth Greenwood goes to the heart of our prisons' modern romantic relationships, and returns with a morality tale about what's gained and lost when America perpetuates the carceral state."

—Vanessa Grigoriadis,
author of *Blurred Lines:*
Rethinking Sex, Power, and Consent on Campus

"Greenwood has unearthed the ultimate American romance story: flawed people loving one another imperfectly, against a backdrop of violence. An important new work by a fearless writer."

—Kerry Howley, author of *Thrown*

"Love can be by turns funny, life-affirming, and heart-breaking; the same can be said about Elizabeth Greenwood's [*Love in the Time of Incarceration*], a warmly engaging look at how relationships find a way (or don't) despite a criminal justice system that stacks the deck against them."

—Rachel Monroe,
author of *Savage Appetites:*
Four True Stories of Women, Crime, and Obsession

"Thorough, empathetic immersive journalism, [*Love in the Time of Incarceration*] is a testament to the power of action, belief, and hope—and urges us to rethink the toll of mass incarceration on loved ones who live free, but with force fields around their hearts and lives."

—Sarah Weinman,
author of *The Real Lolita*
and editor of *Unspeakable Acts:*
True Tales of Crime, Murder, Deceit & Obsession

"With deep empathy, wisdom, and an irrepressible sense of humor that finds lightness even in the darkest places, Liz Greenwood has brought her journalistic brilliance to bear on relationships forged under the most extreme circumstances imaginable. This is a must-read for anyone who cares about the nature of love, both in prison and out."

—Emily Gould, author of
Perfect Tunes

PRAISE FOR
PLAYING DEAD

"A delightful read for anyone tantalized by the prospect of disappearing without a trace."

—Erik Larson,
New York Times bestselling author of
Dead Wake

"Wonderfully weird."

—Deborah Blum,
New York Times bestselling author of
The Poisoner's Handbook

"A beguiling foray into the wacky yet somehow ever-fascinating realm of death fraud."

—Maria Konnikova,
New York Times bestselling author of
The Confidence Game

"Delivers all the lo-fi spy shenanigans and caught-red-handed schadenfreude you're hoping for."

—NPR

"A lively romp."

—*The Boston Globe*

"Grim fun."

—*The New York Times*

"Brilliant topic, absorbing book."

—*The Seattle Times*

"The most literally escapist summer read you could hope for."

—*The Paris Review*

"Mesmerizing."

—*Elle*

Also by Elizabeth Greenwood

Playing Dead: A Journey Through the World of Death Fraud

LOVE
IN THE TIME OF
INCARCERATION

Previously published as *Love Lockdown*

FIVE STORIES OF

DATING, SEX, AND MARRIAGE

IN AMERICA'S PRISONS

ELIZABETH GREENWOOD

G

GALLERY BOOKS

New York   London   Toronto   Sydney   New Delhi

G

Gallery Books
An Imprint of Simon & Schuster, Inc.
1230 Avenue of the Americas
New York, NY 10020

First Gallery Books trade paperback edition November 2023

Previously published as *Love Lockdown* in 2021
GALLERY BOOKS and colophon are registered trademarks of Simon & Schuster, Inc.

For information about special discounts for bulk purchases, please contact Simon & Schuster
Special Sales at 1-866-506-1949 or business@simonandschuster.com.

The Simon & Schuster Speakers Bureau can bring authors to your live event. For more
information or to book an event, contact the Simon & Schuster Speakers Bureau at
1-866-248-3049 or visit our website at www.simonspeakers.com.

Interior design by Davina Mock-Maniscalco

Manufactured in the United States of America

10 9 8 7 6 5 4 3 2 1

The Library of Congress has catalogued the hardcover edition as follows:

Names: Greenwood, Elizabeth, 1983- author.
Title: Love lockdown : dating, sex, and marriage in America's prison system / Elizabeth
   Greenwood.
Description: New York : Gallery Books, [2021] | Includes bibliographical references.
Identifiers: LCCN 2020045850 (print) | LCCN 2020045851 (ebook) | ISBN
   9781501158414 (hardcover) | ISBN 9781501158438 (ebook)
Subjects: LCSH: Prisoners—Family relationships—United States. | Prisoners' spouses—
   United States. | Conjugal visits—United States. | Prisoners—Sexual behavior—
   United States. | Prisoners—United States—Social conditions.
Classification: LCC HV8886.U5 G74 2021 (print) | LCC HV8886.U5 (ebook) |
   DDC 365/.6—dc23
LC record available at https://lccn.loc.gov/2020045850
LC ebook record available at https://lccn.loc.gov/2020045851

ISBN 978-1-5011-5841-4
ISBN 978-1-5011-5842-1 (pbk)
ISBN 978-1-5011-5843-8 (ebook)

For Scott

martha promise receives leadbelly, 1935

By Tyehimba Jess

when your man comes home from prison,
when he comes back like the wound
and you are the stitch,
when he comes back with pennies in his pocket
and prayer fresh on his lips,
you got to wash him down first.

you got to have the wildweed and treebark boiled
and calmed, waiting for his skin like a shining baptism
back into what he was before gun barrels and bars
chewed their claim in his hide and spit him
stumbling backwards into screaming sunlight.

you got to scrub loose the jailtime fingersmears
from ashy skin, lather down the cuffmarks
from ankle and wrist, rinse solitary's stench loose
from his hair, scrape curse and confession
from the welted and the smooth,
the hard and the soft,
the furrowed and the lax.

you got to hold tight that shadrach's face
between your palms, take crease and lid
and lip and brow and rinse slow with river water,
and when he opens his eyes
you tell him calm and sure
how a woman birthed him
back whole again.

CONTENTS

AUTHOR'S NOTE   xvii

INTRODUCTION   1

ONE   Jo and Benny Get Married   11

TWO   Texas   33

THREE   Sherry and Damon   61

FOUR   Maryland   88

FIVE   Jacques and Ivié   106

SIX   New York   142

SEVEN   Crystal and Fernando   150

EIGHT   Georgia   184

NINE   Sheila and Joe   190

TEN   A Reckoning and a Reunion   215

EPILOGUE   235

THREE YEARS LATER   245

ACKNOWLEDGMENTS   251

RESOURCES   253

RECOMMENDED READING AND VIEWING   255

NOTES   257

AUTHOR'S NOTE

NAMES AND IDENTIFYING details of certain people herein have been changed. The words we use to talk about people in the system are potent. Labels like "felon" and "convict" stigmatize and reduce people to their records, without taking into account the circumstances that placed them there or the transformations they may have undergone while inside. Academics widely prefer people-centered terms like "incarcerated person," while some activists use "prisoner" as a political term to delineate an oppressed class of people. There is no universal consensus on terminology among people in prison themselves or those advocating for their rights. I use both terms in this book to reflect that plurality.

People who have served prison time are more than their records. I discuss convictions because they are what landed the incarcerated in the position to be in prison and to meet someone on the outside.

All the stories are true.

LOVE
IN THE TIME OF
INCARCERATION

INTRODUCTION

THE BRIDE WEARS black.

An atmosphere of momentous occasion permeates Room 315 at the Rodeway Inn, nestled between two highways outside Salem, Oregon. It's the morning of the wedding. Mary Kay cosmetics, SnackWell's popcorn, errant shoes, and water bottles are strewn across the room, where the bride awoke at four this morning, ready for her day. She spent some quiet moments of the morning outside, smoking, watching the sun come up over the highway, feeling the presence of her grandparents looking down upon her.

But now, Journey, or Jo, as she's known to friends, is a ball of nervous energy, pacing in bare feet, losing and being reunited with her cigarettes, phone in hand, overwhelmed by the messages of love and blessings coming through every few minutes. Friends have sent a bouquet to commemorate her nuptials, which the bride receives in grateful hysterics, so much so that Lisa—who has flown in from Missouri to attend to all the bridal details, like forcing Jo to eat a slice of buttered toast and running out to buy a forgotten razor blade at the gas station across the street—has to redo her eye makeup.

Lisa is then tasked with fashioning an updo free of bobby pins, as they'd surely send the metal detectors howling.

Afterward, Jo practices walking in her high heels, up and down the carpeted hallway. She has brought two backup outfits in case the guards deem her black sheath too formfitting, or the color too close to navy blue, the shade worn by inmates and therefore forbidden to visitors. Her wedding band, which she'd selected and bought herself, fits the prison's specifications—no gold, no embellishments.

Today, Jo will marry Benny Reed, who is serving a ten-year sentence for attempting to murder his then-girlfriend. Their wedding will take place at the maximum-security Oregon State Penitentiary, in the visiting room decorated in white and pink streamers and paper wedding bells strung up by the prisoners themselves. Their wedding cake will be powdered doughnuts, and they will toast each other with blue Powerade from the vending machine. It will be the third time they have seen each other face-to-face. It will be the first time they've ever gotten to sit next to each other.

WHATEVER IMAGE COMES to mind when you think "prison wife," Jo ain't it. She is in her mid-forties but looks like she's twenty-nine and seems to be in perpetual motion. She's a mother of three sons: twin seven-year-olds and a twenty-one-year-old. She often keeps her light brown hair pulled back when she's running around doing errands and shuttling her kids to Boy Scouts. Her years in the military have given her a knack for organization, ball busting, and punctuality. She stands five feet four inches, but her presence makes her seem taller. She's a survivor: of multiple combat tours as an Army medic; of PTSD, pill addiction, and the fibromyalgia she came home with; of an abusive first marriage in her twenties. She runs on Jesus, coffee, and cigarettes. She reads novels and nonfiction and watches documentaries for fun.

Jo does her research before making up her mind. She'll crack a joke in line behind you at Target. She has a sardonic, self-deprecating sense of humor. Known to friends as Mama Jo, she is the sage older aunt who will help you get your head screwed on straight, and she'll do it without judgment. "I give such good advice because I've done so much stupid shit," she says. She doesn't, however, consider marrying a man with a felony record whom she met on the internet and whose current address is prison to be among that stupid shit. Rather, the very strictures of prison have allowed for a level of connection Jo had never experienced before.

In a way, I get it. Over the course of reporting my book *Playing Dead*, about faked death and disappearance, I acquired my own guy on the inside, or "prison stalker," to use his jokey nickname for himself. Sam Israel III is currently serving a twenty-year sentence in Butner Federal Prison, in North Carolina, for mail fraud and investment advisor fraud to the tune of half a billion dollars. Sam famously faked his death by staging a suicidal plunge off the Bear Mountain Bridge in New York in June 2008, only to turn himself in to the feds three weeks later. That's why I reached out to him.

Most of our relationship has been epistolary, over the phone and through CorrLinks, one of the many third-party for-profit applications that connect those in the free world with those in prison. Sam and I have been exchanging messages nearly every day for more than seven years. Though interviewing him for my book wrapped in 2016, Sam is still one of the people with whom I correspond most frequently and consistently. We have never met in person.

Typically, I don't offer up much information about myself to the people I interview, because it's irrelevant (not to mention boring). But with an interview subject who's in prison, who has lost much connection to society, the rules seem a little different. It seems unkind not to open up a bit more. So, with Sam, I did, and soon came to know firsthand the laserlike attention that a man with a very long day and little to fill it with can lavish on a lady.

He gets an allotted number of monthly phone minutes, and once he has spoken to his family and lawyers he spends the remainder on his stalkee. My phone once documented eight missed calls from the prison over the course of one evening.

CorrLinks emails max out at thirteen thousand characters, and Sam, if his energy is up to it, will send a half dozen a day. He remembers little details about me and asks perceptive questions about how I'm feeling, about what I'm thinking, about my friends and family. When he was in solitary, he sent me a twenty-two-page double-sided handwritten letter, with stories of his past life on Wall Street. He's offered life advice, which I have found thoughtful, even comforting. His vantage in the slammer and the time to reflect on his past give him a unique perspective on what really matters. He asks questions and listens with an unhurried patience that's rare in our busy, digitized world.

He has sent me innovative cell-spun tokens of his affection: a copper chain-mail choker fabricated from metal pieces of his mattress and wrapped in toilet paper ("It may not be Harry Winston however it is Big House Benson!"); photos of himself posed in the prison yard, in shorts and a T-shirt with the sleeves cut off, revealing his sun-cured skin from long afternoons napping in the grass, his gleaming bald spot flanked by long, graying locks down to his shoulders. He has created colorful tableaus collaged from pages ripped from luxury catalogs and travel magazines, with captions narrating our future together. A private jet: "Ready to go?"

Throughout the half dozen years I've known Sam, he has gone from my subject to my stalker to my friend. His story is often featured on cable crime shows like *American Greed*, and, like clockwork, each time he gets a slice of the spotlight, he gets a new batch of mail from women intrigued. When he first told me this, I was fascinated and perplexed. This hit on just the kind of paradox I adore. In my first book, I explored the idea of how one could "die" in this lifetime, yet never escape one's essential self. Here, I saw a similar impulse: Could you find love and vivacity in the ugliest of places? And what are the prisons we erect for ourselves?

While it's jarring at first, most of us have heard about this phenomenon: people (usually women) pursuing criminals (usually men, always famous) whom they've learned about on the nightly news. The higher the profile of the criminal, the more Heloises to the Abelard. When Scott Peterson, who murdered his pregnant wife, arrived on San Quentin's death row, stacks of fan mail awaited him. Ted Bundy, with a body count of at least thirty people, boasted scores of groupies at his trial, and married one of his staunchest defenders. Before he died, in 2017, Charles Manson got engaged to Afton Elaine Burton, a woman fifty-three years his junior. His name also calls up the iconic "Manson girls" he kept under his control. Infamous patricide twins Erik and Lyle Menendez both married women they met while in prison, one a former *Playboy* model and another a magazine editor turned lawyer.

These women—part groupie, part lonely hearts—are who we imagine as prison wives. But "prison wife" is more than a stock character. So why go looking for love in a prison cell?

———

THE INCARCERATED THEMSELVES are rarely stock characters, either. There are currently 2.3 million people incarcerated in the United States, a disproportionate number of them Black and Brown. In 2020, men accounted for 93 percent of the total number of people in prison. Though African-American and Latinx people make up approximately 32 percent of the US population, they accounted for 56 percent of all incarcerated people in 2015. If these groups were incarcerated at the same rates as whites, prison and jail populations would decline by almost 40 percent.

The United States has the highest incarceration rate in the world, and we have the highest rate at any moment in our nation's history. These skewed numbers are a result of policy choices from the War on Crime and the War on Drugs in the past forty years rather than an indicator of unprecedented crime rates, or reflective of who actually creates harm in our society. Street-level crimes like burglary and theft, for example, account for an annual $16 billion of losses. White collar crimes, like fraud and embezzlement, rob victims of $300-$800 billion a year, according to the FBI. The vast majority of white collar criminals are white men, and they rarely face the same level of consequences Black and Brown people do for lesser offenses.

In addition to those in prison, there are millions more, mostly female partners, experiencing incarceration alongside them. Prison wives form their own communities, and, sometimes, hierarchies emerge. Couples who were in a relationship before incarceration are at the top. Those who knew each other before one went to prison—as classmates or co-workers, with some kind of free-world experience—and then reconnected once one went away are in the middle. And those, like Jo and Benny, who met while incarcerated, or "MWI," are at the very bottom. They didn't know each other out in the free world, where they would've gone out to eat, bickered over household chores, Netflixed and chilled. To the prison wives who have long histories with their men, MWI women can be seen as pathetic losers or, worse yet, prison groupies. Women dragged into this life by their law-breaking partners look side-eyed at the MWIs and wonder: Why would you ever step into this world of your own volition?

Jo met Benny the way many a MWI couple connect: through a prison pen-pal site. Though these sites have slightly different bents—humanitarian, religious, fetishistic (see: jailbabes.com; loveaprisoner .com; cagedladies.com)—all roads lead to romance. When Jo was looking to brighten a prisoner's day, one of the sites she checked out was writeaprisoner.com, which has more than thirteen thousand active prisoner profiles and gets seven thousand unique page views daily. The site matchmakes pen pals, and members exchange handwritten letters. (Depending on the facility, you may also be able to send emails at a cost. But in prison, snail mail is a sure bet.)

Inmates pay $40 a year to post shots as smoldering as anything you'd see on Tinder and fill out profiles stating their backgrounds, their interests, their likes and dislikes. You can select for your prisoner pen pal's age, ethnicity, astrological sign, and gender identity. Site founder Adam Lovell designed his service for platonic connections, as he has witnessed much heartbreak from members over failed relationships. Still, he recognizes the inevitability of romance. "It's human nature," he told me. "Who doesn't want to fall in love?" He recently penned a guidebook for prison relationships, advising couples on navigating long-distance with tips like "Have a recent picture of your partner in your hand when you talk on the phone."

In the free world, the progression of love's first bloom would lead to physical exploration. But the likelihood of getting that opportunity with an incarcerated partner is slim. None of the country's 102 federal prisons allow conjugal visits. Only four states officially allow conjugals—New York, Washington, Connecticut, and California. And not every facility in those states offers them. For the vast majority of prison wives in America, getting physical in any way is not an option—at least if you're following the rules. Some find creative ways to get intimate, from inmates staging fights in visiting rooms to distract guards so couples can quickly go at it to tracing one's penis on paper to create an ersatz dick pic. Since her soon-to-be-husband is in prison in Oregon, Jo will have to wait almost four years to consummate her marriage.

During the time between her wedding day and the end of Benny's sentence, Jo will make sacrifices of the flesh, heart, and checkbook to be with him. She lives on the east coast and visits Benny in Oregon only twice a year, at great expense for her, after which she returns home with credit card debt. "We are literally as far apart as it's possible to be," Jo exclaims, bemoaning the cruel irony. "The United States is 3,280 miles across, and I am 3,276 miles away from him!" So why does she persist?

THIS IS WHAT I set out to learn. Who are these people who are also tangentially imprisoned, who choose this fate, by seeking out a person serving a sentence? How is being a prison husband a different experience from being a prison wife? What about people on the inside who met while doing time together? Can these relationships last in the free world? Can this kind of relationship, where one person is away from the daily grind of errands and work and kids, be a real relationship? What makes a relationship real, anyway? Is it mere proximity? Could a deeply devoted prison relationship be more "real" than a loveless free-world marriage? And what might these relationships tell us about our own more mundane arrangements? What does this particular experience—of support—within the criminal justice system reveal about the system itself?

These questions led me to prisons all across the country, to a conference for self-identified prison wives, to living rooms where binders of laminated love letters were pulled out. They led me to countless conversations—in visiting rooms and diners and parking lots and living rooms, over vending machine chips and enchiladas and fruity cocktails and appetizers and cigarettes and coffees—all about the kind of romantic connection most people (prison notwithstanding) long for.

I met and interviewed dozens of people who were in a relationship with a person in prison, as well as people who were incarcerated themselves with their beloved outside. I saw people coming into themselves. After standing up to society's and friends' and families' judgments over their incarcerated partners, I saw a whole world of opportunity open up for them. I saw women go back to school, start businesses, set boundaries. And, sometimes in the same breath and sometimes years later, I heard stories of heartbreak, deception, and hurt. As a writer, it has been a privilege to listen to people's accounts of their most intimate moments, hopes, and desires. I hope these relationships illustrate the privileges many free-world people take as the air we breathe, in daily life and in love.

Love Lockdown tells the stories of five couples I met over the course of five years, who each illuminate different aspects of the met-while-incarcerated experience. They vary in age, race, gender identity, sexual orientation, length of sentence, and the type of crime for which the person in prison was convicted. We'll follow Jo and Benny's relationship, which I got to know the best, as it unfolds from their prison wedding until his release. Sherry and Damon are serving time together in the Midwest; she is a trans woman in a male facility, and he identifies as bisexual. Ivié and Jacques met on a pen-pal site and married while she was serving two consecutive sentences totaling at least fifty years for her involvement in two homicides. Crystal and Fernando met early in his eighteen years served for a wrongful conviction and had three children together while he was kept in prison, as they lost appeal after appeal. Sheila was an editor at *The New York Times* when she married Joe, who was in prison for murder and whom she met while volunteering for her church's prison ministry. Each of these stories answers the question of "Why?" from a distinct vantage. What makes people stay? What makes this love unique, vexing, worthwhile? What makes it enough?

This is not a book about the millions of couples who knew each other in the free world before one of them was incarcerated. This is not a book about the children, family members, and other loved ones of people behind bars. This is a book about people who found love with someone they did not know before logging on to a pen-pal site, or volunteering for a prison ministry, or becoming incarcerated themselves. This is about people who took the greatest leap of faith to develop a relationship in an environment that is, by design, meant to keep love out.

This is not a polemic on prison reform, though I came to witness the singularity of American prisons: their horror, their inhumanity, how domesticated into our culture they are, even though there is nothing normal about how we treat people who have (or in some cases have not) committed crimes in this country. I'm not an activist or an academic, nor have I experienced incarceration firsthand. You can find recommendations for further reading from those crucial perspectives at the back of this book.

I'm a person who, maybe like you, is interested in the lives of people who reside in the country within a country of prisons in the United States. I seek to know why people put themselves in seemingly untenable predicaments. Why pursue a relationship with someone who is (at least physically) unavailable? What I uncovered was far more complex than I ever could have imagined.

Jo is about to marry the love of her life. One woman's dream is about to come true. So what does happily ever after look like for a prison wife?

ONE

JO AND BENNY GET MARRIED

"I DON'T KNOW HOW the fuck I got here!" Jo shouts.

It's the eve of her wedding. I'm in a motel room with Jo and her friend Lisa. Lisa and Jo met a few years back in an online support group for the prison wives of Oregon State Penitentiary. Lisa has a blond wedge haircut and blue-gray eyes the color of baby seal pelts. When the two women met, Lisa was involved with Paul, who is serving time for four felony DUIs. She has since broken things off with him but is nonetheless thrilled for Jo's nuptials tomorrow.

A director and a cameraman are here with us, too, to feature the couple in a Canadian documentary about MWI relationships. We've created a buffet on top of a dresser, a makeshift rehearsal dinner of Mexican takeout in Styrofoam containers. Lisa made room by pushing aside the small altar she's constructed for the upcoming ceremony: a bottle of Cupcake champagne, two flutes—reading "Mr." and "Mrs."—heart-shaped tea candles, and an array of chocolate and baked confections, all presided over by a portrait of the happy couple taken at their engagement. It was snapped by the prison photographer, another inmate, at their last visit, almost a year ago.

Though Jo describes her relationship with Benny as the happiest she has ever known, being here today still feels surreal. It's not as though Jo is walking into this marriage blindly. There's nothing anyone can say to her that she hasn't mulled over herself. Namely: "What am I doing marrying a man who, in a fit of rage, tried to run over his girlfriend?" she says, before biting into an enchilada. "Like, what is wrong with me?" she laughs. "But at the same time, so much time has passed, and he has worked so hard to rewrite his story."

Jo has rewritten her story, too. In January 2014, she was finalizing her divorce from Kyle, a man she still calls her best friend, father to her boys. He was active-duty military at the time. Jo felt racked with guilt for breaking up her family and ending her marriage to a decent man, so different from her two previous husbands. She was on VA disability from working as a combat medic, the job she believed she was put on this planet to do. She found herself in crippling pain from fibromyalgia and living day to day, caring for her sons, just trying to put one foot in front of the other.

She was donating old clothing at a friend's church one day when she passed a prison ministry table. She picked up a brochure that encouraged people to send an inmate a cheerful message—holidays are especially hard for people in prison. Her friend asked if she was interested. She was not. "You know I used to be a corrections officer, right?" Jo reminded her.

Jo had worked as a guard at a Kansas City county jail in the early 2000s. "It paid really well for the area, eleven dollars an hour. It was the most money I had ever made," she says. She liked the work because it was something different every day, and it kept her on her toes. She developed a rapport with her charges. When one called her "cracker," she deadpanned back, "That's CO Cracker to you, inmate," to hysterics down the block. She also saw firsthand the games prisoners played. Some guys had a rotation of women, visiting on different days, each woman buying snacks from the vending machine, sending dirty pictures, putting money on his books—each thinking she was the only one.

Jo had no illusions about getting involved with a guy behind bars. Which is why she didn't want to participate. Not at first, anyway. But she was going through a hard time herself. She thought it might be uplifting to send some sunshine to a stranger, even one in prison, who might also be feeling low. That evening, she logged on to Meet-An-Inmate.com, a prison pen-pal site.

The site posts profiles of incarcerated people with their pictures, indicating whether they are looking for friendship or something more. Jo came across a profile of a shaved-headed, goateed, bespectacled, broad-shouldered man posing before a muscle car, reassuring his potential interlocutor that he hadn't stolen the vehicle. The photo had been taken at the annual car show the prison hosts. His caption made her laugh out loud. She scrolled down. He wrote about his future goals, his job at a call center, and the college classes he was taking. *Here's a guy who is trying to better himself,* Jo thought. Plus, his profile indicated that he wasn't looking for a relationship. He just wanted friends to write with and pass the time. *He's safe,* she reasoned. *He isn't going to want anything from me.*

Jo sent her first message to Benny on January 2, 2014, which was, coincidentally, exactly six years before his release date, January 2, 2020. She used the email application GettingOut, a messaging system that charges both inmates and civilians to use: emails cost $20 for a thousand credits, and each message sent deducts thirty credits. She responded to Benny's query asking for study tips, as he was earning his associate's degree in business administration. "Noise-canceling headphones," Jo offered. Now she could tell her church friend she'd done her good deed and that would be that.

A few days later, Benny responded, writing that she looked so pretty in her profile picture. She felt him testing the waters and immediately shut it down.

"I told him I'd been a CO and I know the moves," she says. "I told him I wasn't going to send him money or sexy pictures."

Honey, he replied, *I have other women for that.* Four or five of them, it would turn out. He was playing the exact games Jo was aware of with those other women. *I just want to be your friend*, he said.

And a friendship did indeed ensue. They cracked jokes, told stories, opened up to each other. They enjoyed the pleasant distraction from their respective lives that this new kinship provided. Their messages gave them both something to look forward to, and they'd smile with each notification of a new email. After a few weeks, messages turned to phone calls, and the ease they shared online came through in conversation, too. "It felt like we'd been talking forever," Jo says.

But over the July 4 holiday weekend, she didn't hear from him, which was unusual. She learned through the prison's Facebook group that there had been a fight and the facility was on lockdown, during which all inmates had to stay in their cells without access to the phone or computer. She was sick to her stomach waiting to hear from him, her phone glued to her hand. Her reaction made her realize that perhaps she cared for Benny as a bit more than just a friend. "I'm not thinking about this like a buddy," she remembers. "I'm like, *What happened to my person?* That was a wake-up call."

When he finally got in touch, she yelled at him. She'd been freaking out the whole time. He asked her to calm down—what was really going on here? He finally managed to drag it out of her. Jo came clean with her feelings. There was a long silence on the other end of the phone.

Did you really think it was just you? Benny asked.

They decided they needed to see each other face-to-face, to determine whether these stirrings were real. In late October, she flew out to Oregon.

Walking into the prison the first time was terrifying. "I'm voluntarily walking into a prison like, *What the hell am I doing?*" she remembers thinking. "*People are trying to escape from this place. Why am I here on purpose?*" But her trepidation dissolved upon seeing Benny in the visiting room. The burly, tattooed prisoner's face lit up, and he engulfed her in his embrace. "He cradled me against him like I was made of glass," Jo recalls. "It was perfect, that moment. It also scared us half to death." The pair realized that with a connection this strong, half measures wouldn't cut it. They'd have to be all in.

"I remember driving away from that first visit thinking, *Am I strong enough to do this?*" Jo says. "He still had five years at that point."

Benny proposed on her second visit, a year and a half after Jo first wrote to him. He sent her money out of his paycheck from working at the call center, which, as the highest-paying job in the prison, at $1.81 per hour, earned him $291 per month for four forty-hour weeks. He told her to pick out her ring. She selected a blue stone on a silver band from Etsy. Jo brought the ring to the visit and, after obtaining permission from the guard on duty, Benny got down on one knee.

THE PHONE IS never far from Jo's reach, lest Benny should call. That's one of the surprising asymmetries I notice: he can reach her, but she can't reach him with the same ease. You can't just call up the prison and ask to speak to Inmate #3987. You'd think that, being the one in the free world, Jo would hold all the cards. But she's the one waiting by the phone.

The phone rings during our rehearsal dinner buffet, and Jo lunges for it. "He's real mad at you!" she teases as the automated "This is a call from a prison" message plays. "He says it's really rude to come to the wedding of someone you've never even talked to before!" I'm sheepish about this. Benny has tried to call me collect several times in the month leading up to the wedding, but I haven't been able to set up the complicated system. You have to enter personal and credit card information, which can take ten to fifteen minutes, and then you have to wait for approval for a few days before even being able to talk to the person on the other end of the line. Whenever these calls have come through, I've been out walking the dog, or teaching, or at dinner. I see the 800 number, which I know is the price-gouging third-party system, and my heart sinks.

Jo hands the phone over to me now, and I take the call out in the hallway, to speak to the groom on the eve of his wedding. I ask him how this week's visits with Jo have gone.

"Really cool!" he says with a light Pacific Northwest twang. "Usually, I can only register her emotions through her tone of voice when we talk on the phone. But when we are together, I can see how Journey expresses herself with her hands, or blushes when I say inappropriate stuff. Those are the things I drink in."

The meaning he distills from these simple gestures makes me smile. He always calls his wife-to-be by her full name, Journey.

"What are you most looking forward to about tomorrow?" I ask.

"That I will just get to be a normal person. I get to stand up there with the person I love and share that moment with her."

I ask him if he's bummed out that they won't get to spend their wedding night together.

"Of course," he says, as if this is the most obvious question that has ever been asked, because, duh. "This might sound crazy, but I'm actually just looking forward to getting to sit next to her without worrying about getting in trouble. You look forward to any little difference, anything that makes life a little better."

BENNY'S PARENTS WERE high school sweethearts. His dad was in the Air Force, and Benny grew up in Northern California, around Travis Air Force Base. His parents divorced when he was four years old, and his mother took up with another man in the Air Force. "He wasn't any good, so he got sent to Guam to wash bird shit off airplanes," Benny tells me. He, his mother, and his older sister followed his mom's new

husband to the island for a few years. As a child, he witnessed eruptions of violence and discord in his home.

She eventually left him and they moved back to the States. She
managed a beauty supply company and worked long hours, leaving
Benny and his sister, in first and second grade, alone and unsupervised from ten in the morning until nine at night. When she'd come
home and see they hadn't done their chores, or that they'd spilled
water on the floor, or any number of kid behaviors, she would yell at
them, send them to bed, and then wake them in the middle of the
night to continue the tirade.

But it was her new boyfriend, Gene, who would come to play a
big influence in the trajectory of Benny's life. "He was tall, dark,
handsome, fresh out of prison, and a drug addict, but I didn't know
that at the time," Benny says. "She was head over heels for him." As a
kid, Benny had shoplifted here and there, but never had he committed "crime for profit," as he calls it. In the summer before sixth grade,
Gene took Benny steelhead fishing. In this kind of fishing, once you
get a bite, you have to fight for twenty minutes, sometimes longer, to
reel in the catch.

"We were there with other people on the bank, and one guy got a
fish. As soon as he got it on, Gene was like, *Come on, we gotta go*. I remember us going to the truck of the guy who had caught the fish.
Gene reached in and grabbed his wallet, his vest, and a bunch of fishing poles. I was like, 'Did you just steal from that guy?' He said something like, 'He left his stuff out—he had it coming.' That was the first
time I ever saw crime. And I thought it was the coolest thing." (Gene
has since gone into recovery and been sober for more than twenty
years.)

School was challenging, as Benny had an undiagnosed learning
disability. He wouldn't learn how to work with his particular challenges until he got to college, in prison. He got his first gun when he
was fourteen, and soon became uncontrollable. He got kicked out of

his house at fifteen and would spend his days at the mall with a friend, charming girls into giving them money. They spent their nights at twenty-four-hour diners. He ended up living with an older woman who grew marijuana and had a crew of underage wayward boys, like Benny, crashing with her and selling drugs. She encouraged him to commit armed robberies so he would have money to contribute to the house. She used sex to control Benny and the others. "I didn't look at it as abuse until Journey pointed it out to me," he says. He started getting sent to county jail at eighteen, and did his first prison bid in his early twenties.

Benny moved on to more sophisticated crimes as he got older—credit card fraud, check forgery. He makes a kind of prideful distinction between robberies and burglaries: "Robbing places is like sticking up a liquor store. That's for people with zero intelligence, zero skills." Eventually he graduated to burglaries, which required more "strategy," more "creative innovation."

When Benny got out of prison in 2004 after a nineteen-month stint for residential burglary with a stolen vehicle, a buddy turned him on to a guy who bought stolen digital cameras. "The easy part is stealing," he tells me. "The hard part is selling without getting into trouble." By studying the electronics store's rotation of security cameras, he figured out the perfect one-minute window where he could get in after hours and not be caught on tape. He stole a car to do the job. "You don't want to go in your own car," he explains. If you're going to get busted, might as well not lose your own ride in the process. He threw a rock through the window and dragged in several wheeled garbage cans to fill with merchandise. The one detail he hadn't considered, however, was how to break through the glass of the display case to liberate the cameras inside it. So he used his own fist.

Two years later, he was meeting with his probation officer when he was informed that detectives wanted to speak to him. A DNA match had come back from the blood he'd left at the crime scene. In the intervening two years, he had quit doing drugs and left his ex-wife, whom he characterizes as "crazy." He started going to court for hearings and sentencing for the camera robbery but decided that returning to prison did not particularly appeal to him at that moment. He heard from a friend that the State of Arizona carries no extradition to Oregon (not true), so he lit out for Lake Havasu, where he was on the lam until he got a DUI that landed him in prison in Phoenix for twenty-two months. A few years later he returned to Oregon, where he was pulled over for not wearing a seat belt. Being on probation, he was taken to prison, where he finally ended up doing the time for that fated fist-through-glass burglary in 2004. He again served nineteen months.

Shortly after, in the early-morning hours of New Year's Day 2010, he woke up in the hospital. He'd caused a pileup on the highway when, very intoxicated, he had driven his car down I-84. He had been going back to pick up his girlfriend, whom he had left on the side of the road after attempting to run her over with his car. He was convicted of attempted murder and second-degree assault. His release date was set for January 2, 2020.

ON THE PHONE with the groom, I ask him what he loves about his fiancée, what attracted him in the first place. Benny cites Jo's southern drawl, her intelligence, her military service. He likes that she enjoys his sense of humor, which he concedes can be "hit-or-miss." He loves that she is strong-willed and takes no shit, which is a departure from other women with whom he consorted in the past. He says that Jo is the first woman who has demanded a certain level of respect, which made him come correct. In his past relationships, when he was active in his drug and alcohol addiction, he did not offer women the respect he says they didn't seek. He could be verbally and physically abusive. But since his sobriety and time in prison, along with Jo's higher expectations, this relationship is the first one where he treats his partner as an equal. I ask about that fateful hug the first time they met.

"Oh, yeah. That hug changed everything." he says. "We just fit together perfectly. I'm really glad she felt the same thing."

Benny tells me that their connection is particularly unique because they've had two and a half years to get to know each other without the distractions of sex, physicality, the endless pressures of the outside world. They've written letters of longing like soldiers overseas at war, though Benny recognizes, "I'm not a soldier at war. I'm in prison, so I guess that kind of takes away from it." The couple has learned to communicate, because communication is really all they have. "Anytime one of us doesn't feel right about something, we talk about it, no matter what it is." He cites an example about the time he asked why Jo didn't have a French manicure, which she took as a slight about her regular manicure. (I totally would've taken it the same way.) Benny was just curious. "You may think you say one thing, but they hear something completely different." True in any relationship.

As I pace the hotel hallway, Benny sounds proud. He's telling me how he's on the path to success, as he puts it, working as a trainer at the prison call center and studying for his degree. Then the call cuts out. Those fifteen allotted minutes go fast.

I FIRST MET Jo a few weeks ago, at the Deptford Mall, in New Jersey. She was shopping for visiting-approved outfits for her wedding week with her best friend, Ro. Ro and Jo, it's true. Ro lives in North Jersey, and Jo outside of Baltimore, so this mall, near Philadelphia, is about halfway for them. Ro is one of the most heart-stoppingly beautiful people I have ever encountered in real life. A onetime Ms. Fitness New Jersey, she looks like an Italian movie star, with long, dark hair, olive skin, and wide hazel eyes.

Ro and Jo connected through Strong Prison Wives & Families, of which Ro is the founder. She started SPWF, a nonprofit and social network that boasts more than sixty thousand members worldwide, when she reconnected with Adam, a friend from high school. He's currently in federal prison in Pennsylvania, serving a 213-year sentence for armed robbery. (That's not a typo. The extreme number comes from mandatory minimum sentencing guidelines under Section 924(c), a federal tough-on-crime provision whereby judges can dole out "enhancements" based on previous criminal records and "points" assigned to certain features of the crime. Under this provision, the years do not have to run concurrently.) Ro and Adam fell in love in 2009 and they have been appealing this unfathomable sentence together. Ro started SPWF in part because she wanted to create a forum where prison wives of all backgrounds—couples who knew each other before incarceration and those who met during a prison sentence—could exchange information and lend support to one another as they navigate the intricacies of the system, while expressing themselves in a judgment-free space.

Jo found her way to the organization when she got involved with Benny. "I wanted to find a place where I could just be happy about my relationship, without having to explain or defend it," she says.

Still, not all solidarity comes unconditionally. Even among prison wives, Jo has encountered negativity because she's a "met while incarcerated" (MWI) wife. "We shut that down on the site real fast," Ro says, "but judgment of MWI couples definitely exists. Women who have been doing this for years"—living in the world of prisons by fate rather than by choice—"just can't understand why people would walk into it." Jo admits that at first she lied and told people she and Benny were a reconnect, that he knew her brother back in St. Louis. Even that small thread of connection felt more respectable than saying she'd met him on a prison pen-pal site.

That day at the mall, we had lunch at Ruby Tuesday, with Jo's twins, Davin and Elijah, in tow because their dad had been unexpect-edly called into work. Jo seemed a bit deflated to be missing out on a girls' afternoon unencumbered by kids, but the boys were quiet and sweet—indeed, the most well-behaved human children I've ever en-countered. We ordered salads and iced teas, and as they discussed the logistics of what Jo would wear on her prison visits during her wedding week, it became clear why she needed a friend in the know, beyond the banter of girlfriends passing a Saturday at the mall.

"Jo will go for her visit four days in a row, so it's hard to pick out that many cute outfits that will work, given the rules," Ro explained. "Each place is different. Where I go, I can't wear sleeveless; my shoul-ders have to be covered because they are super sexy and hot," she said, with a sarcastic laugh. "Shirts can't be too low-cut. I've gone in with leggings before, which you can sometimes get away with, depending on which cop is working. Then there was a time when you couldn't wear black jeans because those were now considered leggings. I always bring five backup outfits just in case, which means I have to bring backup shoes . . ." She shook her head at the thought.

Jo chimed in with her specifications. "I can't wear blue, because it's what the prisoners wear. Nothing with camo print, no blue denim jeans, no skinny jeans. Right now I stay kind of boring—maxi dresses, cardigans, tank tops with extra-wide straps. Female COs are worse—they'll make you change. I bring a backup outfit I know is safe and keep it in the locker." As I listened to the details of these logistics, it occurred to me that they were really circling something bigger. The mental load required to keep all of this straight is just one of the costs of being a prison wife. The women laid it all out:

"You can't bring anything into visiting besides your money for the vending machines," Jo said. And even that has to be specific: "I'm not allowed bills of any kind; I can only bring change. I always get a roll of quarters from the bank in case the machine is out."

"Our visits are six hours, so we're allowed to bring in tampons if we need to. But they went through a phase where they were like *Nope! You figure it out*," Ro said.

"At Benny's facility they don't allow you to bring in tampons, only pads," Jo said. Nothing like announcing the status of your menstrual cycle to a roomful of strangers.

"No ChapStick, no chewing gum," Ro said and sighed. "But we're just used to it. People bitch and complain, but you just know you're going to make it worse for everybody. So you deal."

"If you make a stink, you won't get your visit," Jo said.

"That whole process of getting in," Ro said, "I've been doing it for so many years and I'm not used to it yet. I get anxiety every time I go through the metal detector."

"I hold my breath every time!" Jo squealed. "Until you're through the metal detector and standing in the hallway ready to go on, you're like, *Okay, I made it*."

Just entering a prison, even as a civilian, means you can be treated with the same hostility and presumption of guilt as the people inside. Jo's and Ro's experiences reflect not just the constant paranoia of being turned away and the ubiquitous checklist of having brought everything, and in the right way, but also the stigma they endure—the judgment of being associated with someone in prison. Beyond the mental stress, prison relationships come at a literal high cost as well.

"That's why I live at home with my parents," Ro said. "The cost to visit, putting money on his commissary, phone calls, messages, travel . . . I'd say I spend about $2,000 a month."

"It adds up really quickly," Jo concurred. "At Benny's facility it's $5 for a thirty-minute phone call. They have video chat, and that's $9 for half an hour. If I want one phone call a day, that's $150 per month. And I send him $100 a month so he can have toiletries and snacks from commissary."

Jo's semiannual trips to Oregon end up costing a few thousand dollars every time, between the plane tickets, the rental car, the hotel, food, and prison-approved visiting outfits. And she's socking away savings for when Benny comes home.

As things started to feel heavy, Ro took the opportunity to pivot us back to the reason we were here:

"But you're getting married!" she exclaimed. "What do you still have left to do?"

"I have my outfit for the wedding," Jo said. It's a slim black sheath with red and white accents, from Rent the Runway. "I have the preacher. We had to find our own because the chaplains at OSP don't do it." She paused. "Here I am, across the country, trying to find somebody to go into the prison and officiate. Most people I contacted didn't even bother to write back when they saw it was a prison wedding. At first I was offended, and then I thought, *What did you expect?* Sad to say, but I think you get used to a certain amount of discrimination."

This stigma is why the SPWF support group is a vital lifeline for women in Jo's position. She has a group of friends, women from all over the world, who understand precisely what she is going through. It's an experience that feels alienating, until you realize there are masses of people facing the exact same challenges.

"People approach you with a morbid curiosity once they find out you have a husband in prison," Jo said. "You wouldn't believe the questions you get."

What's the most offensive?

"Conjugal visits!" both women screamed simultaneously.

"When I explain to people that we don't get those, they freak out," Jo said. "But it's *their* issue. We're okay, it's you that's not okay! People think we're so desperate we have to go fishing in prison."

"People are shocked," Ro said, "because we speak well, we dress well, we're not what you'd expect."

"People have a preconceived notion of what we're going to be like," Jo said. "I tell them they watch too much TV."

"That's why the stereotype exists," Ro said.

"Sorry to disappoint you, I don't wear stripper heels everywhere I go," Jo said and signed the check.

ON THE MORNING of the wedding day, I hear a knock on my door. It's Jo. She has been up since before dawn, pacing, smoking. We lie on my motel bed like girls at a sleepover and I ask her what's on her mind this morning.

"Two and a half years ago, everybody was convinced I had lost my goddamn mind and needed to be committed. Now, I spent all morning responding to texts and messages with people sending blessings for my marriage. Benny was asking me why so many people had changed their minds. And I think it's because they see how happy I am. It just pours out of me."

If a woman tells you she's happy and in love, and she seems happy and in love, then maybe she is, in fact, happy and in love?

Not everyone has changed their mind, however. Jo's own mother (technically her stepmother—her biological mom died when Jo was a young girl) doesn't approve of the marriage.

"My mom, God bless her, is the most judgmental person I've ever met," Jo says.

None of Jo's family or friends will be attending today's ceremony. Lisa is in town for emotional support, but since she visits Paul, another prisoner at OSP, she is ineligible to visit Benny and therefore to attend the ceremony. One civilian to one prisoner—that's the rule at this facility.

Many friends and family members have asked the question hanging in the air: *Why get married?* One can see what's in it for Benny—steadfast support, someone to help him soften the time—but what's in it for Jo? Why not just be in a committed relationship and marry when he comes home, if you're still together?

"We just got to the point where 'girlfriend' didn't seem deep enough to show our commitment to one another," she says. "We knew we were in this for life." But friends still ask, "Do you *really* have to get married?" Jo is quick to counter: "I don't ask why *you* married *your* partner!"

There are pragmatic considerations, too, in changing relationship statuses. Because prison relationships notoriously come and go, marriage carries more heft both within the system and among other prison wives. Being a wife affords you rights that are denied to mere girlfriends. You can be listed as his official next of kin. If your husband is ill or transferred to another facility or goes into surgery, the prison will notify you. (Or is supposed to, at least. I heard too many stories of women not being able to locate their loved one for days, sometimes weeks or months, due to transfers they were never informed of.) In order for inmates to earn parole, they need an address to return to, and living with a girlfriend or a friend won't cut it.

"Nobody wants to say, 'Well, I had to marry my husband before he came home from prison so we can live together,'" Jo says. "You tell people that and they say, 'Oh, that's why you married him.' No, I married him because I love him. But," she admits, "it was a factor."

Why marry now when you'll still have to wait so long to be together?

"Because he's everything I've ever wanted," she says quietly. "He's everything I never thought really existed in a man. He's perfect for me. He's not perfect—neither am I—but we're perfect for one another. How do you not wait? If somebody came to you and said that everything you've ever wanted is at the end of this four-year wait, how do you not wait for that? So, no, I don't have any problem waiting for him to come home from prison. Because he's my husband. He's mine. He's the person I'm supposed to be with. So of course I'm going to wait. What else am I supposed to do?"

Next to me in the motel bed, like any bride-to-be, she is a ball of nerves, but happy, excited. She says it's a sharp contrast to the Jo of several years ago. "Iraq really changed me. It made me a deeper person, but I was broken," she says, referring to the PTSD and fibromyalgia the war left her with. "I thought a part of me was too damaged to ever love anybody again. My friend thanked Benny the other day for bringing me back. Me and Benny saved each other."

Serving in Iraq was a critical turning point in Jo's life. It was the catalyst that changed how she viewed the world. She was in the Army Reserves when 9/11 happened. "It fueled a righteous sense of indignation," she recalls. "I thought they were horrible people who deserved to die, and that we should just go over there, kill 'em all, let God sort it out." She served as a medic and went in with clear lines of demarcation. She was there to help her boys, not local civilians. But once she got to Iraq, things changed: "I met people. I met mothers and fathers and children who weren't any more a terrorist than I was. I met good people who had a passion for their country, the same as I had for mine. And it just really changed my perspective on a lot of things."

She believes that a clear line can be drawn from the open-mindedness she cultivated in her time in Iraq to her wedding today. "I learned how to see the heart, and nothing else," she says.

We go outside so she can smoke and, with the morning sun beaming down on us, cutting through the thick Pacific Northwest clouds, she tells me a story that gives me pause. The other day, Benny went over to a friend's "house" (prison slang for a jail cell) and got offered a puff of a cigarette. Even though he hadn't smoked in years, he took one, nonchalantly. Only then did he realize that the cigarette was laced with Spice, the highly toxic synthetic cannabis known to induce psychotic episodes.

"Not only did he threaten his sobriety, he could lose everything," Jo said. "It bothered me at lunch, so we talked about it. It was the underlying attitude of *I haven't done it in a while, I can take a puff.* But you're an addict." Jo understands his struggles firsthand because she is in recovery herself. She became addicted to pain pills in Iraq, self-medicating to deal with grueling back pain and grief from losing a friend in combat. As a medic, she could write her own prescriptions and get a doctor to sign off on them. But she has been clean for more than a decade. Sobriety is nonnegotiable for her. The couple talked it through, and Benny was receptive to Jo's concerns. "I feel safe expressing my emotions with him. Sometimes he gets defensive, but not yesterday. We discussed it, he acknowledged it, and we moved on."

The story unnerves me. Yes, the couple is working together on a real-life problem, creating frameworks and using tools to discuss pressing issues. Still, it's a story in a vacuum. Once Benny is out in the world, he'll have access to all the cigarettes, all the Spice, anyone could wish for. What then?

THE TRIP TO the prison for the ceremony is calamitous. Lisa is driving us there because Jo's hands are trembling and she's also applying last-minute touches to her makeup. We can't find an ATM, so I lend the final $40 due to the officiant for his services. Jo scrambles to write her wedding vows on a sheet from my notebook.

A handful of brides-to-be are waiting in the reception area of the prison. Twice a year the facility cancels regular visiting hours to hold wedding ceremonies. A middle-aged woman in a red dress and glittery shoes, with blond tendrils cascading down from her bejeweled headpiece, tries to keep her young son entertained while maintaining her bridal composure.

When we meet Anthony, the judge who will administer the vows, and Mona, the only guest on the groom's side, I realize I am the only guest on the bride's side. Mona is a curvaceous Iranian woman who was Benny's manager when he worked at McDonald's. She routinely comes into conflict with guards when she visits Benny, because, no matter how matronly her outfits, her curves will not be quelled. Mona once told them as they suspiciously eyed her outfit, "I cannot cut off my ass." I myself am wearing a sports bra under my dress to this wedding, as I've heard that underwire will set off the metal detectors, and I've draped a travel shawl that I wear on planes over my shoulders, just in case.

Walking through the metal detectors and having one's very person evaluated is, in a sense, the ultimate experience of surveillance. No matter how innocent one may be, no matter how virtuous, there's a feeling of being caught, of guilt by association. And being scrutinized by the guards—who tell you whether you'll pass go or not, if you need to go back out to the parking lot to change into one of the backup outfits you brought—is humiliating and degrading. A guard comes over to Lisa, who has simply escorted us in, to inform her that she would be forbidden from the visiting room because of the cut of her shirt. It makes you feel like a criminal.

Jo removes her jewelry and shoes, trembling. She makes it through and does a celebratory dance on the other side.

The prison is a maze of industrial cinder blocks coated with layers of thick gray-green paint, a shade you encounter only in institutional settings. We walk down a long, sloping hallway and several clanking metal doors lock us in little holding pens before the next one opens. We turn another corner and walk into a large room with vinyl-covered chairs, vending machines, and bookshelves of tattered board-game boxes that all look like they're missing a few pieces.

And there is Benny, waiting for his bride. He wears his standard-issue prison uniform—baggy jeans emblazoned with an orange OREGON STATE PENITENTIARY logo, a navy blue T-shirt, and Timberland work boots. The effect is wedding casual. He's bigger than he appears in pictures, gray-scale tattoos coiling up his thick forearms. He got them here in prison, from a fellow inmate who used a gun cobbled together from a CD player motor, a rubber band, a guitar string, and the ink cartridges from several Bic pens. Since the tattoos are technically illegal, during each of the inking sessions, Benny held up a two-way mirror outside his cell to spot guards patrolling the unit. The tableau on his left arm symbolizes his past: skulls, a set of dice with the faces adding up to the number of years he's serving (nine), a harlot sucking a lollipop above the caption "Man's Ruin." On the right, his future: an angelic yet sexy woman in glasses who bears an uncanny resemblance to Jo.

He immediately embraces her and tells her how beautiful she looks. He is flushed, and jittery. We walk, escorted by a guard, to the room next door, which has been decked out in crepe paper and wedding bells and a white plastic tarp lying on the floor, covered with silk rose petals, all leading up to a white archway with green plastic ivy coiling around its trellises. Given the limited resources, it's an impressive feat of decor.

A few inmates are waiting for us, ready with institution-sanctioned cameras and video to document the moment. ("The photos and the videos cost thirty-five dollars for regular people, less if you know someone, and I always did," Benny tells me later.) Anthony, our officiant, is now standing under the archway in a finely pressed suit. Benny is up at the front, awaiting his bride. It's a charged moment as Mona, Jo, and I stand at the back of the aisle, waiting for some kind of cue. Benny hums the first few bars of the bridal march. Out of pure reflex, Mona and I each grab one of Jo's arms and escort her to her groom.

In my line of work—witnessing, documenting, and sculpting life through a personal and therefore biased lens—I often think about ethics. I spend a lot of time with the people I write about—years, in most cases—and our relationships come to resemble a rather one-sided friendship: we go out to eat, I meet their families and friends, they tell me their most intimate secrets, hopes, fears. I always keep my notebook and recorder out as a silent reminder of what we are doing. But when the bridal march begins, and you see the bride caught deer-in-the-headlights, journalistic protocols go out the window. You grab her by the arm and walk her up to her man.

Anthony reads from a script about love and commitment with a gravitas fit for St. Patrick's Cathedral. Jo and Benny exchange their customized vows. They entwine both hands, and it seems as if they are holding each other up. Benny's prison Toastmasters class pays off in his perfectly memorized speech. He speaks about communication, and weaves a metaphor about learning all of Jo's translations. Jo gets teary.

I don't forget for a moment that I'm in a prison. But I see two people declaring love for each other from the depths of their souls. I see two people commit to a life that will not be easy, and not just because marriage is never easy. They seal their vows with a kiss, and it is a kiss of two people who don't get to do it very often. It's a real kiss, not stagy. It's a kiss with some oomph behind it. They grin like mad.

I CATCH UP with Anthony Behrens a few weeks later to ask about his experience officiating prison weddings. He started out as an attorney and then became an administrative law judge. Judges, along with religious leaders and county clerks, can perform weddings in the state of Oregon. Anthony has since left the bench and mainly practices public policy law. Weddings are his side hustle, and not just in prisons. He's one of the highest-rated wedding officiants on Yelp in the state of Oregon.

But prison weddings are special to him. "When you have a wedding in a fancy place with a lot of people, it ends up being more about the production than the couple. Prison weddings are all about the couple." Anthony lowers his typical fee of $195 to $95 for these nuptials. "My assumption is that people who are getting married in prison don't have the same resources."

He generally enjoys performing these ceremonies. "Sometimes

you can feel the love coming off of them," he says. But on occasion, he admits, it's a little strange. "Sometimes I'm curious as to why they are doing this. I always want to know what happens when they get out. They don't know each other, or you feel this isn't the best idea. But I've never had anyone stop or not go through with it."

Anthony loves his job and says that if he could do it full-time and maintain his lifestyle, he'd do it in a heartbeat. "Sometimes I feel guilty charging people at all, because I have such a good time."

AFTERWARD, WE SIT on vinyl benches in the visiting room while the newly minted couple fills out the required paperwork. I sign as Jo's witness, Mona as Benny's. Benny's arm is securely around Jo and they are wedged as close as two people could be. They look pretty natural, if overly excited, like teenagers in the back seat of a car.

"Other than the days my children were born, this is the happiest day of my life," Jo says.

"This is the happiest day of my new life," Benny agrees. "In my old life, it was when I robbed a lottery store for $12,000!"

"That's my husband!" Jo says.

We all laugh.

You never know how the marriage of any wedding you witness will turn out. But on this day, the couple is happy. It's time to take my leave. Jo insists that I can stay for the rest of their three-hour visiting block, but it seems important that these two get some hard-earned alone time. Because tomorrow they will be back on opposing sides of a table. And today they deserve every possible latitude.

TWO

TEXAS

A WEEK AFTER JO'S prison nuptials, in the spring of 2016, I journey to Dallas for the InterNational Prisoners Family Conference. She and Ro will be giving a presentation entitled "Doing Time
on the Outside: Success Strategies for Families of Those Incarcerated."
Jo is thrilled to submit her new married name, Journey Reed, to the
conference program.

Nestled alongside the Lyndon B. Johnson freeway, the Wyndham
Garden Dallas North appears to have recently undergone a perplexing
face-lift, as if overseen by a Real Housewife of New Jersey, or any
other doyenne with jewels studding the butt pockets of her jeans. Inside, the lights are dimmed as if in a nightclub, every surface is bedaz-
zled, and the vibe is very key-party-on-a-cul-de-sac. We will attend
sessions in over-air-conditioned conference rooms named "Couture"
and "Vogue." I am offended upon discovering that all the toilet bowls
have been painted black. That's just wrong.

This annual conference provides a rare opportunity for the few
hundred attendees here who are supporting an incarcerated loved
one—whether a mother, father, husband, wife, or child—to come together and not just hear speakers but also feel at ease among strangers.
Everyone here has a person in prison. They don't have to explain,

qualify, or amend their stories. When we collect our name tags, we are given heart-shaped stickers to put on them, representing the people behind bars who aren't here. I put one on for Sam Israel, my friend and "stalker" in federal prison. I notice some attendees have a cluster of hearts by their names.

Over the next few days, participants can attend panels of academics and nonprofit leaders and the formerly incarcerated themselves, on topics ranging from criminal justice reform to improving outcomes for the children of prisoners to the impact of the sex offender registry on families, with breakout groups on topics like reentry and supporting those with life sentences. In between sessions, there is time for networking and perusing information tables, and to vote in a fine arts competition of prisoner-created pieces. Prison wives are well represented here, particularly a contingency from Strong Prison Wives & Families.

On the first afternoon of the conference, Jo and Ro hold court at a table of women in the hotel's restaurant. They all appear to have known one another forever. Each of them has a boyfriend or husband doing time, some serving life sentences. There's Heather, with dark eyes and a no-bullshit demeanor, whose husband was her teenage sweetheart. Samantha, a pretty blonde from Oklahoma, met her boyfriend when she was running a dog-training program in his facility. Regina, with cat-eye glasses and cowboy boots, knew Manuel when they were kids, and reconnected with him on this bid. Cat, from the Niagara region of New York, who speaks with the flat vowels to prove it, has also known her boyfriend since childhood; they got together six months before he went to prison, for a crime that landed him on the sex offender registry. Lauren, a mom of two from Florida, was set up with her fiancé, Spencer, by a friend who was dating his cellie.

All characterize themselves as fiercely independent. They are doing the double duty of holding down their men in prison while single-handedly supporting themselves and their families. They are all around the same age—thirties and forties—and most have children. Everyone but Ro has already been married, some several times. All are middle-class but feel the squeeze of finances from supporting a man in prison. Several say they used their tax refunds to travel to this conference. Everyone, save for Regina, is white.

These prison wife demographics present a sharp contrast to what I observed in visiting rooms, where the majority of both visitors and inmates are Black or Brown. When I started this research, I'd had a hunch that the MWI experience was a primarily white phenomenon. Looking at the ladies gathered here today, I think back to a conversation I had with another prison-wife support group administrator. Shani Dee is a young woman in the Bronx who runs a group called Love Lockdown (no relation). In her profile picture, she is wearing a fiery red wig and a sly smile, and her bio states she studied Minding My Business at Minding My MotherFucking Business. She knew her boyfriend before his incarceration, and they reconnected once he went in.

I told her I was interested in speaking with women of color who were MWI, as I was having a hard time finding this particular demographic. I speculated that I could very well be biasing my own research, as I'm a white woman and, consciously or unconsciously, it was easier for me to find women who look like me. But I was casting a wide net, and it seemed to be mostly white women who were getting scooped up in it. She suggested that this was because Black women were more likely to be judged by their community: "The thing with African American women and prison relationships is you'll hardly find any MWI . . . It's frowned upon in a way, especially here in New York City."

I noted that I'd found the same attitude in my reporting. "What do you think is behind it?"

"Shoot, I knew my man for almost twenty years and I'm being

called stupid. We're called stupid or we're wasting our lives waiting for a guy who's in prison or we're being used. Then the question is posed: *Will he wait for you the same way?*"

"Right. That's gotta be very frustrating. What do you say back?"

"It's beyond frustrating. I just ignore them. Or I don't talk about my relationship to my friends . . . Especially my male friends. They're the worst to talk to about it. They say, 'He's using you and he wouldn't do the same.' People will literally hook you up with someone else."

"Meaning they don't consider it a 'real' relationship?"

"Yup. Nothing counts. Not until he comes home."

I asked the same question to Dr. Ish Major, a psychiatrist and dating expert who hosts *Marriage Boot Camp* on WE tv. He is also a consultant on *Love After Lockup*, a reality show about how couples fare post-release. He did his early clinical work in a state prison where he witnessed many relationships. I asked him why it seemed as if so many of these MWI relationships are initiated by white women. He had a differing opinion from Shani, saying this might have more to do with perceptions than facts:

"The key word there is 'seem,' " he said. "The truth is that there are more African American women than Caucasian women in relationships with men in prison. White women in relationships with prisoners ping higher on our radars because that somehow doesn't fit with the image of white women pop culture portrays. If that's the pen-pal dynamic we are shown most often, then our brain's natural tendency is to assume that's the norm when, in fact, it's not," he said. But, like the prison wives represented here in Dallas, that perception might derive from financial realities, too.

"If you're from a classically disenfranchised minority group," he said, "you become proficient in prioritizing your needs and allocating resources, what little they may be, accordingly. Often, single Black women and mothers simply don't have anything extra financially to offer anyone else. But there is a huge wealth gap in this county, so in white communities there's typically some extra kitty in the bank in terms of money and time. When you're not stressed with the day-to-day concerns of survival, you tend to have some extra resources. If you have extra bandwidth in terms of time, money, and emotions, then you'll be more apt to spend those resources in other areas, such as commissary cards and cigarettes, for a return on your investment in the form of a relationship."

But the fact remains: if you've been sheltered from prisons, you're more likely to be tantalized. As Dr. Major said, "If you've never seen firsthand how awful prison is, through a parent or loved one being caught in the system, or if you are not acquainted or even aware of the country within a country that is American prisons, then meeting a prisoner might hold some intrigue. *What is this parallel universe within our own, where the rights and privileges afforded to citizens do not apply? What is this language to learn, this bureaucratic maze to navigate?* For people who have not been in or exposed to the prison pipeline, that world might seem novel, interesting, compelling. There is no sense of romance to prison for Black and Brown people. You know how dark and ugly it is."

The women here in Dallas are all joking, hugging, sharing pictures of their kids and husbands on their phones. What I don't immediately realize is that this is the first time many of them are meeting face-to-face. They've bonded through the online community fostered by Strong Prison Wives & Families. Each state has its own chapter, where members exchange intel on visiting procedures at local facilities and arrange carpools. They sign up for Mother's Day card exchanges. The site has forums for women to exchange words of support and inspirational stories, and tips for sustaining long-distance relationships. One of the most popular tabs is "After Dark," which is for discussing sex—how to satisfy your own intimate needs as well as your partner's under these peculiar circumstances.

Despite the grim facts—long sentences, separation, uncertainty—

the women are laughing, nodding in recognition, shouting in agreement. They are revealing that which they often keep obscured, and the urgency with which they are laying it all out over glasses of white wine and baskets of fries feels like a great catharsis. For once, they are in a place where people understand. They needn't pretend or defend. They are staunchly committed to purifying their perceptions of themselves, however.

"There's so much stigma against prison wives," Ro explains, "which is partly why I wanted to start the organization. These are some of the strongest, smartest women I have ever met. That's why I'm so protective over our image."

"We are not those groupies you see on TV," Jo says. "Our lives are actually quite boring."

"But the stereotype exists for a reason," Heather is quick to counter.

The prison groupie is a nightmare to these women. She is the first thing that pops into the minds of many people when they meet someone whose significant other is in prison. These women take pains to distance themselves from her. She is the one writing love letters to the serial killer, declaring his innocence, reveling in the dark celebrity. She is one reason for the judgment that prison wives face.

And, as Heather says, she does exist. And she is not at this conference.

I MEET HER at her home in San Francisco. It's a large, light-filled apartment in Pacific Heights, teeming with makeup, books, bongs, and strewn high heels. In 2010, *SF Weekly* declared then-nineteen-year-old Samantha Spiegel "the most successful murder groupie." Today Sam is an easily excitable woman, with long, dark curls cascading over her shoulders and a big, lipsticked grin. A decade ago, she was the woman of prison-wife nightmares.

"Oh wow, here it is!" she shouts, stumbling across a torn-out page from a journal, bubbly handwriting flourished across the page. "These are all the people I wrote to!"

She recites the names:

"Charles Manson, Bobby Beausoleil, Tex Watson, Ted Kaczynski, Sirhan Sirhan, Richard Ramirez, Richard Allen Davis, Ramon Salcido, John Anthony Silva . . ."

When Sam was nineteen, she was in a deep depression and using hard drugs. She sought out people who wrought the kind of destruction she was feeling inside. She wrote frequent letters to the aforementioned, whose names read like a who's who of America's celebrity murderers: members of the Manson family, the Unabomber, Bobby Kennedy's assassin.

She became particularly friendly with Richard Ramirez, "the Night Stalker," who was responsible for the murders of at least fourteen people and for the rape and torture of dozens more. He was apprehended in 1985 and died awaiting execution on San Quentin's death row in 2013. Sam shows me original artwork he mailed her, including a drawing of a T. rex and a stegosaurus fighting before an exploding volcano. The T. rex is kicking the stegosaurus in the head. When they first began corresponding, Ramirez sent her a form questionnaire in a scrawl of all caps to get to know his new fan, asking about her "WORK/SCHOOL/FAMILY/LIKES/DISLIKES/WHAT GETS YOU EXCITED/DESCRIBE UPBRINGING/AVERAGE DAY LIKE?/BEST MEMORIES?"

Sam long ago moved on from Ramirez, but she defends her choice of correspondent:

"I had standards!" she laughs ironically. "I hate Scott Peterson—he's a douche! But when I saw old footage of Ricky Ramirez in court in the eighties, wearing his aviators and all black, and he's a Satanist with all these groupies, I was like, *Yeah, that's my type!*"

At twenty years old, Sam was engaged to another prisoner at San

Quentin, Richard Allen Davis, who murdered twelve-year-old Polly Klaas in 1993. Sam would visit Davis in prison every few weeks and sent him pictures of herself in her underwear. He attempted to pay her back in kind, but, lacking resources like a camera or cell phone on death row, he was forced to improvise. "He sent me tracings of his dick on paper!" Sam says.

She lifts her tank top to show me a purple splotch covering the better portion of her right rib cage. It's a tattoo, in the process of laser removal. It's hard to make out the words:

BODY HEART SOUL

RICHARD ALLEN DAVIS

XOXOXO

The words are in Davis's handwriting, and these are the words with which he would sign his love letters to her, a kind of mantra, a pact of their belonging to each other. "I was on heroin when I got the tattoo, and for like my whole relationship with him," Sam says. She's clean now and hasn't written to any of these men for years, but she still wears the scars of that time in her life, quite literally. "Am I the ultimate serial killer groupie or what?"

While Sam may have closed this chapter of her life, the prison groupie archetype is not going anywhere. See: prison hunk du jour Jeremy Meeks, who boasts 1.6 million Instagram followers. Meeks's 2014 mug shot went viral in a matter of hours, owing to his golden skin, smoldering gaze, pillowy lips, and cheekbones up to his eyeballs. Meeks, whose popular aliases include "the blue-eyed bandit," "prison bae," and "Dreamy McMugshot," was arrested as part of a gang sweep. The Stockton, California, police department likely did not anticipate the responses the thirty-year-old prisoner's photo would elicit when they posted it on their Facebook page—comments like "Mama, I'm in love with a criminal!" and "Dat bone structure doe."

Since his release from prison, Meeks has become a model, walked in fashion shows in New York and Milan, and left his long-suffering wife for the twenty-six-year-old heiress of British clothing retailer Topshop.

Americans have always been fascinated with criminals, dashing ones in particular. An 1874 article entitled "A Handsome Murderer," in the pseudoscientific *Phrenological Journal and Science of Health*, asked, "Can it be that one may be comely and yet be a murderer? May one have a tolerably symmetrical face and very bad head?" The author of the article visited Emil Lowenstein (who, the author noted, was "of foreign parentage") in prison and determined: "His phrenology indicated that he was capable, at least, of committing the crime for which he was executed."

New York police detective Thomas Byrnes popularized our ability to gawk at criminals' symmetrical faces and bad heads in his 1886 tome *Professional Criminals of America*, a compendium of mug shots of famous Lower East Side marauders. In the opening essay, "Why Are Thieves Photographed?" Byrnes emphasized the value of gazing into the faces of criminals: "The very cleverest hands at preparing a false physiognomy for the camera have made their grimaces in vain . . . What has to be studied in the Rogues' Gallery [is] detail . . . The skilled detective knows all this and looks for distinguishing marks peculiar to his subject." Offenses in Byrnes's taxonomy include: sneak, pickpocket, swindler, confidence man, forger, butcher cart thief, and window smasher.

The criminals who get anointed into the public imagination often coincide with anxieties specific to the zeitgeist. *The Police Gazette*, founded in 1845, established the tabloid model of following crime, celebrities, and hotties that we see today in *People* and *Us Weekly*. The column "Criminals and Beats" reported on legendary no-goodniks with the glee and schadenfreude of modern celebrity journalism. Western outlaws like Billy the Kid and Depression-era bank robbers like Baby Face Nelson and John Dillinger were populist heroes in their respective moments. It's easy to see the appeal of these Robin Hoods. More confounding, however, is the obsession with men who kill women.

The 1894 trial of Will Myers, a "youthful" and "stolid" heartthrob who was convicted of murder on circumstantial evidence, in an attempted robbery that went wrong, drew a sideshow of ardent female supporters in the gallery. *The Atlanta Constitution* reported on the response to the verdict: "The feminine portion of the audience was more demonstrative. One lady, the moment the word 'guilty' was pronounced, threw herself into the arms of another lady, and the two wept together."

In another murder trial across the country, Theodore Durrant drew his own contingent of admirers. Known as "the Demon of the Belfry," Durrant was the assistant Sunday school director at Emmanuel Baptist Church, in San Francisco's Mission District. In 1895, he killed and mutilated the bodies of two young women. One of his victims, twenty-one-year-old Minnie Williams, was found inside a church storage cabinet on Easter Sunday by parishioners who were decorating the sanctuary. And yet Durrant drew the admiration of legions of young women, many of whom resembled his victims. *The San Francisco Call* reported breathlessly on "the Sweet Pea Girl," a young woman who attended court daily, a bouquet of flowers in her hand, to support the defendant. "The Sweet Pea Girl is rapidly becoming quite a celebrity," the newspaper contended in 1895. She demonstrated so much emotion during the court proceedings that "an enterprising theatrical manager . . . conceived the idea of offering her an engagement." She reportedly sent "books, flowers and sweetmeats to [Durrant's] lonely prison cell." Her profile grew so great that courtroom journalists began reporting on her regularly, and sought to identify this curious fan. Readers were scandalized to learn that the girl, who "resided in a pretty flat in Oakland," was actually twenty-seven years old and married to an insurance salesman. Why was a respectable married woman obsessing over a cold-blooded killer?

One might ask the same of the millions of female true-crime fans today. Women consume the vast majority of true-crime programming, from reality procedurals like *Forensic Files* and *CSI* to supermarket paperbacks like Ann Rule's *The Stranger Beside Me* (1980). In 2017, the Oxygen Network, previously a lesser Lifetime, rebranded itself as an entirely true-crime cable channel. White women are the principal audience of such true-crime, as the victims whose stories get elevated in media are also white women. The interests of their female viewership made this programming shift to all true crime all the time seamless. CrimeCon, a three-day convention billed as "a true-crime theme park," draws thousands of women every year.

Why is it that women in particular are attracted to true crime and criminals, notwithstanding Jeremy Meeks's remarkable cheekbones? Sheryl McCollum, the founder of the nonprofit Cold Case Investigative Research Institute, in Atlanta, theorizes, "Women are detail-oriented. We like the nuts and the bolts. We run with the stories. We run with them to the point it makes no sense." But why recapitulate these horrors, why comb through the autopsy reports and crime-scene photos of women in pools of their own blood?

Lucy Fitzgerald, cohost of the *Wine & Crime* podcast, thinks it might have something to do with control: "Women so often feel like helpless victims when it comes to crime, especially the boogeyman who breaks into a single woman's apartment and rapes her. We see the same scenarios played out over and over again, and we feel helpless. Women being so into true crime speaks to how we cope with those anxieties." Maybe fetishizing criminals is a reversal, a way for women to gain control. If a killer can be objectified as a sex symbol, then the fear falls away. Played out to its greatest extreme, Sam's relationship with serial killers allowed her that control. "I could decide if I was going to visit San Quentin or if I was going to pick up the phone," she says. "These guys may be murderers, but they are locked up in a tiny cell and can't really do anything to hurt me."

In a 1925 *Vanity Fair* article entitled "The Fascination of Murder and Murderers," Aldous Huxley observed, "We are interested in [murderers] for precisely the same reasons as those for which we are interested in great actors, virtuosos and all exceptionally gifted or fortunate beings—because they actualize and carry to perfection in a startling and dramatic way certain tendencies which we feel to be latent in ourselves, because they really live through the scenes and act the parts which we only live through and act in some obscure corner of our minds." This psychological (even aspirational) reading of the perplexing criminal mind intrigued Huxley in the 1920s as much as it does Sam a hundred years later.

Even among the most depraved and perplexing criminal minds, however, there are still discrepancies in relative appeal. Murderers who get sent to maximum-security prisons like San Quentin are the ones rolling in the groupies. But those who are sent to the state hospital for reasons of mental illness, rather than the state prison, do not boast such fans. Dr. Stephen Seager has worked as a physician and psychiatrist at California's Napa State Hospital for ten years, treating people with mental health disorders who have committed crimes—people found not guilty of their crimes by reason of insanity, or found incompetent to stand trial.

"Once you add mental illness, the allure disappears," Dr. Seager tells me. And it's not because the crimes they commit are generic. The worst of the worst brutalities attract the most attention—people who hack up their parents, skin their victims, etc. "Mental illness scares people. If Charles Manson had come to Napa, nobody would have been interested." Most of his patients don't get any visitors, Dr. Seager says. In his time at the hospital, he has seen only two weddings. One was between an inmate and a staff person, who had to quit her job in order to marry. "There are fifty thousand incarcerated people in California who are mentally ill. They don't get love letters," Dr. Seager says.

The serial killer groupie herself might serve a social utility. Criminologist Scott Bonn, author of *Why We Love Serial Killers*, writes that "the social construction of the serial killer identity is symbolic and helps to clarify the moral boundary that separates good and evil in society." Perhaps the serial killer groupie, too, serves a function, an extreme example of romance gone haywire, someone to measure our own standards against. *Hey, my love life might be a hot mess, and I seem to always be drawn to the wrong people, but at least I'm not writing to serial killers, right?* In an episode of the sitcom *30 Rock*, Liz Lemon chastises Jenna Maroney, saying, "You don't get to give dating advice—you wrote a letter to Scott Peterson." Jenna counters, "After he dyed his hair and got super thin from all the stress."

While Sam is still intrigued by the criminal mind, in that she loves true-crime documentaries and forensic psychology, she hasn't been in contact with these incarcerated men in years. She has quit hard drugs, gone to therapy, and reckoned with the trauma in her early life that attracted her to these people in the first place. During her murderer groupie phase, she was depressed and drawn to people who could access that darkness with her. People like Ramirez and Davis. She is quick to point out how different she is now: "I laugh all the time! I'm all about the feels. My friends call me Bucket of Giggles. I mean, I do yoga, I cook, I get massages. I take care of myself."

After leafing through Sam's pieces of serial killer ephemera, we walk to a small park next door to her house so she can smoke. I ask her what she'd tell her younger self today. She takes a drag off her Camel Light.

"That you deserve a lot better, and these guys don't give a shit about you. These guys have no capacity for caring about anyone. If you're locked in a twelve-by-five cell twenty-three hours a day, you're just desperate."

A seventeen-year-old girl recently reached out to Sam over Instagram, asking her advice on how to get in touch with serial killers. "I told her not to do it."

I tell her that I find it ironic that she was particularly drawn to Davis, who murdered a girl not much younger than her.

"It's what I thought I deserved," she says.

IN DALLAS, RO and Jo are at the front of a frigid conference room, ready to deliver their talk. Ro has blown out and curled her hair to Jersey girl perfection and is wearing a fitted black jumpsuit. Jo has her cue cards in her hand, ready to go. They tag-team back and forth, and Ro begins by telling the audience of about thirty people, "Whether you are a fiancée, a girlfriend, a friend, a pen pal, or a partner, you are living the prison-wife life."

"My goal for today," Ro tells us, "is to empower each one of you to find your tools for successfully doing time on the outside."

"The emphasis isn't going to be on our partners," Jo chimes in. "We are going to focus on us for a change."

Last week, at her wedding in Oregon, Jo told me that being in a prison relationship had helped her to find her voice and her passion again. This is evident throughout her presentation. She laughs knowingly, sharing her trademark self-deprecating humor about her foibles, big and small. Through her work with Strong Prison Wives & Families, she has become a counselor to women, helping them evaluate when a relationship is healthy or not. If her relationship has helped her get here, it seems the antithesis of the kind Sam Spiegel engaged in.

Ro and Jo polled thousands of their members to determine which relationship issues they struggle with the most. The top one, they tell us now, is cheating. I had assumed infidelity in this specific arrangement would entail hooking up with other inmates, as seen in many pop culture representations of what goes down in the big house. Not so. The biggest fear plaguing this particular streak of prison wife is that he has other girls on the outside writing and visiting him. Other women like them, about whom they are none the wiser. "We all know there's a guy who always has a different girl visiting him," Jo says, to nods of recognition in the audience. This is also surprising to an outsider, as I had assumed that one of the biggest benefits of dating a guy in prison would be that he could never step out on you, literally. But, as ever, enterprising fellows will find a way.

Men on the inside, meanwhile, often fear that their women are messing around on them. And how would they know? As a man in a Rhode Island prison told me, "She knows that after 9 p.m. I am locked up in that cell and the phone will not be ringing. When you're in here, you're not in touch with reality, and your mind takes on a funny way of thinking. You go to the worst-case scenario." There's actually a term for the man taking care of your woman's needs while you do time: "sport coat." Urban Dictionary defines a sport coat as "a guy who is screwing your girl while you are away, especially in prison."

This worse-case-scenario thinking, coupled with insecurity from feeling powerless, can result in incarcerated partners getting aggressive: demanding more attention or money, threatening to end the relationship. When this comes up at the conference, Jo cuts any trace of humor from her voice: "Being a good wife or partner does not mean sitting and taking abuse."

The survey found that the second most pressing issue for the prison wives is setting boundaries regarding time and money. A big part of the prison-wife identity is sacrifice: giving up the normalcy of everyday togetherness, of holidays at home, of stretching the emotional bandwidth to accommodate the cruelty of the system. Perhaps they are natural caretakers, people who truly thrive on doting upon others. Caring for a man in prison can become all-consuming. There's so much to learn in navigating the labyrinthine prison system, in driving and sometimes flying miles to visit, making oneself available for phone calls. It can be like caring for an additional child, one who is away at a very high-security summer camp and often finds himself desperately homesick.

A few weeks after the conference, I speak with Dr. Fred Berlin, director of the Johns Hopkins Sex and Gender Clinic. Dr. Berlin is a psychiatrist specializing in sexual disorders, and he was an expert witness in the trial of Jeffrey Dahmer, who murdered and dismembered seventeen men and boys over a thirteen-year period. He tells me he has seen this trait of intense mothering in prison wives. "I think these women tend to be very nurturing," Dr. Berlin says. "They have a sense of wanting to be caring for someone else, and men in prison, for obvious reasons, are often quite needy." Dr. Berlin insists on not pathologizing these women. "If women *want* to provide for these gentlemen, and the men appreciate them, then there doesn't seem to be any harm."

But where does one draw the line when nurturing others at the expense of oneself becomes its own pathology?

Jo is very determined to help her ladies see the difference: "It's necessary to create space to stay healthy and whole, so your life does not center completely around your partner." And she gets specific about how to do that. "The first thing a lot of you need to do is take the words 'I'm sorry' right out of your vocabulary." Jo speaks firmly: "You're not the one who did the knuckleheaded thing that landed your partner in the joint. Not to put too fine a point on it, but that's their own damn fault."

I adore Jo in this moment, commanding her audience's attention, telling it like it is. Her words strike me as very feminist, though I'm not sure the members would use this term themselves. I've heard some women say that they defer to their husband as the head of the household, even though he is behind bars. I've heard them describe these guys as demigods and Adonises. I've witnessed women who are beautiful, competent, and wickedly smart spending their hard-earned money on men who simply cannot return the favor. Even meeting Benny, I couldn't quite see what all the fuss was about. (But, in fairness, I usually feel this way upon meeting my friends' boyfriends.)

Jo is keen to get women to recognize emotional manipulation itself as abuse. She continues: "We are the ones working, taking care of the kids and all the responsibilities. And I know there are people sitting here in this room who are putting themselves into debt to take care of a partner who not only doesn't appreciate it but demands you do more of it." She provides examples: "I'm talking about a man who throws a temper tantrum when you tell him he can't call nineteen times a day because he's bored, or you don't have an extra fifty dollars to replace what he lost in a poker game, or you told him the car broke down and you can't visit and now he's yelling at you." She pauses. "Listen to what I'm going to say, because I am dead serious: that is abuse. He doesn't have to hit you."

The presentation ends with some exercises about setting goals to use our time wisely, just like the institutions encourage the incarcerated to do. In prison, the men can watch TV and sit at the poker table all day or they can go to school, take advantage of rehabilitative programs, better themselves. Same goes for the wives: "We can put our heads under the covers and comfort ourselves with junk food," Ro declares, "or we can use this time to get a hobby, educate ourselves, enhance our lives." It's real talk, with a smidge of Oprah thrown in, about how the life you want is the life you make, and about how that life is possible. Even in the face of the Bureau of Prisons.

These women were brought together by the men they support, and yet, here they are, cementing an identity unto themselves. Independent. Hardworking. Reliable. There for their sisters in the trenches. But what does it mean that a large part of their identity still centers around the choices and fate of someone else?

THAT NIGHT, WE pile into the courtesy van to go to dinner and drink heavily to celebrate the girls' presentation triumph. They take a big group selfie on the way over. Adam calls, and Ro puts him on speaker. After he hangs up, the women speak passionately about the phone calls and the stress that they bring. Regina reveals that she doesn't shower after the gym if Manuel hasn't called yet. Heather asks, "Do you all have the one-minute bitch?!" to cackles of laughter. She's referring to the automated voice recording that comes on all prison phone calls at the fourteenth minute, warning that the phone will hang up in sixty seconds, the voice severing these women from their beloveds. Ro is embarrassed when we get out of the van, and asks the driver if we freaked him out. He assures us we did not.

We grab a table on the outside patio of the Tex-Mex chain Pappasito's Cantina, which overlooks a parking lot and a series of box stores in the distance. Soon a bunch of margaritas the size of kiddie pools arrive. We lift them up with two hands and toast Jo's nuptials and Ro's presentation. They all comment on what a relief it is to finally be around people who don't question their relationships. "If you have a friend who's supportive, they still don't get it," Lauren says. "The best ally is only an ally. You need someone who is living this." All the women whoop in agreement. Regina explains that level of understanding: "I don't have to apologize when I disappear for fifteen minutes," she says. "I got my phone call. Everyone here gets it."

In the van on the way back, I sit next to Regina. "Did you see the couple at the other table?" she asks me quietly. "They were on their phones the whole time, not even looking at each other. That's the kind of thing that drives me crazy." She constantly notices couples who don't realize what a gift it is to be in each other's physical presence, free of guards and regulations, people who take for granted the simple act of being together, sharing a meal.

The party continues back at the hotel, where we claim a cabana by the pool. Glasses of white wine get refilled, and in the Dallas night air, with the hum of the freeway in the background and the stressful part of the conference behind them, the prison wives let their hair down.

They talk about the split in their lives. Most of the women have two Facebook accounts: one for their regular life and one for their prison life. They keep the accounts separate so as to protect themselves against the judgments of family members, or the fear that they may lose their jobs or even their friends if they are known to associate with a person with a criminal record. Ro and Samantha are still fully "in the closet." That is, they both go to lengths to keep their relationship a secret from people outside their most intimate circle. Their use of the term is striking—I've never heard it used by straight women. Heather, Jo, and Lauren have "come out." Regina is open with select people—not family or her employer. Cat describes herself as "half out," because of the extreme stigma of the sex offender registry.

"Were any of your fears about coming out realized?" Samantha asks the women.

"No!" they all shout, possibly wanting to reassure, possibly because of the chardonnay.

No one here who has come out about their prison relationship has lost friends, family, or their jobs. If anything, some friends were hurt that the women had kept such a profound part of their lives secret for so long. Heather says that setting the tone for people has been critical: "When I portray myself as proud and excited instead of vulnerable and scared, that allows people to be excited with me. You teach people how to feel about it." She went to her gay friends for counsel on how to come forward with her relationship. She respected their insight into living in nontraditional arrangements. *Give it a year*, they told her. That's how long it takes to go through holidays that look different, and for some staunch naysayers to come around.

That's Jo's plan, because for now, her mom "won't acknowledge Benny's existence." In the eyes of her mother, Jo threw everything away. "I was married to a man who is an officer in the military," she says, referring to her ex. "He was perfect on paper. Now I'm at the opposite end of the spectrum. She couldn't deal with my divorce. Now, after two and a half years of Benny being in my life, she realizes he isn't going anywhere. And she's pissed." Jo is trying to be patient, but it's frustrating.

"Would you ever allow your daughter to get into a relationship like this?" Ro asks the group.

"Hell, no!" Jo says, to a resounding chorus of consensus. "In some ways, I understand exactly where my mother is coming from. You don't want your children hurt."

She's still pretty guarded, she admits, about who she tells. You have to have boundaries, they all agree. Boundaries, as Ro and Jo schooled us earlier in the day, are critical in maintaining one's prison relationship, too.

"I'm always so impressed with Lauren," Ro says. Lauren has positioned her fiancé to be purely life-enhancing.

"I tell Spencer my schedule," Lauren says. "*Here's when I'm at football practice, here's when I'm at PTA. My life hasn't stopped because you are now in it.* That's always worked for us. I've also tried not to let it consume me."

"But that asymmetry has got to drive you crazy," I say. "You're the one who has to make sure you can get to the phone, you're the one traveling, and spending all the money . . ."

They all insist it's not this way. But I'm still straining to understand what they get out of the relationship. Lauren describes the feeling of acceptance Spencer has provided for her: "I told him, 'This is who I am, take it or leave it. Either you love me or you don't.' I've adapted to the prison lifestyle, but I've never changed who I am."

They all acknowledge a kind of old-school chivalry from the men inside prisons that they don't experience outside. "I've never had so many doors held open for me," Samantha said.

And there's a respect—maybe even a fetish?—that the toughness of prison inculcates for their men. These men have to be constantly cognizant of their surroundings in order to survive. They have to lobby for the most basic access to education and healthcare. They are present and fully locked into the rhythms of their women in a way distracted men on the outside just aren't. Other women who don't live this life simply don't understand. "My man is a hundred times the man yours will ever be," Jo says to an invisible adversary, though I'm sure she could readily fill in a few dozen real people. "He has to fight to be that man every day." Benny fits a retro image of masculinity that she doesn't see in most men on the outside.

"Has anybody ever asked you guys if you're in your relationship because it's 'safe?'" Ro asks. This is a favorite explanation of armchair psychologists everywhere: women choose these relationships because the man is at arm's length, and therefore they never really have to risk anything, physically or emotionally. It's the rationale Sam Spiegel gave for why she wrote to the men she did.

"What do you say when people ask you?" I ask, turning to Ro, because she clearly has something to say about this, and it's a question I've been wondering about.

"I say no. It's the exact opposite," she replies quietly. "I have to put everything I want in my life on hold."

More than anything, Ro wants to have a family. What she is doing is actually quite risky. She is wagering the best years of her life and a waning window of fertility on the very uncertain proposition of Adam coming home. When I think about her relationship through that lens, it sounds anything but safe. Apparently, my face makes this evident.

"Look at Liz!" Jo says, pointing at me and breaking the spell that had settled over the group. "You can see the wheels turning!"

"Yeah, I'm trying to take it all in."

"You can see the smoke coming out of her ears!" Heather teases me.

And it's true. These women blow my mind. Once I think I have them figured out, someone says something that bursts all my theories into confetti. Any counterargument that I pose, they have already considered and reconsidered a thousand different ways. Ignorant, delusional, they are not.

"I feel like I'm torn in a million different directions trying to keep everyone happy," Ro says. "But *I'm* not happy." Adam has pointed out to Ro that by keeping him secret, she is disrespecting him.

"Do you see?" Heather exclaims. "All of you are saying, *I can't live with how I'm disrespecting him and my relationship if I don't come out*, but you're scared. So who wins? Either you're going to be cautious of your family's feelings and deny yourself or you're going to embrace yourself and give their feelings back to them. Let them deal with it."

Our drinks have been freshened and the conversation turns to a book the women adore, *The Five Love Languages*. The 1992 manual, by Gary Chapman, puts forth a handful of archetypes for the way you best express and receive affection from your partner: gift giving, quality time, words of affirmation, acts of service, and physical touch. I am familiar with the categories, as my boyfriend recently explained them to me and asked which love language I speak. "All of them?" I'd replied.

It turns out the women's partners have also read this book. It contradicts all of my assumptions to realize that tough guys with criminal records are getting in touch with their feelings behind bars.

Samantha says her love language firmly falls under acts of service—your man stepping up to do onerous tasks so you don't have to.

"So how, in a prison relationship, is your love language fulfilled?" Ro asks. "It's not like he can take out the garbage . . ."

Samantha doesn't answer, exactly, but she does say how much it means to her when Michael includes wildflowers that he picked from the prison lawn inside the love letters he sends her. Everyone cites their own small tokens that their men have managed to scrape together. The effort that goes into it. Ro carries an index card from Adam inside her wallet that reads, RO, KIDS, DOGS, BEACH. It is a small talisman he kept on him for years, as if to will this dream into existence.

The tiniest gestures swell with extraordinary meaning. Every little moment in the time they do get to be together during visiting, during their "dates," counts so much, too—hugging, holding hands, sharing food from the vending machine. I think about how Benny and Jo were both so excited for the special wedding day privilege of just sitting next to each other.

For many, physical touch is a love language that is the most difficult to fulfill. And this, of course, is the question the prison wives get asked the most, and the most invasively. Everyone in the cabana agrees that really getting to know someone without the distraction of sex has its merits. The women claim they are fulfilled. Phone sex is a staple. One prison wife says that when she gears up to perform phone sex for her man, knowing the calls are monitored by guards, "I tell them, 'You're welcome!'" Some write letters of erotica. As Regina told me earlier in the day, "I write stuff to Manuel that would put that *Fifty Shades of Grey* lady to shame!"

From what I gather from various Instagram accounts, the women get by with a whole lot of masturbation. Jo says, "When you meet someone and you have that chemistry and you're flirting, that's the fun part. The part where they actually have their dick in you? Usually that's quite disappointing. I'm not interested in anyone but Benny. He takes such good care of my heart and my mind that my body comes in a very distant third. And let's be real: I have two small children and I'm tired. I have a two-hundred dollar vibrator and I take care of myself at the end of the day for five minutes before I go to bed, and I'm thinking about him when I do it."

Some women, I've heard, will take things into their own hands.

Literally. Guys will create elaborate fake fights to distract the guards while getting it on quickly in the visiting room, often in front of children and other visitors. Sometimes guards will even help orchestrate the circumstances. In more lax facilities, you can sometimes rendezvous in the bathroom. And a woman who wants to get pregnant before her man gets out can grab a baggie of his newly minted semen from under the table, excuse herself to the bathroom, and insert. I heard a story from a man in federal prison about a child conceived by baggie. When the plot came to light, he said, prison officials considered the child "contraband" and forbade him from seeing his father.

In order to satisfy their men's physical-touch love language, the wives send racy photos. You can get away with sending lingerie shots as long as your bits are covered. But many of the women are uncomfortable with it. "It's been difficult for me to give him the kind of sex stuff he needs," Heather admits. "It was hard for us to get past. That's not my love language in the first place, and how do you express intimacy when you know your pictures are going to be viewed and your letters are going to be read by corrections officers first? How do you keep something that is normal and beautiful protected in a system made to prohibit privacy?"

Jo was also wary in the beginning when she realized the guards were going to be seeing her photos. She still isn't totally comfortable, but she knows how much it means to Benny. For Christmas, she staged a boudoir photo shoot and sent him the results.

We refill glasses. We talk about the future—the hope that fuels a lot of these relationships, and its shadow side. Hope is a dangerous thing, for all of them. Even with the firmest of release dates, guys can have time heaped onto their sentences for infractions. And then, being in positions like Samantha's and Ro's—Michael has a life sentence, and Ro is desperately trying to appeal Adam's 213-year sentence—hope is all the more lethal.

"Be real with me," Heather says to Samantha and Ro. She is gearing up to ask a question of a decidedly different tone. Everyone senses it, and the chatter subsides.

"When you say Adam and Michael are coming home, do you really believe that? Or do you know it isn't true and that's the facade that gets you through?"

Ro vehemently believes she is close to getting Adam out, or that his sentence will be commuted under Obama. (It won't be. The day before President Obama leaves office, the final commutation list will come out and Adam's name will not be on it. Ro will weep for days.) "But Adam is the first to not get excited. I always have to check myself," Ro admits.

"Michael is coming home," Samantha says, quietly, definitively. "His first parole date is 2043. There is a lot going on in Oklahoma with reform and sentence reduction. I tell Michael, 'You are coming home, I just don't know when.' He has moved a lot more slowly in getting his hopes up."

"They have to be more realistic, or else they will succumb," Heather says.

"He told me that it's actually dangerous for him to be in a relationship with me, because he needs to be focusing on what's going on inside," Samantha says.

"Adam told me the same thing," Ro says. "He feels like he has one foot inside and one foot at home, and he doesn't know how to straddle the two worlds."

"I get it," Jo says. "It's like being at war. You can't be thinking about what's going on at home or you will get yourself killed. They have to stay focused."

"Michael says he's going to live to be 120 years old," Samantha laughs.

"Me and Adam say we are going to live to be 214 years old. Just give us one good year!" Ro laughs along, although a bit plaintively.

In spite of it all, the women all agree that they are in the healthiest, best relationships of their lives. And they went into them constantly interrogating themselves and their motivations.

Jo remembers having to take a really hard look at herself when she got involved with Benny. "*Why am I with this guy?*" she recalls asking herself. "*Am I just with him because he needs somebody to take care of him? Do I have a savior complex? Is this dysfunctional?*"

Samantha talks about the process of introspection she went through before entering into her relationship: "I didn't fall into love. I walked into love."

"Eyes wide open," Heather says.

"How is it that a guy in federal prison makes me happier than any boyfriend out in the world?" Ro asks, bowled over.

Just as I contemplated at Jo's wedding: If a woman declares that she is happy, and she appears to be happy, then who am I or anyone else to say that she is not, in fact, happy? But it does occur to me that a great deal of this happiness is built on a wobbly, hypothetical vision of the future: the dream of what life will be like when he comes home. What then? Can these relationships last once they become 24/7?

"It's almost like having a relationship with yourself," relationship expert Dr. Venus Nicolino tells me later. She has worked with prison wives and has seen this pattern of fantasy and projection. The long-distance desire so present on this night in Dallas is actually a key ingredient in these relationships. "I've often experienced people in this kind of dyad who exhibit a strong desire for a feeling of longing," Dr. Nicolino says. "Longing is one of the strongest, most dramatic, darkly romantic feelings there is. Leaning into that sensation of simultaneous pleasure and pain can be alluring."

The prison wives long for a more equitable future. They joke about the retribution they will wrest upon their husbands. "I told Benny I'm not cooking another meal in my house once he gets home. He's gonna make me pancakes and give me piggyback rides to the kitchen to eat 'em. *You owe me, motherfucker*," Jo laughs.

"When he gets out in seven years," Heather says of James, "the motherfucker is screwed. I'm not doing shit!" They all say they expect to help the men readjust, but they are also looking forward to some return on their investment. I hope it's true. I hope these women receive back in kind the affection they have given and the sacrifices they have made.

Even though they spend days and nights postmorteming visits and marriages and the cost of commissary, seeing these women together, engaging, empathizing, commiserating, I realize that at times the men are incidental. Some part of this is about women's lives and choosing what they want, becoming strong enough to go against the grain. What they want is these men, yes, but they are learning much about themselves and the vast wells of strength they possess. In rejecting society and their families' expectations to go for what they want, they have fostered self-belief. That has translated into going back to school, starting businesses, and, in Jo's case, taking on a leadership role in this community of women. This gives their lives purpose, and in some cases a political awakening. All the women have become more progressive, and some have become involved in prison reform. They have found a voice that was always there. Somehow, prison provided a grammar in which to speak it.

Back when I first met Ro and Jo at the mall in New Jersey, I'd asked them both if they would trade this prison experience, if they could wave a magic wand and their men would never have been locked up. They both said they would not. They'd trade it for a shorter sentence, maybe, but they wouldn't give up the space and the container it provided them to get to know their partners slowly, intimately, free from the pressures of carnality and the outside world. Now, in the cabana, Ro asks the women the same question. They all echo these sentiments.

Because under the stars, obscured by smog, these women have found one another. It feels like a girls' weekend. Tonight, they are not worried about putting kids to bed or cleaning up the house. They have each other, in a way that seems blood-ordained. They are laughing and telling stories and trading bits of gossip in the heat of early summer. It's a night they won't get to replicate for some time, after they return to the world of responsibilities and the grind of the wait. They seem to be savoring it.

But they still grasp their cell phones, just in case he calls.

THREE

SHERRY AND DAMON

S HERRY GLIDES INTO the visiting room of a maximum-security prison in the Midwest like it's her personal runway. She is petite, with long, dark hair flowing behind her as she walks, and has an infectious laugh. Hard and raspy, it comes on at surprising moments, particularly when she's relaying one of her life's many challenges. "You can decide to accept and laugh or you can be sad and miserable," she says across the small table that separates us. "I choose to laugh." Her vibrance stands in stark contrast to the airless beige room.

She wears rectangular glasses and a faint smudge of kohl around her inner eyelids. With guards and prison staff, she gives a *Hey girl, hey*, and is chatty and familiar. She devours a meal of buffalo wings and a bag of Cheetos and wipes the orange dust from each manicured finger. Even in prison, she loves to cook. A concoction of her own design for which she is famous involves packets of beef ramen noodles, Fritos, and three varieties of cheese. Referring to herself and her dairy habit in the third person, she declares, "Mother eats *cheese*, honey!"

When she talks about Damon, whom she calls her husband even though they are not legally married, she gets giddy. She dotes on him, cleaning his cell and making sure he eats and has everything he needs. She loves how silly he is, always dancing in front of her door, especially when she's in a bad mood. She talks about him so much that she thinks her co-workers and the COs at her job in Receiving and Deliveries have grown tired of her gushing. But Sherry doesn't care. She's in love.

When a guard calls us over to have our picture taken together in the visiting room, she summons Sherry by her last name. Sherry's okay with this, because technically they cannot call her by her first name. It's not on her record. Still, she's been going by the name Sherry since she was a kid. Her legal name, the one she was given at birth, doesn't match who she is. Sherry is a trans woman serving her time in a men's prison.

Damon (pronounced Da-Mone) is currently incarcerated along with her. I met with him earlier this morning—separately, since people in this prison can't see the same visitor at the same time. Damon is tall, with leonine eyes, and his multiplicity of faded prison tattoos make him seem menacing at first glance, until you hear his slow, honey-dipped twang. He goes by the nickname Monebone, because when he was young his mother thought he could pass for a member of Bone Thugs-N-Harmony.

Damon proposed to Sherry in the dayroom, and she wears a cross he gave her around her neck as a symbol of their commitment. A former Crip, Damon found Jesus and the woman he calls the love of his life in prison. "We've been together six or seven months now," Damon wrote in a letter when we first started corresponding, "and have outlasted every other couple." They plan on taking their relationship "to the streets" when they're released, and Sherry said that in their free-world wedding, her dress will have "a train so long Monebone will have to carry it down the aisle."

They're both in for the kind of charges poverty sometimes initiates—robbery, gang activity, addiction-related crimes. Both suffered physical and emotional abuse and found themselves in public educational and correctional systems that were not equipped to handle their needs.

They've dealt with unrelenting disturbance and disruption and, in Sherry's case, drug addiction. Both have been in the system since they were kids (Sherry since age fifteen, Damon since age ten) and have spent significant stretches of their lives behind bars. Once they were in, it proved difficult to get out.

Damon and Sherry met while incarcerated, but the old-fashioned way: as prisoners. There was no pen-pal site for them, no Facebook group to vent to. In the prison wives I've met up to this point, women like Jo, Ro, and many of the ladies in Dallas, I've noticed a demographic trend: they seem to be at least in their thirties, heterosexual, and white. But what about the incarcerated themselves? What does a relationship look like inside a prison? For all the free-world pen pals out there, there are people on the inside trying to find love and comfort with one another, searching for humanity in inhumane conditions. And for all the discrimination that prison wives face from prison staff and from society, couples like Damon and Sherry have it harder.

Like the Rihanna song says, these two found love in a hopeless place. But in the eyes of the system, the fact of their relationship is a crime—at least according to the guidelines of the Prison Rape Elimination Act, or PREA. The federal law was passed in 2003 in an effort to deter sexual assaults in prison. On its face, it's hard to argue with. But under its broad language, PREA determines that any sexual contact whatsoever—whether an assault by a guard or a relationship between two prisoners—is tantamount to rape. The underlying premise of the law is that any sex in prison is inherently non-consensual. PREA legislation defines sexual misconduct to include "offender-on-offender sexual assault, sexual abuse, sexual harassment and *consensual sex acts* [emphasis mine]. It also includes staff-on-offender sexual harassment, staff sexual misconduct, and staff misconduct of a sexual nature."

Violating PREA can result in any number of disciplinary measures. These include tickets, which strip away "privileges" such as visits, phone calls, and time out of cell for recreation and jobs, resulting in earning even less money. Accumulating such disciplinary infractions can lower chances of parole or even extend prison time. PREA violations can lead to solitary confinement, a practice that has been deemed cruel and unusual punishment by the United Nations Committee Against Torture. Though PREA legislation is meant to protect the most vulnerable populations in prison—such as the mentally ill and underage people—it can be applied punitively to queer and trans people, which is how Damon and Sherry, respectively, identify. The law makes their consensual relationship, their love, a crime.

I was quite aware of this dangerous paradox when I began corresponding with the couple. As a reporter, I want to protect the people I write about at all costs. I offered the use of pseudonyms for Sherry and Damon, but they insisted on using their real first names. (I have omitted their last names.) Both were released from prison before this book's publication, yet remain in the system on probation. Sherry and Damon are the experts on the risk, as they live incarceration every day, and I do not. As LGBTQ+ people in prison, they have had much of their humanity stripped away. They wanted to use their real names to have their story told, to be validated in black and white. As Damon said, "In my life, I haven't had much acceptance. I want to show people that if I can be myself, you can, too." As Sherry said, "Our names are who we are."

_____

I FIRST GOT to know the couple when I posted a query on Write-A-Prisoner, a newsletter that goes out to tens of thousands of people in prison, asking for stories from the LGBTQ+ community. While MWI stories of white, straight, middle-aged women like Jo were readily accessible to me, I'd had a harder time finding people from other sexual identities. I received dozens of pieces of mail, most of which had nothing to do with anything related to my question. But Damon's eight-page missive stood out for his circumstances, sense of humor, and innovative use of punctuation. He titled it "A Dream Come True."

> I've "lucked up" and found the transgender of my dreams.
> I'm a gay/bi-sexual brother (black man) by the way & proud
> of it. Sherry is the only person I've actually had a committed
> relationship with & I must admit that I'm "happy" with
> Sherry (even though she drives me crazy everyday) & look
> forward to having a life-long marriage with her NOW but
> also when we both get released back into society.

Like many of the couples I've interviewed, Sherry and Damon have a fated origin story. They got together in 2018, but it wasn't the first time they had met. Their paths had crossed seven years earlier, when they were locked up together on a previous bid in the fall of 2011. Damon wrote:

> I remember the instant attraction I felt towards this lil' short
> pretty long haired Hispanic transgender prisoner.

He made a move on Sherry, which in retrospect he considers "corny and creepy." She emphatically turned down his advances. ("I was with someone else at the time, and I am a monogamous person," she tells me in the visiting room.) Loyalty and commitment are huge values for her. She told Damon to back off, that she was spoken for by another person in the prison, someone who was "crazy possessive." Damon took the hint.

When they met again seven years later, in a different facility, Damon wrote:

> My attraction to Sherry is still as strong as it was back in
> 2011. In my eye, Sherry is perfect in every way (especially

physically). At this point I am in love with Sherry to
the point I've come all the way "out of the closet" &
introduced Sherry to my mother & friends on the streets.
Our marriage is like a roller coaster ride but even with
all of that I wouldn't trade my wife "Sherrybone" for the
world. Even in prison where the people are miserable &
the time drags every day, LOVE IS SOMEWHERE 2 BE
FOUND.

Even though they have both spent wide swaths of their lives in
prison, Sherry and Damon have found comfort and solace in each
other.

SHERRY WAS BORN in New Mexico in 1974, along with her twin. Her
twinship was a fierce and joyful connection to another person, who
she said was "like me: gay, we thought, when we didn't have the words
for it, but she was also transgender." She calls her twin Jerrica. The
twins have a sister who is a year older, and in that tight braid of three
they created a world unto themselves, insulated from their mother's
abuse. "We had a camaraderie where we didn't let her destroy us. We
used to play outside a lot, playing house or with dolls," Sherry says.
"But if one of us got in trouble, she would hurt all of us."

Sherry describes abuse that sounds ritualistic in its torture. Her
mother would force the children to eat an entire can of jalapeños or
sit in a bathtub filled with scalding water. "But that was better than a
beating, know what I'm saying?" Sherry laughs, somehow, when she
tells me this. "I don't know what my mother's problem was, but she
was probably mentally ill. I remember that every morning she'd count
out thirteen tabs of aspirin that she would eat throughout the day."

Sherry never met her father, who died when she and her siblings
were young. She remembers her mother bringing her and Jerrica to

his gravesite, where she instructed them to dance on top of it. "When you're born and your mom hates you—the person who is supposed to love you most in the world—you see things differently," she says. "You learn to love yourself."

The kids were always running away, and when they turned ten their mother had had enough. She sent them to live with a family member in a Rust Belt city, in a rough part of town. He forced them to go scavenging on garbage day in rich neighborhoods, where the kids would find small electronics and appliances to salvage and resell. He, too, was abusive, beating the siblings with little provocation, often dragging them up a set of stairs by their feet. They ran away from there, too, but were returned to the house. "I knew jail would be better than living under his roof," Sherry says.

At age fifteen, she decided to commit a crime that she knew would come with a harsh sentence, in order to guarantee that she would be sent away. So it was that she liberated a river barge.

It's a Saturday morning, and Sherry's telling me the story of her early life from a closet-size cinder-block room. This is the prison space reserved for the half-hour video call I pay $10 for each time (not a ton of money for me, but insurmountable for many). She's cracking up telling me this, with her forehead in the crook of her arm, gasping for breath. Not because she thinks it's funny, but because to laugh at her life's hardships and absurdities is how she has gotten through.

"Girl, they charged me with piracy!" she snorts. As in: commandeering a water vessel. Like a *pirate*. She and a friend untied a small barge from a dock and took a short-lived joyride down the river. "They had the whole Coast Guard out after us!"

That was her first stint in juvenile jail. There, she began experimenting—sexually, with other kids who were locked up, and with her gender performance. She told everyone to call her Suzy Q. A guard in the jail pulled her into his office and told her that Suzy Q was "a second-rate name. He told me I should choose a more refined name that fits my personality." *Sherry*, he offered. But he told her to think about it. "I did think about it as I looked in the mirror and said it out loud. Sherry. It fit," she says.

Over the next decade, she and Jerrica lived together, their run-ins with the law mixed with times of relative peace. But in 2005, Jerrica, Sherry's twin, her other half, was murdered by a man she was sexually involved with. He killed her upon learning that she was HIV-positive. That man is now serving a fifteen-years-to-life sentence in the same state as Sherry. (Due to an institutional separation order, they can never be incarcerated in the same prison.) In her grief, Sherry fell into addiction, which led her to the charge for which she's currently serving time: bank robbery.

The first time, Sherry was not so much a bank robber as a person who was high out of her mind on crack one day and decided it'd be a good idea to stick up a bank. She'd been on a bender the night before, and as the sun was rising, she felt keyed up, without a cigarette or a dollar to her name. Across the street from the apartment where she'd been partying, she beheld the answer: a bank. "I'd never steal from a person," she clarifies. "That bank wasn't going to be missing its money."

She went in with a hairbrush poking out of her pocket, meant to look like a gun, and told the teller to give her everything in the till. She scored, and checked into a Motel 6, where she turned on the local news and saw security camera footage of herself, sticking up a bank with a hairbrush. She became so paranoid that she barricaded herself in the bathroom, sure that the vice squad was going to kick in the door at any moment. The cops never showed up, but she turned herself in to the police a few days later.

When she got out of prison on that five-year bid, she stayed clean for a bit. Eventually she relapsed and got into some more scuffles with the law, which landed her in county jail in 2015. It was there that she first met other trans women who were taking hormones. They told her how to get them—go see a doctor and get diagnosed with gender dysphoria—and how to begin her transition. She was still in the throes of addiction and stealing to fund it. So she robbed another bank—this time with a real gun—and ended up in prison again, where she met Damon. Though it is a men's prison, Sherry had started transitioning and taking hormones before this sentence, so this particular prison is legally required to provide them (not all of them are). She says she feels more herself than ever before.

BEFORE MEETING DAMON, I spent the night tossing and turning in a scuzzy motel in a blighted downtown. It's the time of year when the winter sunset casts the abandoned streets into the darkness of midnight by late afternoon. Sleep didn't come to me until an hour before I had to wake up to get to the prison. It didn't matter that I've been initiated into the culture of prison wives and been to a wedding in a maximum-security facility: each prison is a country unto itself. I roiled with every anxiety imaginable—*they won't let me in to visit, my winter coat won't fit in the locker, they'll turn me away for my outfit.* This paranoia is a feeling every prison wife I've ever spoken to has described, and these sleepless nights are a by-product of the guilt by association one experiences when walking into a correctional facility.

To use the vending machines at this prison, for example, you must use a five-dollar bill to purchase the (nonrefundable) card to load money onto it for snacks. Cash, coins, and credit cards are forbidden in the visiting room, the exact opposite of several other places I've visited, which only allow quarters. To purchase photos taken with your loved one, you must have separate money orders in the amount of $5 for each photo. (I don't know who needs to hear this, but: you must obtain those money orders from the post office, not the bank.) While a bag of chips and a low-res digital photo printout might not seem like a big deal to people on the outside, these are tokens that people in prison very much appreciate. I was determined not to mess up.

Inevitably, my Uber got properly lost on the way to drop me off at the prison. I knew this meeting was important to Damon, who hadn't had a visit from his family in some time. "They used to visit me when I was in juvenile jail, but since I've been in prison as an adult, they let me handle it like a man," he'd told me over the phone. When I finally got to the cafeteria-like visiting room, I took the seat closest to the vending machines, as directed by a corrections officer. Off in a far corner were booths with phones and glass partitions for people with higher security levels. Hand-painted lettering on the wall declared, RE-ENTRY MEANS NEVER COMING BACK.

Damon came in, dragging his feet in prison-issued sandals, wearing navy scrub pants and a light blue collared shirt. He had a scraggly goatee and faded tattoos he's acquired on his time inside—MOB, for example, across his neck, meaning "Money Over Bitches." His face erupted into a smile and he gave me a tight hug.

"That's the first hug I've had from a civilian in thirteen years," he said. He's gotten hugs from friends, and from Sherry, of course. But in thirteen years, I was the only free person to embrace him.

The room soon filled with the aromas of pizza pockets and microwaved burritos, and we accumulated a feast that Damon wolfed down: three Reese's cups, two vanilla lattes from the coffee machine, a lemonade, a Crunch bar, a Baby Ruth, a Twix, cheese and crackers, and a salad, for good measure. Damon earns $12 a month from his prison job as the gym porter, where he cleans and takes care of the equipment for at least eight hours a day. He sometimes clocks up to twelve hours a day, because he enjoys being out of his cell and "learning to work," he says. His earnings are enough to buy laundry detergent, a few packages of ramen noodles, instant coffee, and cookies. His family doesn't add money to his commissary account. Candy bars are a luxurious indulgence.

He wears his hair in cornrows that have gone a bit fuzzy, and freckles fleck his cheeks and nose. He pointed out that one of his eyes is acrylic, from an injury he sustained in another facility when he was attacked with a belt with a lock on the end of it. It made him blind for six months. Three tattoos triangulate his face—a teardrop by his right eye, the tiny phrase NO GUTS, NO GLORY by his left eye, and a Sagittarius arrow on his third eye. When I asked about his dreams upon getting out, he said, "I'm just looking forward to being a citizen. I want to walk into a room and for nobody to know I was ever in prison."

"You might want to think about getting some of these tattoos removed if that's the case," I said, laughing. He laughed, too.

Damon's ability to laugh and be lighthearted is one of the most striking things about him. He has spent the vast majority of his life in prison. I asked him what he did in those eighteen months he was out—the longest stretch of time he'd ever been free as an adult.

"What eighteen months?" he asked, puzzled.

I tried to jog his memory. "Like you told me on the phone, you were out for eighteen months once—"

"No," he said, looking a bit sheepish. "I was out for eighteen *days* once."

As Damon tells it, he has had every case under the sun except for rape or murder. They range from grand theft auto to aggravated robbery to arson, his first charge. He was put in a juvenile jail at age ten, when he accidentally set fire to a friend's living room. I told him I couldn't believe how young an age that was to be put in a prison environment.

"They'd lock us up at five years old if they could," he said.

From there, his record is like an encyclopedia of charges, mostly stemming from gang activity as a young person. He was concerned with being the baddest, the toughest. As he explained in a letter, "I'm from the inner city. Fighting & being a gangsta is glorified in my hood. Whoever did the most dumb shit got the biggest reputation."

His parents themselves met as kids in juvenile jail, and married at eighteen. His mom usually had several jobs, but worked mostly as a home health aide. His father didn't live with them, and Damon doesn't remember him having a job, but recalls that he always had money. Damon is the eldest of five. His mother lost custody of the kids when he was ten, and for many years he thought it was his fault. "She was on the phone with her caseworker and she was beating me with a belt at the same time. I yelled to the person on the other end of the phone for help," he told me over our vending machine feast.

Growing up, Damon was concerned with asserting his dominance, partly because he was obscuring his sexuality. He'd been with both women and men but realized in his early teen years that he was particularly attracted to trans women. He remembered seeing an episode of the Maury Povich show, one of those nineties exploitation talk shows where they would parade trans women out. He saw something magical in how beautiful trans women are, the quicksilver alchemy. He personally identifies as bisexual, calling himself a "homo thug."

Like Sherry, his first sexual experiences took place in juvenile detention. He had many girlfriends with whom he was publicly attached, but also hooked up with guys privately. He grew up in a homophobic culture, and he himself once used every gay slur in the book. Until very recently, he kept his sexual identity and activity shrouded in secrecy. But being with Sherry, someone who is so authentic in who she is, even in the face of grave danger and discrimination, has given Damon the confidence to be open. If he has any regret, he says, it is "not being me for so long."

Sherry's trauma originated from the abuse she suffered as a child, and the loss of her twin, which sent her into addiction. Damon's is from prison itself: at thirty-six, he has been in the system for twenty-six years. The perpetual trauma of institutionalization is all he has ever known. Damon and I are the same age. Those twenty-six years aren't just conceptual to me. I see the movies of our lives playing in split screen: he locked away at ten, while I, a middle-class white person, was taking after-school recorder lessons and watching *A League of Their Own* on repeat. I see us at eighteen: me, graduating high school and setting out on a backpacking trip across Europe; him, graduating from juvenile jail to the adult penitentiary. Now, both at thirty-six, we are both making commitments to marriage and family.

Damon has tried to make the best of what he has, where he is. As he slowly chewed a Baby Ruth, in a maximum-security prison, he told me that this year has been the best of his life.

"In the last prison I was in, I was locked in my cell twenty-three hours a day. Here, I can be out doing my job from eight in the morning till nine at night if I want to. I can move more freely. I have my Sherrybone. I've never been happier," he said.

When he talked about Sherry, he lit up. A smile stretched across his face and his eyes got squinty. He said he admires her strength in everything she's been through. "She's the one who's had the crazy life," he told me. "I love her so much, even when she's at her most evil." He pulled down his collar to show me the scars of bite marks and scratches Sherry has left from play fighting. They make the fighting seem more real than play. This is a major dynamic in their relationship. Sherry will get upset with something Damon has done, whether it's flirting with someone he shouldn't be or not spending enough time with her. She'll cuss him out, and hit, scratch, and bite him to make her point.

By the end of our morning together, Damon had grown weary. "This is the most I've talked to anyone in a long time," he said. Before the visit concluded, we took a photo in front of a hand-painted mural of the skyline of this rusted-out city. Damon hugged me from the side and rested his head on my shoulder. He hadn't had a real picture of himself, other than his ID badge, in many years. As I walked out of visiting, I glimpsed him staring at the pictures we'd taken. A small thing like that, seeing yourself smiling, can prove you're still here.

———————

DAMON AND SHERRY experience one advantage that other MWI couples do not: they have time together and proximity on their side. I've come across numerous prison-wife memes about yearning to be locked up with him, to be his cellie. Sherry and Damon aren't locked in the same cell, but they're next-door neighbors. Separate yet together. The rooms are connected by an air vent, which they spend a lot of the day talking through. They sit next to each other in church once a week and eat all their meals together. During their recreation time, they play long games of Scrabble. Sex is a given, which they usually sneak in one of their cells during rec time, when the bars are lifted for an hour.

The intensity of their environment amplifies the intensity of their relationship. "One day in prison can feel like four days in the community," Dominique Morgan tells me. Morgan is the executive director of Black & Pink, a prison abolition and advocacy nonprofit serving system-impacted LGBTQ+ people and people living with HIV/AIDs. Morgan was incarcerated herself and served eighteen months in solitary confinement at Tecumseh State Correctional Institution, in Nebraska. She knows firsthand how intense prison relationships can be.

"You can spend an entire day with someone, hearing their whole life story," she says. "There are no cell phones, nothing to interrupt you. In a week, it's like this is the love of your life. There is such a hunger for connection in prison. You want that one person you can share everything with. And the little things become so important, like holding hands when you haven't held hands with anyone in years. It's grazing skin walking past each other in the chow hall. Or sitting closely on the same bench. Or exchanging a look across the yard. These relationships can move very quickly, and they can become all-consuming."

So what happens if one partner gets out before the other? Can that intensity be sustained? Morgan's own relationship ended once she left prison and her partner was still inside. "I experienced trauma every day, just trying to navigate the system to communicate with him and visit. I had found liberation. But to love and support the person I had promised to love and support, I was still experiencing incarceration," she says. "It reached a point where it was just unhealthy for me." Practical considerations made it hard, too. "It's very difficult when you get in the real world and you're busy and working. You're not going to spend ten hours a day to stay in love."

Of the many prison relationships she witnessed in her time inside, she can't think of one that survived on the outside. But she is quick to qualify that she doesn't believe that this just has to do with people who have been incarcerated. "Let's keep it real," she laughs. "I know people who have never been locked up and *they* can't have healthy relationships! I've seen the most 'well-adjusted' adults who don't know how to love without misusing power."

EVEN THOUGH SHERRY and Damon get to spend many waking hours together, they still go through challenges in their relationship. Jealousy is a big one.

"Oh, these girls are scandalous, honey," Sherry tells me, crossing one leg over the other, as she perches on the edge of a plastic visiting-room chair. "I'm not friends with any of them, because they will try to steal your man." Earlier today, Sherry had caught wind that Damon was chatting with the one other trans woman in the prison. Sherry had heard that they "were laying all up on each other" and that when Damon stood up, he had an erection. Rumors in prison catch like wildfire.

" 'Have less to do with her,' " she says resolutely. "That's what I'm going to tell him later tonight."

Sherry blames her sensitivity in part on the hormones she takes, which make her edgy. Damon tries to be accommodating, but "every little thing makes her mad," he says. One thing guaranteed to make her mad, however, is keeping company with another woman. Sherry perceives a lot of people to be jealous of their relationship. They've been together for almost a year, which in prison time counts for a lot. Sherry has "titties like a woman," as she describes them, which makes other men lustful. And Damon is handsome, built, a catch. She thinks people maliciously mess with their relationship.

Sherry experiences bigotry every day, so others interfering with her relationship is no different. Sherry is HIV-positive. Her status is widely known because, in an effort to humiliate her when she first arrived, a guard announced it to her entire cellblock. This made her a pariah. "In the line for dinner, people make a big gap to stay away from me," she says. "I don't care, I don't like them anyway. But it does hurt." She is routinely called the F-word and other slurs. Sometimes she claps back: "I tell them, 'I respect you, so you have to respect me. I hear you when you say those things.'" Her admonishment makes little difference, but she takes pride in sticking up for herself.

Sherry has to fight to be who she is. For her husband, gaining acceptance is less fraught. Damon, with his muscles and tattoos, fits the mold of someone who has spent a great deal of his life in hypermacho environments. Even though their relationship is widely known, he comes off as masculine, as a man who looks more like the majority of people in the prison. When people say hateful names around Damon, he doesn't get ruffled. "Sherry takes things personally," he says. "They might just be talking like that around her, but she takes it like it's about her." He explains it in a letter:

The homophobic guys use words like "faggot/fag"
"dicksucker" & "weirdo" to insult us but like I said . . . they

never say it directly to me or Sherry, just loud enough for us to hear 'em. It doesn't bother me though. I'm a man. Whatever I do with my dick (excuse my language) is my business. If someone doesn't like who I penetrate then I advise them NOT to indulge in same sex relationships.

The different levels of privilege the two experience, even in prison, affect their dynamic. Damon is friendly, and because his job as a porter allows him lots of time in the gym, he knows a lot of people. He is always stopping to chat with someone or do a favor. This frustrates Sherry, because she thinks Damon can't see through to their real motivations. "Everyone always wants to talk to him," she says. "But they are using him to pass notes and get them things. They don't actually care about him."

No one cares about Damon more than Sherry does. But fulfilling her deep emotional needs can be taxing for him. She always wants to talk through the vent, for example, and sometimes Damon doesn't. On his last bid, when he was locked in his cell for twenty-three hours a day, his conversations were limited, to put it mildly. This new level of stimulation with Sherry at his side sometimes becomes overwhelming, and he'll just want to lie down. "I'll tell her I don't want to talk, but then she'll hear me rapping to myself and get mad as hell," he explains. But he understands where her needs come from. "I don't think Sherry got a lot of love or affection growing up," Damon says, "so now she wants all of me."

Sherry is aware of this codependency and its dangers. "I feel like I have put Damon as the focus of my every day," she tells me. "I got to figure out how to be stronger. I got to figure how not to want to be loved, how not to worry about nobody but myself. It's real easy for me to be selfish during active addiction. However, when I am clean it is very hard to put myself before everyone."

Morgan has seen this pattern among incarcerated LGBTQ+ people, from her firsthand experiences inside to the hopes and fears she hears Black & Pink members express. "You just want to know someone loves you," she says. "You feel like the world has forgotten about you. If organizations like ours are doing our jobs, we should be loving these folks in a way that makes them feel seen and supported. So when they decide to invest in a relationship, which is normal and human, it's based on a positive. That they would want to be in this relationship whether they are inside or not. Folks are just hungry to be loved."

Surprisingly, given the challenges Sherry and Damon face being in a relationship while in prison—being right next door to each other yet still separated; the rumors and instigation; living with the constant trauma of incarceration—it does not sound as if PREA, the law that forbids sexual contact in prison, is one of them. They are careful to keep their hookups private, but their relationship is out in the open. "We don't do anything in public, but everyone knows," Damon tells me. For example, guards will let Damon know if they've recently seen Sherry while Damon is on his cleaning rounds. "'Your girl is over there,' they'll tell me."

I find myself quite nervous to interview the couple and write about their relationship through the mail, as incoming letters get read by prison staff. I don't want to jeopardize them in any way. Damon is unconcerned:

PREA has nothing to do with me and Sherry's relationship. PREA was implemented to prevent rapes, sexual harassment and things of that nature. It can be used against staff or inmates. PREA is rarely even used in prison nowadays. This place done changed so much. All the raping and stuff like that is "non-existent" in 2Day's prison system.

I wonder if this has to do with their prison justly interpreting the law in its proper spirit, or if their luck just hasn't run out yet.

———————

SHERRY AND DAMON'S relationship stands in sharp contrast to what I hear experts say about how PREA is implemented in prison. Chase Strangio, deputy director of transgender justice at the American Civil Liberties Union and the attorney who represented Chelsea Manning, the transgender U.S. Army whistleblower, describes the plight of trans prisoners: "For trans women housed in facilities for men, you see the overuse of solitary confinement for 'their own protection.' For all LGBTQ+ people in confinement, there are expectations of hypersexuality, and people are regularly policed and punished just for existing as themselves." In terms of relationships, that has been even tougher. "I've worked with hundreds of trans people in prisons, and very few have consistent and stable relationship support on the outside. More often, I have worked with people who form intimate bonds with other people who are locked up." Like Sherry and Damon. "But then those relationships are criminalized and punished within the facility," Strangio says.

Losing a core part of one's humanity—to experience emotional and physical intimacy—must be destabilizing. So how do PREA proponents see the benefits justifying these losses?

Dr. Mary Ellen Mastrorilli worked as a PREA auditor for three years. She began her career in the 1980s as one of the very few female corrections officers, starting out at MCI Walpole (now called MCI Cedar Junction), in Massachusetts, one of the most violent prisons in the country at the time, because she "wanted to be where the action was." As a female officer, she was relegated to soft duties: working the visiting or patrol rooms, not interacting with the men inside much. But over her seventeen years working for the Massachusetts Department of Corrections, she climbed the ranks to high-powered supervisory positions. She has been a criminal justice professor at Boston University for almost two decades.

I ask her whether, in her time as a CO, she ever saw any relationships develop between inmates. She recalls one between an infamous bank robber and a trans woman. "They were roommates and had a relationship. Our investigators looked into it and we were convinced it was consensual. The trans inmate was small, effeminate, skinny, needed protection. The other inmate was protector and lover. This was back in the nineties. That would never, ever fly now, in light of PREA standards."

As a PREA auditor, she went into institutions to evaluate the extent to which the guidelines were being enforced. She explains the definition she upheld: "Corrections professionals and the Justice Department believe there is no such thing as a consensual relationship behind the walls. It's really resulting in a culture change in corrections." Mastrorilli says that, before the ratification of PREA, there was no protection or recourse for people who were sexually abused while incarcerated. "If an inmate was sexually assaulted, raped in the shower, what we used to think was *You can't do the time, don't do the crime. That's part of prison.* No more." When Dr. Mastrorilli spins it this way, PREA sounds progressive, because who could argue against decreasing the incidences of rape?

In 2012, almost a decade after PREA was signed into law, the Justice Department issued its first set of national standards, requiring facilities to provide inmates a variety of ways to report abuse while also giving facilities a wider range of options to investigate every allegation. That resulted in an exponential increase in claims, a 180 percent jump from previous years. The rise in reporting suggests that the law is effective. But while there were 61,316 investigations into sexual assault allegations in detention centers from 2012 to 2015—covering city, county, and Indian reservation jails; federal, state, and private prisons; military lockups; and ICE facilities—only 8.5 percent of them were found to be true, a number that seems too low to be telling the whole story.

Depending on the nature of the assault, it can be handled as a criminal case or an internal disciplinary case, one distinction being whether the parties involved are inmates or corrections officers. The incentive for facilities to enforce the guidelines is federal dollars. Becoming PREA-certified makes institutions eligible for federal grants.

Mastrorilli describes the acts that institutions consider to be under their jurisdiction: "Even if two inmates say their relationship is consensual, we still treat it as a PREA incident. We probably wouldn't bring criminal charges, but you investigate. I really believe that behind the walls, there is no such thing as a consensual relationship. The dynamic is so steeped in power, coercion, control. Even if it truly is consensual, we can't sanction it." I ask about how the law may in fact unfairly punish queer people in prison. "There are unintended collateral consequences with any policy and program," she says. "But that has to be balanced against the benefits. It's my belief that the incarcerated LGBTQ+ community is a very vulnerable population. I believe PREA, on balance, has made life safer for them."

Yet under the lens of PREA, Sherry and Damon's consensual and loving relationship is tantamount to rape.

I MEET WITH Jason Lydon, the founder of Black & Pink, on a bright spring morning at a coffee shop in the Jamaica Plain neighborhood of Boston. He is bald, affable, and an ordained Unitarian Universalist minister. Lydon started the organization as a letter-writing group in 2005. He had been released from federal prison two years earlier, after serving a six-month term for an act of civil disobedience protesting the Western Hemisphere Institute for Security Cooperation (formerly the School of the Americas), in Fort Benning, Georgia, in 2002. Since its founding in

1946, the School of the Americas has trained more than 83,000 Latin American security forces in how to quell uprisings through the use of torture, disappearance, and the displacement of communities. Lydon and his codefendants were charged with trespassing.

As an openly gay man, he was placed in a queer-segregated cell for "his own protection" while awaiting trial in county jail in Georgia. There, he was sexually assaulted by a guard. Part of Black & Pink's mission is connecting people on the outside with incarcerated LGBTQ+ and HIV-positive people. "When I got out," he tells me, "I wanted people on the outside to care about what was going on with gay and trans folks on the inside. So I'd make dinner for my friends, and they could eat if they'd respond to letters from prisoners. Letter writing is a harm-reduction tactic. Mail call usually happens in the dayroom, and if your name never gets called, then people know no one is looking out for you. But if your name is getting called on a regular basis, people will know *If I fuck with that person, maybe someone will pay attention.*"

When we first speak, it's 2017, and PREA is a top priority. "Many claimed PREA was intended to protect the most vulnerable," Lydon explains. "But in fact it's being used as a tool to penalize the LGBTQ+ community, and gay men in particular, for engaging in any kind of sexual activity. Anytime you put people together, anywhere, people are going to develop romantic relationships. And if you penalize those relationships, they might get in trouble, but they are not going to stop."

PREA sets up impossible paradoxes. The Marriage Equality Act of 2015 states that all same-sex unions are to be recognized, yet PREA stands in direct opposition to that right for prisoners. In 2014, Black & Pink conducted a sweeping survey of 1,200 incarcerated LGBTQ+ members, the first of its kind. They found that about one-third of respondents had experienced intimate partner violence while incarcerated, similar to numbers on the outside. So someone could be in an abusive relationship with a partner in prison but have no recourse. Because they are already considered guilty of breaking the rules under PREA, reporting it would open them up to punishment.

In step with the great variation in rules and their enforcement from prison to prison, PREA, too, is carried out at the discretion of individual facilities, by individual wardens and guards. It all comes down to the enforcer's whim, their definition of words like "consensual" and "sex." So, while this legislation may have been intended to halt sexual violence, it can be used to stop anything from hand-holding to kissing. "My friend got a ticket for touching his boyfriend's thigh!" Lydon tells me. "But straight people do it all the time—hug each other, high-five after playing sports. These kinds of tickets are targeted against LGBTQ+ people. My assertion is that we will see a giant drop in parole rates for queer folks." Disciplinary infractions of the sort Lydon describes can result in parole being denied.

While PREA may have been rolled out with good intentions, in many cases it has been used as yet another tool of oppression against queer prisoners. As Lydon contends, "They're failing to address the culture of sexual violence, and actually trivializing the reality of it. I know women in prison who treat it as a joke. They'll tickle each other and say, 'PREA! PREA!'" When I ask him to say more about what the culture of sexual violence in prison looks like, his answer gives me great pause.

"Think about strip searches," he says. "That is sexual assault. If you and I were walking down the street and someone stopped you and said, 'You are not allowed to move any further until you allow me to take off all your clothes and examine your naked body,' you'd be like, *I was sexually assaulted.* But in prisons we say that's just a part of the security of the institution, even though we know the guards bring in at least half, if not the majority, of the cell phones, drugs, and weapons."

Studies back up this assertion. According to *Prison Legal News,* a journal of the Human Rights Defense Center, "Often the people doing the smuggling [into prisons] are guards or other corrections employees, who, motivated by greed, accept bribes from prisoners." A policy paper from Columbia Law School states, "Poor pay and low hiring standards have made guards particularly susceptible to corruption." An internal investigation of Rikers Island Jail, in New York City, found corrections officers making between $400-$900 per day smuggling drugs and other contraband into the complex, and in California a prison guard confessed to making $150,000 a year bringing cell phones into his facility. Another guard in the same facility was found to have fifty phones in his car, parked in the prison lot, labeled with the names of various inmates. Prison employees walk through metal detectors and have to show the contents of their bags upon coming to work, but they are searched by their colleagues, who may be willing to turn a blind eye. Only inmates are subjected to strip searches.

When I visit Sherry and Damon, each time they return from using the restroom, they are strip-searched. This deducts valuable minutes from the visit, and enduring the humiliation of standing naked before a person with power is nothing short of traumatic. This is especially true for Sherry, whose body is the source of much commentary in her facility to begin with. Sure, we think, prisoners get strip-searched for drugs and other contraband. That's just part of the deal, right? But why do we assume that strip searches are a given? When I stop to consider the humiliation, I reassess the whole practice; it makes me question what other assumptions are baked into our psyches.

I ask Lydon if, like with the other prison pen-pal sites, romance ever blooms between Black & Pink letter writers. He says it happens. "Letter writing, especially in this day and age, is such an intimate act. There's an aspect of vulnerability people can be in when writing letters, or visiting without the ability to really live in the same space." He is quick to contradict the judgments many prison couples receive.

"There's nothing fake at all about the relationships that happen through writing and visiting. If we say that's imaginary, then we devalue the experiences." He also finds dubious the claim that people who date prisoners are desperate and couldn't find somebody on the outside. It discounts demographic facts: "Those assertions are unfair, and even if that was true, it doesn't make the relationship any less valid. There are over two million people in prison—that's a lot of people!"

———————

DAMON AND SHERRY'S luck runs out around Christmastime, a few weeks after I met them in person.

On December 23, Damon gets into a fight with another prisoner in the dayroom, where they can use computer kiosks. The fight is over a tablet used for sending messages on GTL, another third-party prison communications platform. When the other guy thinks Damon is taking too long, he starts making threats, shouting, "I'm getting sent to 4B"—the unit where you're put if you've done something violent. "I can take a lot," Damon tells me, "But don't threaten me." I ask if he feels concerned for his safety. He says no. "I'm scared about what I might do to someone else."

After the fight, he's placed in limited-privilege housing, in a part of the facility away from Sherry. She had been looking forward to the holiday, since it would be their last Christmas together on the inside. She was planning on cooking a commissary feast, with the three types of cheese she loves. "It was hard on me," Damon says, "but it was harder on her."

The couple write long notes to each other to stay in touch during their separation. "I write to him about my daily activities, about how much I love him," Sherry says. "He writes me and tells me how much he misses me, that he never thought he'd miss me this much. It's all that stuff that makes you love a person even more." But she's still angry at him for getting in trouble. "I cursed him out in the first letters! I wish I could beat some good into him," she says with a laugh.

Damon starts going to the medical center every day to get some time out of his cell. Sherry is getting her urine tested because she is diabetic. They run into each other. "Monebone came up behind me and hugged and kissed me. I tried to get him to stop, but hey, I wanted my kiss! It was just a little kiss on the forehead, it was nothing."

Another inmate reports them to a CO. Damon describes that person as an older man who is jealous of his and Sherry's relationship. "He told them we were making out to sexually gratify each other, and it wasn't like that," Damon says. "It was a man and woman who missed and finally got to see each other."

"They know me and Monebone are husband and wife," Sherry tells me. "But these people are so homophobic. They can get away with targeting us. I didn't even know you could get in trouble for something as small as a kiss on the forehead!"

Damon reads the disciplinary ticket to me over the phone:

Rules violated: consensual physical contact for the purpose of sexually arousing and gratifying either person.

Inmates were kissing and engaging in other sexual acts in the waiting room. After reviewing the cameras, the inmates were in fact making out in the waiting room. They can be seen kissing several times, hugging and needing to adjust their clothes. These acts among others took place for almost 30 minutes.

Damon admits to adjusting his clothes, but not for the implicit reason of arousal the ticket suggests. "Sherry had heard I was stabbed"—the person Damon fought with had attacked him with a sharpened toothbrush, but it didn't puncture his skin—"and I was just showing her it wasn't that bad, just little scratches."

The couple has a hearing. "Sherry went in like a little lawyer and got the charge thrown out," Damon says. They still end up receiving a punishment of seven days in limited-privilege housing, where they can't work or interact with the general population. For Damon, this is an extension of his time, since he was already there from the fight. Sherry is let out of the restrictive housing early. "That's Sherry!" Damon says with pride. "What Sherry says, goes."

Soon Damon will be moved back to his usual cellblock, but while they were away on punishment, their cell assignments have been shuffled and they won't be next door to each other. Talking through the vent won't be an option. "It's just an inconvenience now," Damon says. "But we will be together again. We'll get it done."

———————

SHERRY WRITES ME a letter on pink notebook paper, dated Christmas Day 2019. She says her New Year's resolution is to put herself first in all that she does. She also writes, "This is what I would like for you to put as the conclusion of me and Monebone's story."

> Sherry and Damon are growing in their relationship and their individual lives. We are both focused on success but know that tomorrow is not promised. We are two totally different people trying to align our lives to an everlasting partnership. It is a never-ending learning experience that Sherry is fully committed to.

She ends with this:

> The most important thing right now is surviving this prison time.

FOUR

MARYLAND

I'S THE SUNDAY after the Women's March of 2017 when I meet Jo at a Panera Bread in suburban Baltimore. The last time I saw her in person was nine months ago, at the conference in Dallas. It will be the first weekend that we hear the phrase "alternative facts," which will shade our moment and then fade into the background as ubiquity, our new reality. The day's drizzle suits my mood.

I'm happy to see Jo. I have so far seen only the extremes: her prison nuptials, the prison conference presentation—blips in the rhythm of her life. I want to get a sense of her every day. What is it like to be married to someone who is far away yet omnipresent, to try to manage the stresses of life inside while staying connected across great distance? What does something as mundane as marriage look like given those unusual constraints?

Jo is now forty-two and, while attending to Benny and taking a leadership role in the organization Strong Prison Wives & Families, she's also pursuing her B.A. online from Southern New Hampshire University, in psychology with an emphasis in addiction counseling. Her other main job is raising her seven-year-old twins, Davin and Elijah, whom I had met as guest stars shopping at the mall.

Today her brown hair is pulled up in a topknot and she is in a comfy daily uniform of plaid button-down, ripped jeans, and slouchy boots. We catch up over massive sandwiches and then climb into her stick-shift Jeep, which has a bumper sticker proclaiming Tolkien's maxim NOT ALL THOSE WHO WANDER ARE LOST. She tells me what our itinerary for the next few days will include: homework and hanging with her sons; a friend's baby shower; errands at AutoZone, Michael's, Target, the post office, and the Boy Scout shop. She's trying to quit cigarettes, which means she is pulling on a vape pen, making her typical edginess a bit spikier. As she starts the engine, a text comes in from Benny through their prison messaging app, which she reads aloud:

> Hi baby girl, just got done with a mean ass workout, finally got a good one in. Hope work was okay, gonna find out who is in the Superbowl . . . I've got to work on my stats homework, heard it was easy but we'll see. Game starts at 1 so if there's a good time to talk between 11:45 and 1 let me know, otherwise it's gonna be much later, I love you boo.

She messages him back on her phone, quickly telling him she has me in tow but can talk when he can talk. She tells me how busy Benny is, which seems surprising for someone ticking off the days of his sentence. But Jo is ticking off days, too. On the same phone, she has a countdown app with two clocks running: one for how many days left until their next visit (178 days, just under half a year) and another for how many days until he is released (1,075 days, just under three years). Between the errands, the twins, the classes, the whole messy business of living and taking care of oneself and one's family, the minutes of his phone calls and the erasure of another day down are what carve up the time. The specter of the one who isn't there weighs most heavily on the hours of the day.

Benny's absence is a presence, and I feel it most acutely in Jo's bedroom. She lives in a massive apartment complex—in the same unit as her ex Kyle and their sons. Their place is comfortable and spacious, with wall-to-wall carpeting and a lofted play area for the boys. Her two small dogs patrol the scene. A child-size table with containers of colored pencils and markers is below a kitchen window looking out onto a parking lot full of SUVs and minivans. Kyle and Jo sleep in different bedrooms at opposite ends of the apartment. Kyle has his own bathroom; Jo shares with the boys.

"I haven't dug all this out in a minute," Jo says as she unpacks a shoebox full of Benny memorabilia. Letters from Benny; cards from Benny; many, many photos of visits with Benny and the wedding that took place nine months ago, which is also the last time she saw him. She spreads the artifacts across the electric blanket on her bed, which covers an enormous U-shaped body pillow she has nicknamed "my husband." We sort through the pile delicately and lovingly, like archaeologists panning for fossils. We are amassing proof of something that's hard to see.

She shows me pictures from Benny's Toastmasters class and weight-lifting club. Here is the man I met on his wedding day, not so long ago. He has a wide, friendly smile, a shaved head, sharp rectangular glasses, and a body that all the time in the world in a civilian gym cannot buy: broad shoulders, a thick neck, and biceps his baggy blue prison T-shirt can't hide. Even though she hasn't looked upon these in a while, they afford her the opportunity to talk about him, which animates him, brings him into the room with us. It's a live-action version of what happens online in prison-wife Facebook groups. If you can't be with him, at least you can talk about him.

The boys get home from church with Kyle and they barrel into their mom's room, jumping on the bed, jumping on Jo. They are at the age when calling each other "butthead" is the apex of comedy, and they are cultivating personality quirks, like sharing a Koosh ball they've named Harry. This is the outer limit of their naughty behavior; having two parents in the military will do that. Jo is perpetually drinking coffee from a cracked "Starbucks: Kuwait" mug, a little souvenir from time overseas. Kyle, who is still active in the military (his exact position remains obscure to me, though it involves a high security clearance), has a blond crew cut and is clearly the one from whom the boys inherited their coloring. He is polite yet withdrawn and regards me with skepticism before retiring to his bedroom.

Fellow prisoners have told Benny he is foolish for marrying a woman whose life is still so enmeshed with her ex's. *She's playing you, bro* has been the general consensus. When Kyle and Jo divorced, just a few short years ago, around the time she started writing to Benny, they decided to keep living together because it would be best for the boys. Neither wanted to live away from their kids, and since Jo's principal income is disability insurance from the VA and Kyle receives a military housing allowance, the arrangement made sense. "And he is a great dad," Jo says with pride. At the beginning of Benny and Jo's correspondence, this unorthodox living arrangement didn't pose a problem, because their budding relationship was not yet romantic. "He didn't care that I still lived with my ex, and I didn't care about the other girls he was writing, because we were just friends," Jo reports. "I told him flat out, 'This is my living situation, and it's probably not going to change, because it's what's best for my boys.'" As things got more serious between them, he struggled with it.

But not as much as Kyle struggled with his ex-wife finding love in a prison cell across the country.

KYLE'S COURTSHIP WITH Jo had been somewhat underwhelming, but still, it was on the outside, between two citizens with no criminal records. The wife of a mutual Army buddy had tried to set them up in 2005, but Jo was dating someone else at the time. "He was firmly in the friend zone," she says. They became best friends over the next three years, while Jo was deployed in Iraq.

Jo had enlisted at age eighteen, simply to get out of town. "I was working at Burger King and life sucked. This was three meals a day and a roof over your head," she says. Ironic, I think, given that chestnut conservatives like to use about prisoners having it easy: *three hots and a cot.* Joining the Navy as a corpsman, she provided medical aid in combat hospitals and on the battlefield, a set of skills somewhere between "a paramedic and a registered nurse," she explains. After basic training, she was assigned to Parris Island, South Carolina, home of the famous Marine Corps Boot Camp. She wasn't the first female corpsman ever to serve on the island, but she was the first in a long time.

She recalls being very keen to set the right tone among her men, both brass and recruits, when she started. She introduced herself as the guys were reporting to the battalion after road watch. They were taking their boots off in the middle of blister check, half with their pants down. The fact of this new female colleague spread through the room, and they all looked at her with curiosity and confusion. Jo dropped her bag and looked straight into the eyes of the senior drill instructor. "I said, 'I'm Doc. I'm here to fix you, not to fuck you. Any questions?'" Her announcement was met with ten seconds of dead silence. As time dragged on, she wondered if she would be fired on the spot. Then she saw the corner of the drill instructor's mouth start to quiver, and all the other recruits busted out laughing. From that moment on, she had found her place.

She talks about her service with warm nostalgia and refers to her colleagues as her brothers. "I don't doubt that there are women who experience sexism in their career, but that was not my experience, ever. You've got to have thick skin and a certain level of tolerance. After all, you're working with frat boys who know how to kill people really well."

When she came home, in June 2008, she was "broken," she says. On top of the challenges of reentry into civilian life, she was kicking the prescription drugs she had become addicted to. She had been in an emotionally abusive relationship that left her "without a shred of dignity." That relationship had now imploded. She told Kyle that she was done with men. "Well, before you're done with men entirely," he said, "I kind of have a thing for you." Jo was initially resistant, not wanting to screw up an important friendship. "He didn't push it," she says. "But gradually, you get to the point where you're like, *Fuck it, whatever.* I was pretty honest with him from the get-go. I told him, 'I am not in love with you. I don't know how to be in love with anyone anymore.'"

Jo calls fibromyalgia a "garbage bag" diagnosis for the host of symptoms she'd acquired, ranging from extreme fatigue to severe joint pain. She was also rattled with PTSD from serving as a medic in Iraq. She is much better today, but she is still nervy, her jumpiness rooted in having spent so much time in the immediacy of combat. Jo always knows where the exits are, watches hands in a crowd, and has to fight the urge to cut the steering wheel when a piece of trash blows across the highway. But even when it was worse, Kyle understood what she had witnessed in her clinic and in the emergency room, what it's like to wring out your socks at the end of the day after standing in blood up to your ankles. ("How do you ever get over something like that?" I ask Jo. "You don't," she replies.) Here was someone who could see in her what she no longer could when she felt like a husk of her former self: someone beautiful, someone worthy of love.

She found being with Kyle—even if she wasn't in love with him— preferable to being alone. It didn't seem so bad to spend the rest of her life with someone she genuinely trusted to take care of her. "I hoped that I would heal and grow to be in love with him, the way you hear about it happening in arranged marriages. You just convince yourself you're too broken to know what a good man is, so you just shut up and take what you get. And rationalize not having any kind of passion or romance."

The couple married in July 2008 at Fort Rucker, Alabama. They had decided together that they wouldn't have kids. Kyle would be happy being a stepfather to Dylan, her son from a previous relationship. They were able to take a short honeymoon before Kyle left for training at Fort Gordon, Georgia. Jo had made an appointment to get an IUD a few weeks later, and insisted on using condoms in the meantime. But she got pregnant with the twins, quite by surprise. By 2012, after four years of marriage, she and Kyle were separated.

The decision to end the marriage was a gradual one. Her diagnosis forced her to give up her career, which led to simmering resentment toward Kyle, who was still on active duty. So active, in fact, that he was working sixty-hour weeks, leaving Jo to raise the twins alone on a tiny Army base where she didn't know anyone, far from her family in Missouri. This was after a complicated pregnancy, months of bed rest, and an emergency C-section to save the lives of the babies, who were born prematurely. After giving birth, she was fighting severe postpartum depression and anxiety, on top of the depression she'd brought home from Iraq. For a few years, "we were just in survival mode," she says.

But as things in their lives calmed down, she began to see clearly the chasm between them. "We had no business being married, that's the long and the short of it," she says now. Even though they were mostly miserable and ended up divorcing, their marriage is of the type that society considers "normal": a gainfully employed (and non-criminal) husband, two kids, a stay-at-home mom. She's had that experience, the one we often think prison wives must be incapable of. Jo lived it. And it didn't work.

Later, I run this story by relationship expert and author Tracy McMillan. McMillan's father was in and out of prison her whole life, so she is familiar with the dynamic of love behind the walls. Given Jo's trajectory—being with abusive men, then with a good one, then with one in prison—McMillan posits, "When you get out of the honeymoon phase and into long-term attachment and the person is available, you're like, *What's wrong? What's missing? This feels weird*," she says. "What's missing is the drama you've become accustomed to. The person is actually there, emotionally available, and, to people who have been traumatized, that can feel foreign and overwhelming."

Jo had told me on the eve of her wedding that her time in Iraq had opened her eyes to the variety of experiences in the world, and complicated her simplistic view of good and evil. As a corpsman, she met mothers who brought their children in with "diseases like rickets, [which] we haven't seen in first-world countries in hundreds of years." Already a mother herself (Dylan was eleven and living with his grandparents in Missouri), Jo would spend her sleepless nights rocking sick babies to sleep. "It wasn't hard to look at those kids and see my son. It wasn't hard to look at a mother and think, *What if that were my child? What would I need right now?* I'd need a drink of water and a hug." The enemy, she soon realized, was as often as not a mother just like her.

This understanding of people and the limiting labels assigned to them helped open her mind to Benny in prison. It also gave her a singular insight into the kind of mindset he must maintain to survive the dangers in his midst. Whether from fights, simple illnesses, or suicide, people die in prison all the time. The latest official figures date back to 2014, when the Bureau of Justice Statistics reported 4,980 deaths among prisoners in correctional facilities, a 3 percent increase from 2013. In state prisons, 275 people out of every 100,000 died, the highest rate since they started compiling data in 2001. According to the Marshall Project, one in five inmates has tested positive for the coronavirus, and more than 1,700 people have died from COVID-19 behind bars, where social distancing proved impossible.

"You get dead from being distracted," Jo says. "If you're thinking about the fight you got in with your wife or that your home is being foreclosed, then you don't see the copper wire stretched across the street or the guy with the cell phone. So you put that stuff away." She can hear it in Benny's voice when she asks him how things are and he says he can't talk about it. She knows not to pry, and can anticipate the kind of PTSD he will come home with.

She will understand Benny in just the way Kyle understood her—or the way he once had. When, shortly after their divorce, Jo mentioned offhandedly that she'd sent a prisoner a message online, Kyle shrugged it off. But when Benny and Jo's relationship started progressing, he was less than enthused. Soon he seethed with jealousy. And it came out in hostility. When Jo would take a call from Benny, Kyle would loudly tell the boys to come with him because their mom was busy on the phone again. Or the phone would ring and he would slam stuff and mutter under his breath. Finally, when things became serious with Benny, Jo confronted Kyle: "I said, 'I'm sorry I hurt you. And I'm sorry I don't feel about you the way you wish I felt about you. But I am done feeling like I need to apologize for being happy. Whether you like it or not, this is happening. Either we can respect each other or make plans to live separately.'"

They decided to respect each other. As we lounge on Jo's bed, she points out, "You'll notice how there are no pictures of Benny in the common areas of the house." Here in her bedroom, though, they are everywhere.

———————

"OKAY, WE SHOULD get ready for the baby shower," she tells me. We swipe on some lip gloss and say bye to the boys, who are reading books on opposite ends of the window seat while Kyle plays a video game in his room. We walk through the apartment complex in the rain. Jo uses a key card to access various hallways and buildings. The vastness of this place feels something like a city unto itself. She shows me the gym and the outdoor pool, now closed for the season. She and the boys will be there every day once school is out, she says. In the claustrophobia and redundancy of the towering apartment buildings, this feels like the kind of place where at least people know each other.

Like this baby shower Jo has been invited to on this rainy Sunday afternoon. Though we have arrived at the appointed time, friends and moms and aunts are still hanging up streamers and laying out a buffet in the party room of the complex. Many of the women in attendance are the Bus Stop Moms, as Jo has anointed them, women whose kids all go to the same school. I remember her telling me way back that several of the BSMs had shunned her upon learning of her new husband's whereabouts. That said, given what I know of Jo, I have a hard time picturing her skating comfortably on the surface of things. This is the woman who recently told me, "I don't do small talk. I want to talk about sex and existentialism and death and what makes you tick. *Tell me who you are. Tell me what you dream about at night and what scares you and what keeps you up at night.*" So, not exactly morning pleasantries.

Like Jo and Kyle, many of her neighbors are active military and/or military wives. She sees the similarities between prison wives and military wives, having been both: "Whether you have a husband on a prison yard or on a battlefield, he may never come home," she says matter-of-factly. "The big difference, of course, is that I can't brag on what my husband does," she says. She quickly offers a caveat: "I mean, I'm not ashamed to be a prison wife, or to be Benny's wife. I'm so dang proud of who that man is! But I choose not to broadcast our reality to strangers." I ask her what she tells people, like these neighbors, for example, about Benny, should inquiring minds demand more intel. "I'll say we are a bicoastal couple. He's in Oregon attending college on a scholarship. He's getting a business degree and he'll come home when he's done," she says, taking a bite of pasta salad. "All the details therein are true." (The college "scholarship" is being footed by the taxpayers of Oregon, but I don't mention it.)

I'm eager to get Jo's opinion on the identity that is Prison Wife. Since walking her down the visiting-room aisle nine months ago, I've become more immersed in this world, mostly through the voyeuristic following of prison-wife Instagram accounts and Facebook groups. I've noticed a certain dynamic threaded through many a prison-wife profile: *I, prison wife, am his queen. He, prisoner, is my king. I am chaste and devoted, counting down the days until he comes home, tending to his needs in the meantime. I'm saving money. I'm writing letters and showing up looking my best on visiting day. I'm holding him down. I am ride-or-die.*

"I do not want to ride, nor do I want to die," Jo deadpans. "I want to be in bed by 8 p.m." She laughs. "Don't get me wrong, I love my husband. But to walk around bragging that you're a prison wife? That's not something to brag about. You're not a gangster. You're not hard because your man is. You're going to brag because your husband got coked out of his head and did some dumb shit?" She punctuates her monologue with a slow clap. "Go, you! Try working for a living. Try being productive in your life. I know women my age who say, *Oh yeah, he's my king and I'm his queen.* Shut up! You are having trouble paying your light bill because your man is in prison. You are not a gangster queen. Stop glamorizing it."

This is the kind of tough-love advice Jo is known and loved for in her community. I ask her what questions she gets most, and one is about money. Money, in any relationship, is tricky. The prison framework only amplifies what is already complicated for couples on the outside. And when incomes are so disparate—no one on the outside is earning mere cents an hour; even working a minimum wage job is an exponentially bigger paycheck than anything you can make (legally) in prison—money can become more of an issue. "For a lot of women, money is a big form of control," Jo says. "Some guys want to know that you are spending every penny on them. That's not behavior I would tolerate in any relationship."

I ask her how money breaks down in her marriage. She says she and Benny keep to a very strict budget. Bills get paid first, then she socks away a few hundred for savings, then operates on whatever is left for the rest of the month. But whatever is left is still a significant chunk of money. And it mostly goes toward making their relationship feasible.

In prison, communication costs are staggering. Their phone calls average about $150 a month. "I don't want my phone calls to go away!" she says. "They are a huge part of our relationship." They text every day, which is another $100 a month. A thirty-minute video visit, or "a date," one where she can wear sexier outfits like spaghetti strap tank tops and boy shorts that wouldn't pass muster in the prison visiting room, costs $9. And often the connection is crap and that money gets thrown into the abyss. Jo also sends Benny $100 a month for commissary, little comforts of food and hygiene products "to take the edge off," she says. "Everything costs money. But I'm not going to put myself in debt because of it. I tell him, 'You can't have cupcake money if I have life insurance payments to make.'"

Some months are better than others. A while back, Jo spent $700 to get Benny's name in his handwriting tattooed on her hip. They had to cut back that month, but both were happy with the result. If Benny were still working at the call center—a plum prison gig and, at $181 a month, one of the highest-paying—he'd be able to contribute more. But he recently got fired for getting "too big for his britches," as he put it: getting into conflicts with management, talking back to the people training him. He has since been working as a unit orderly, taking out garbage, sweeping floors, or "working fast food without the free burgers," as he describes it.

If Benny weren't in the picture, Jo says she'd spend the money saving for a tricked-out minivan, or more scuba lessons, which she has been enjoying when she can. She says she doesn't deprive herself, but her aggressive frugality in the name of her relationship suggests otherwise. "I'm in charge of my money and my life," she declares. "Partly that's because I am so independent, but also because that's not how a marriage is supposed to work. But Benny has never tried to manipulate me for money. If he asks me for something, I'll say yes, we can do it, or no, we can't. He's never pitched a fit."

I note how infantile the negotiation sounds. As the person on the outside taking care of all the dreary business of supporting a family, paying bills, and planning for the future, she essentially shoulders all the adult responsibility. And she herself has seen how often women fall into the trap of being manipulated. When I ask her if she'd be upset if she found out Benny was writing to other women on the side, she said she'd be far more devastated to learn that she'd been getting scammed for money.

We go home, and she makes dinner for the kids. I read them a book on extreme weather and they ask incisive questions about air pressure. After they're asleep in bed, we grab our coats and head to the car so Jo can drive just off the perimeter of the property, where she's able to smoke without breaking the rules. The vape just hasn't been cutting it. She lights a Marlboro and we sit in the dark with the engine off but the radio and windshield wipers on as the rain comes down.

For a rare moment, Jo is quiet. She's enjoying a hit of real nicotine, the victory of getting the kids to bed, the hard-won peace of another day down. Having spoken to Benny, she can loosen her vise grip on her phone. She had sounded upbeat and slyly flirtatious on their fifteen-minute phone call, the lightness in her voice a sharp contrast to the feeling of having to manage all the life details that arise throughout the day. Now she can exhale. But the peace feels hollow. The real payoff is still so far away. It's like Benny's ghost is with us in the car, a visitation.

I think about the metaphor I've often heard from prison wives: It's like being pregnant. At first, I thought they meant that prison is akin to a period of waiting. It wasn't until I got pregnant myself, while writing this book, that I actually understood what they meant. It's not just the waiting. It's the constant presence of a person who is always with you but not yet here.

"I sometimes have to wonder if I'm crazy," she says softly. "There are days when I am the spokeswoman for all things prison wife. And there are others when I drop the boys at the bus and crawl into bed and cry, I miss him so much. And then I have to make sure I'm not just living in a fantasyland." It's not just the cruelties of time and space that get Jo down. As much as she knows and trusts Benny, she hears the external chorus of judgment that says *This relationship is not real* and *You won't last* and *Oh yeah, easy for you to be in love when you've never lived with the person.*

But it would be crazier *not* to let those voices creep in. Who doesn't understand toggling back and forth in matters of love, even in the best of circumstances? Anyone who claims absolute certainty is suspect to me. Jo opening up about her doubts reassures me more than when she postures about how confident she is about Benny. Worrying that you're insane is a mark of sanity.

IT'S STILL RAINING the next morning. We herd the kids onto the bus and get in the car to run errands. "If I wanted to be in cold and gray, I might as well live in Oregon," Jo says. We return a battery to AutoZone, stop at the post office to mail a friend an old Kindle she's had lying around, and go to the Boy Scout shop to have the boys' latest badges stitched on their uniform shirts. When we enter Michael's, Jo announces that she must put figurative blinders on even to walk through. Even then, her eye catches on a nautical-themed photo box. On the drive over to Olive Garden for lunch, I ask her a question that's been plaguing me since I first met her and the other wives.

"It's really easy for me to see the ways you support Benny. How would you say he supports you?"

"Oh my goodness, that man puts up with so much crap from me," she says.

"But like what?" I ask. "The obvious counterargument is that he's stuck in prison for the next three years. What else does he have to do?"

"Do you have any idea how many men who are in prison don't support their women at all? Who expect it to be all about them?" she says. I can't see her eyes because she's driving, but I sense her anger building. Her cheeks are turning red. She pounds the steering wheel emphatically. "There are plenty of guys who will sit in there all damn day and tell you exactly what you want to hear, how beautiful and lovely you are. Benny calls me on my bullshit. He tells me I'm beautiful and lovely and perfect, but he also tells me when I'm being a huge pain in the ass or ridiculous about stuff."

"That makes you feel supported?"

"Yeah, because he is doing the real work of the relationship and making me the best possible version of myself."

"And in past relationships this hasn't been the case?"

"Yeah, because they were too busy doing their own thing. They didn't care enough about me to help me improve in any way. Not because he wants me to be different than I am, but because he loves me enough to refuse to accept behavior from me that's less than, and I do the same for him. The biggest way I feel supported by him is that if I tell him what I need, there's nothing he won't do."

"But what can he actually do? Right now?"

"He's been known to get up at work and walk out to call me, which could cost him a write-up and his job. He will tell his boss, 'I have to call my wife, she needs me.' He puts me ahead of everybody in his life. He can't send me gifts or support me financially, and maybe that's what women on the outside are accustomed to thinking of as support."

We stop at a red light and she turns to look me directly in the eyes.

"When is the last time your boyfriend sat down and spent half an hour dedicated to just you if you're having a bad day? No Facebook, no TV, no game on in the background. Just sat and said, 'Talk to me. What's going on in your head, your heart? How do I make this better for you?' When is the last time most of us just took our partner's hand and looked into their eyes and talked to them for half an hour?"

I think what I can't bring myself to say: this isn't that rare, or at least it shouldn't be. It seems like the bare minimum, to listen and be present for the people we love. But the truth is, it did take me a long time to find the right partner, and not for lack of trying. And not everyone does.

At lunch, we order two glasses of white wine, partly to cut the tension lingering from the previous conversation and partly because it feels decadent to indulge in all-you-can-eat salad and breadsticks washed down with Barefoot chardonnay. We joke that Jo had a destination wedding, but not on purpose. We talk about some of Jo's previous relationships, before Kyle, before Benny.

"Nobody needs any reminder I've been married four times," she laughs. To summarize: she had valid reasons for leaving her marriages—her first husband was an abusive alcoholic, the second couldn't keep his dick in his pants. The third didn't have any egregious problems, but they didn't work as a couple. But what strikes me most about Jo is her resilience. It sometimes seems superhuman. She told me about leaving a violent marriage with her first husband and living in a homeless shelter for six months when Dylan was two years old.

"I worked two or three jobs at a time back then. I sold plasma, worked construction, worked as a preschool teacher, a boat mechanic, security, day labor. Anything that would pay me. That's why I joined the reserves: I needed the extra two hundred dollars a month to eat. I was twenty-three, twenty-four. Eventually I saved up enough money to move into government housing. I had daycare vouchers for Dylan and I was a daycare teacher during the day and a pharmacy tech at night. I slept three to four hours a night for three to four years. Then I got a job working at the county jail and started making good money, eleven dollars an hour, for the first time in my life. That's when I met Brian, my second husband. Dumb—so dumb. God, I was dumb. But that's what happens when you have no self-esteem. You accept behavior you shouldn't."

I ask her how she got her self-esteem back.

"It was a long process," she says. "I got tired of being married to a guy who constantly sticks his dick in other people and said I wanted a divorce. I think the biggest piece was being married to Kyle and having a safe spot to heal, learn who I was. Another big part was getting to a thought process not of *What is wrong with these guys?* but *What is wrong with me?* Not in a self-condemnation way, but *What am I doing that is contributing to this big neon sign above my head that says 'Treat me like shit?'* I was the consummate people pleaser—whatever you needed me to be, I would do. I was the exact opposite when I met Benny. I said, 'This is it. Take it or leave it.'"

This renaissance in her self-esteem coincided with finding the Strong Prison Wives community, which was a game changer. "I discovered girlfriends for the first time that centered around building each other up. That's why I'm so passionate about supporting other prison wives. Having conversations with girls like, *What are you learning? How are you paying your bills? Where do I help you get stronger? How do I build you up?*"

It seems counterintuitive that dating a man in prison would be the key to building one's self-esteem. But for Jo, it was just that. It was a coming home to herself.

We order chocolate cake for dessert.

"Yay, I'm a fat kid!" Jo exclaims, and laughs off the previous conversation like it's nothing.

———

THE NEXT MORNING, the sun finally breaks through the clouds. We get the boys ready for school and drop them at the bus stop. Jo drives me to the train station. Her day will entail more errands, maybe a workout, maybe a nap, depending on how her fibromyalgia is behaving. She and Benny are coauthoring a workbook for prison couples, and she may work on that. She'll see what she feels up to.

At the conference in Dallas, I had gone to see a lecture by Dr. Avon Hart-Johnson. She's a leading academic researcher studying the plight of prison wives and has given it a name: vicarious imprisonment. Over the course of hundreds of interviews and surveys, Dr. Hart-Johnson has found that women who are tangentially connected to the criminal justice system because of their romantic relationships can exhibit symptoms of trauma, depression, and withdrawal that become their own kind of punishment. They may experience "social loss." As she writes in her book, *The Symbolic Imprisonment of African American Women: A Legacy of Mass Incarceration*, a prison wife "may feel singled out as different and somehow tainted by their mate's incarceration." As a result, she might not make friends or go out. Feeling guilty that she has freedoms her lover does not, she will "emulate the mate's state of incarceration (reduced food intake, restricting television, no sex, and reduced social interactions)." Whether out of guilt for enjoying the free-world pleasures that her husband cannot or shame because of his situation, she can end up in a self-made prison of isolation.

What I see in Jo isn't that. Not quite. She is still very much involved in the wider world, in being a good friend, in studying for her degree, in being a mom. But Benny haunts her. He's the ghost butting in when she debates whether she can afford to get a massage or if that money would be better saved for when he comes home. He's in the phone, ringer always on and within arm's length. He's in the countdown app, in the moments on the clock ticking by till bus stop pickup, till bedtime, till she checks to see if she got a good-night text. He's another day down. Jo hasn't stopped living, but life, real forward momentum, feels on hold. The waiting itself is a kind of prison, isn't it?

FIVE

JACQUES AND IVIÉ

THE EVENING I meet Jacques is one of the first in summer's full bloom. We rendezvous for an early dinner at Rosemary's, a corner trattoria in New York's West Village. The sun casts a warm glow through the restaurant, glinting in the pitchers of water and the mason-jar flower arrangements on the worn wooden tables. The hostess informs me that Jacques is already seated and waiting for me. (Jacques is not his real name, as he requested the use of a pseudonym.)

A dashing figure rises from the table to greet me, pecking me on each cheek. Jacques is tall and slim, with close-cropped salt-and-pepper hair. He's wearing dark jeans and a button-down shirt and has the easy bearing of many a middle-aged man in this affluent neighborhood.

I've heard so much about Jacques that meeting the man feels like encountering a minor celebrity. His reputation precedes him. He is a former diplomat of Belgian extraction who's worked for the UN and the Canadian government and has traveled all over the world, making quite a bit of money. (His most recent annual salary was a quarter of a million dollars, a stat I've heard on many occasions.)

This was the thumbnail I got from Ivié (pronounced Ee-Vee-Ay), his wife of six years. She resides in Bedford Hills Correctional Facility for Women, in upstate New York, one of the few maximum-security women's prisons in the country. The couple met on WriteAPrisoner .com and married a year later. And, having the good fortune to fall in love in New York State, every six weeks they get to spend a glorious forty-eight hours together on a family visit, or conjugal. This type of unsupervised, overnight visit is commonly known as a "trailer," because the encounter always takes place in a mobile home on prison property. Since women account for only 7 percent of the total U.S. prison population, Jacques and all prison husbands are a minority. He's one of the even fewer who met their brides while incarcerated, and one of the fewer still who has consummated his marriage.

At this stage, several years into my reporting, the partners I've spoken with on the outside have been exclusively prison wives. I know their values, their concerns, their identity. I feel much more skeptical meeting a man who went on a pen-pal website to meet a female prisoner—perhaps because the dating pool on the outside seems more robust for men, or maybe because a woman behind bars seems more vulnerable. So what of the prison husband? And what of *this* prison husband, an accomplished, handsome man with a French accent and a spy novel career, who married a woman serving at least fifty-five years behind bars?

———

I FIRST BECAME acquainted with the couple in the roundabout way that had become familiar to me. In my interview with the criminologist Scott Bonn, who studies popular fascination with serial killers, I had posited that there were more women who go for famous murderers than there were male admirers getting starry-eyed for murderesses. He quickly disavowed me of the notion. "Why are we fascinated with Jodi Arias?" Arias was twenty-eight years old when she stabbed her boyfriend, Travis Alexander, twenty-seven times before shooting him in the head. She claimed self-defense but did not convince the jury.

"She's young and beautiful and looks like she's supposed to be the victim, not the perpetrator," he said, referring to the media's distorted portrayal of victims as young white women. "Same thing with Pamela Smart."

Pamela Smart was a twenty-three-year-old teacher when she was convicted of conspiring with a fifteen-year-old student paramour and three of his friends to murder her husband. She is currently serving a sentence of natural life. The 1995 movie *To Die For* is based on her story, with Nicole Kidman portraying a Smart-esque character. Smart has been in Bedford Hills prison for almost thirty years. After hearing Bonn's argument, I had figured she had probably received groupie fan mail in her time. I had sent her a letter to ask, and she'd written back.

"Yes, I have received 'amorous' letters over the years," she affirmed. "I do not encourage any of them though, and purposefully keep things on a friendship level. I think some of the men who have written are just lonely or feel they might find a 'captive' audience in me but I'm just not interested in having a relationship through visits and the mail."

She also had a view on the MWI experience: "I think that it's selfish to expect someone else to have to go through the pains of loving someone in prison. I mean, if one was already in a relationship, and then the person ended up in prison, that would be different, but I just can't imagine starting something new."

She told me, however, about a woman she knows on the inside "who wrote a book about her relationship." The book, I would soon find out, is a self-published memoir called *25 to Love: A True Pen-Pal Fairytale*. "She'd been in prison for at least ten years when she put an ad on an inmate pen-pal site. Long story short, a man in Canada who used to work for the UN answered her ad, they corresponded, he visited, they got married, and he moved to Connecticut to be closer to her. They are very much in love. I spoke to Ivié and she said you could write her."

And so I did.

ON THE COMMUTER train to Bedford, a posh suburb in the Hudson Valley, I read more about Ivié's crimes. The person described in news articles from the time doesn't jibe with the friendly letters and phone calls I've been exchanging with the fifty-two-year-old woman. A *New York Daily News* article from the time, "Hooker Led Trio on Spree," proclaims:

> She led a gang of born killers who robbed, beat and on two occasions, murdered suburban men looking for sex in the city as part of a get-rich-quick scheme, police said. Cops believe [the] Manhattan call girl and her bloody threesome robbed "more than a dozen" Johns before they were nabbed after sticking up a midtown hotel. "You remember the movie 'Natural Born Killers?'" said Detective Michael Duggan of the NYPD. "They were like that. They were very cold-hearted, very separated from reality. They were more brazen, more bold-faced than anything I've ever seen . . . Sociopaths was the only way to describe them."

It sounds like the plot of the 2019 film *Hustlers*, also based on a true story, in which strippers drugged and robbed men from Wall Street, but with a body count. I feel nervous.

But not nervous enough, it turns out, to read the visiting guidelines of this facility closely enough. I make what turns out to be the very wrong assumption that dress code protocol at a women's prison is more relaxed than at a male facility. Having set out in the morning when it was still dark, I had pulled on a pair of leggings and a massive sweater that covered any part of me that could be construed as sexual (unless you're really into calves), thus turning my figure into something of a bell.

I'm stuffing my bag into a tiny locker when a maintenance man eyes me and says they probably won't let me in. "Leggings," he says. Leggings are deemed inappropriate for their form-fittingness.

I stand in an unoccupied children's play area, waiting to be summoned to reception by the corrections officers. The walls have construction paper flowers taped all over them to herald spring's arrival, but they somehow have the effect of making the already sad room, absent of children on this day, feel that much more depressing.

The guard buzzes me in. She looks me up and down and confirms it's a no-go. The maintenance man was right. I ask if I can just keep my long parka on to obscure the objectionable leggings. The sergeant on duty, along with three other male guards, comes over and assesses my outfit. Even though I'm completely covered up, their eyes make me feel as if I'm being undressed. The jacket is not an option. All jackets are required to be stowed in the locker, even though the walk from reception to visiting is outdoors and not short.

I feel foolish, having broken a prison-wife cardinal rule: always bring a backup outfit. I inquire if there's a Target or some such close by. They tell me of one several miles away, which deflates my hope, since I arrived by taxi. I debate just going home, but then I decide to hoof it back up the hill toward the train station to see if I can find a store that might sell pants inoffensive to the guards.

The town of Bedford is designed more for SUVs than for pedestrians. After heaving up the side of a highway for about a mile, like a mirage on the horizon there appears a sports screen-printing and trophy store. After pawing through racks of children's soccer team jerseys, I'm delighted to find a pair of women's XL sweats with the name of a local rec softball league emblazoned on them. I explain my plight to the store owner (though for simplicity's sake I tell her I'm visiting a friend at the prison) and inquire whether I might purchase these voluminous pants.

"Those are samples," she informs me. My face does not change. "I can't sell you those." My face changes. Taking pity on me, she sighs. "Let me see if I can find something in back."

She returns with a dusty pair of men's sweatpants she's dug up. She charges me five dollars for the detritus. As I'm leaving she asks, "What did your friend do?" Obviously, this woman has not been initiated into the customs of the incarcerated. In prison-wife circles, it's impolite to ask.

"Oh, it's a long story," I call back over my shoulder. I run back down the hill, hoping the window for visiting hasn't yet closed. Back at the prison, I pop into the restroom and pull the billowing maroon pants over my leggings. I saunter back to reception. The same guards are leaning on the counter.

"She's back!" yells the one who had banished me. She smiles. "This will work." She tells me now that she had actually tried to help, telling Sarge it was my first time visiting and I didn't know the rules. They copy my ID, take my picture, print out a visitor pass, send me through the metal detector, pat me down, stamp my wrist with ink visible only under a special light, and direct me through the double doors to the main facility. Even though I feel victorious after the pants episode, the sound of the heavy metal door locking behind me still makes my stomach drop.

Every prison visiting room is a little different, but also exactly the same. You've got the high school cafeteria feel, the worn board games and decks of cards soft at the corners, the elevated platform where the guards stand, a giant clock to ensure you never forget your time is limited. Here at Bedford Hills, one of the walls is mostly windows, letting in natural light, which makes all the difference in the world. I sit at my assigned table and wait for Ivié. I get some funny looks from the other clusters of prisoners and their guests but chalk it up to my enormous pants.

I'm greeted with a big hug from an arresting woman with expressive eyebrows, big hazel eyes, and unlined caramel skin. Ivié. "It's so nice to meet you," she says. Then she leans in and whispers, "But you're sitting on the wrong side. This is the side for inmates." Ah. We swap places.

Over the course of our three hours together, she tells me long, detailed stories, each punctuated with "to make a long story short." She often gets up and waves to other women and prison staff. Having been inside for twenty-four years, she knows most everyone here. I want to get a sense of who this woman is, beyond the tawdry tabloid headlines. More than anything, I want to understand how her marriage works. We start at the vending machines—a fruit cup and water for her, chips and soda for me—and she tells me the story of her life.

Ivié grew up in East New York, a poor Brooklyn neighborhood. She was close with her mother and her siblings, and proud of her Puerto Rican heritage. After graduating from high school, she went to secretarial school and moved to the city. "I lived in a fifth-floor walk-up in Gramercy, a tiny matchbox apartment. But it was *mine*," she tells me, still beaming with pride almost thirty years later. She was a young, beautiful woman, making good money as an executive assistant for a firm on Wall Street. It was the early nineties in New York, with the excesses of the 1980s still flowing. She went out every night, dancing at iconic places like the China Club, Palladium, and Limelight. If she woke up hungover and craving her mother's chicken soup, the only cure-all, her mom would send a container to the city in the back seat of a cab. Ivié's young life looked promising.

Then, at age twenty-five, she reconnected with a family member in California. She had flown out because another family member was having a medical emergency. During this reconnection with a man she hadn't seen for years, a long-suppressed memory became unlocked. Her body remembered that this man had sexually assaulted her as a child, between the ages of six and seven. Tapping into that trauma sent her down a dark path. She self-medicated to numb her pain. "I became addicted to crack and alcohol and became a prosti-tute," she tells me, without decoration.

She didn't become just any kind of sex worker. She became a dominatrix. This choice of profession was connected to the anger she felt toward her abuser, and her desire to punish men, she says. And, of course, the money she earned. "I was once paid six hundred dollars to walk around a guy's block six times and then let him snort coke off my toes," she tells me.

She was making a ton of money and spending most of it on drugs. In the summer of 1994, she hatched a plan to rob several of her for-mer clients. Ivié, going under the name Erica, and a young accom-plice who called herself Alexis promised sexual favors to get into the men's apartments, where the victims were then restrained and robbed by two male accomplices—Ivié's brother and her boyfriend at the time. In the end, a New Jersey man, James Polites, and a Long Island man, Joseph Fiammetta, were murdered. Ivié tells me she never in-tended for anyone to die. Though she herself did not kill anyone, the jury considered her the mastermind behind the operation. She was convicted of attempted assault, robbery, and burglary.

Even though she was not the killer, "nothing reduces the degree of my participation," she says today. "I made a terrible mistake that I have lived with every day since and will continue to for the rest of my life."

Her childhood sexual abuse was never made public nor was it mentioned at trial. She now believes that contextualizing this experi-ence for the judge might have resulted in a lesser sentence. She de-clined to give this information at trial because her mother was in the courtroom, and she wanted to spare her feelings. Since her victims were from New York and New Jersey, she was tried in both states, with each handing down maximum sentences: twenty-five years to life in New York and thirty years to life in New Jersey, to run consecu-tively. At the time of her sentencing, she was under the impression that these years would run concurrently. There is a chance that she could stay in the New York prison system for the rest of her life, or that she could get transferred to New Jersey at some point, to begin serving that thirty-year to life sentence. The future is unknown. She went into Bedford Hills in 1994, at age twenty-eight. She has served twenty-four years thus far. The earliest she could hope to get out would be at age eighty-three.

"Getting arrested saved my life," she tells me. "If I hadn't been, I would've died of drugs."

For the past two and a half decades, she has been making the best of her time. A prolific artist, she has had her paintings in shows for prisoners and created the backdrops for musical revues the women put on, the most recent being "Bedford Sings Broadway." She participated in the dogs program, where inmates live with and train dogs who will become service animals. She trained the Labradors Athena, George, and Tiki. She works as a Spanish interpreter in the law library, and facilitates workshops for the Alternatives to Violence Project. She earned her GED, and this coming May she will graduate with her B.A. in psychology from the College of New Rochelle, through a satellite program they offer inside. She insists on staying positive and busy. "It makes the time fly," she says.

In 2010, she posted an ad on WriteAPrisoner.com. A friend had had some luck on the site and urged her to do it. She initially resisted, thinking it would be "crazy people from Craigslist." But she relented, and wrote:

> I'm NOT looking for any Pity.
> I'm NOT searching for any Pennies,
> NOR, am I looking for a Pen-Pal . . .
> What I NEED, are lots of Prayers &
> A POTENTIAL PARTNER!
> So, IF you're between the ages of 29-50, Disease

& Drug Free, Healthy, Intelligent & Preferably Tall . . .
TO BE CONTINUED . . .

The ad posted on April Fool's Day. The irony made her laugh.

Her prophecy about getting attention from loons was realized, at least at first. One correspondent was a giant bald man who in her estimation "looked like a child molester." Another asked her to send him her pubic hair. The ad was about to expire and, given the response, she was not keen to renew. In her memoir, she writes that she prayed for one more letter, a letter from Mr. Perfect.

And a letter arrived. It was from a six-foot-tall, twice-divorced, multilingual, physically fit Belgian, now residing in Canada. He prided himself on his relationship with his three daughters, with whom he had never missed a visit or a child support payment, he said. He told her he'd come across her ad, and wrote, "I know that you don't want any pity, I get that, that much sadness and loneliness were expressed, very poetically it is true, but expressed nonetheless. And it made me sad, too. If I write to you though it is not because of that, but because of who you are. You sound proud and artistic and I like it."

He rattled off a bit of his résumé, including the far-flung locales of his travels in Europe, Africa, and Asia: "I could take you on a guided tour of these places trying to turn perfumes, images and sounds into words, with anecdotes included."

God had answered her prayers.

———

GOD, PERHAPS, BUT also the World Wide Web. After my first conversation with Ivié, I feel very curious to square her image of Jacques, sophisticated continental diplomat, with that of a man who writes to female prisoners via pen-pal sites. Not to generalize (well, to generalize a little bit), but he doesn't seem the type. First of all, he's a man. From what I've seen in various prison family support groups, the vast majority of people (at least vocally) supporting loved ones on the inside are female. This is borne out by the raw numbers: 93 percent of the U.S. prison population is male. (Yet the number of women being imprisoned has been growing at an alarming clip. Women's incarceration has increased by more than 700% between 1980 and 2019, according to the Sentencing Project.) Though of course there are same-sex couples within that number, and people who are unpartnered, the lion's share of romantic partners on the outside are female.

The number gets whittled down even further, though, when it comes to straight men who pursue women in prison. Men seem less likely to endure the hardships of a prison relationship—navigating visitation, yielding to having one's world revolve around the axis of phone calls, the lack of sex. Men don't have the same pride in holding down somebody in prison, in sacrifice, in staying home on a Friday night and writing letters, in being a "good man" the way ladies I've met strive to be "good women."

And, according to Dr. Danielle Rousseau, a Boston University professor of criminal justice, specializing in gender and justice, who has worked in both male and female prisons, "it is far less likely for women to be on the pen-pal sites. Women are more relational, and the female prison environment makes it safer to do that. It's quite social. Women are much more willing to seek out connection within the institution, whether that's through platonic or romantic relationships inside." Eighty percent of women who are jailed or imprisoned are mothers. These women spend their emotional resources reconnecting with their children. "Women who go to prison are far more likely to be primary caretakers of dependent children, versus men, who are not," Rousseau says. "In my research and clinical practice, the women's first drive as far as connection is to stay connected to their children. Perhaps they are less concerned with finding outside connection with a male pen pal instead of writing to and getting visits from their children."

The challenges facing female prisoners are distinct from those of their male peers. In addition to the vast majority of incarcerated women being mothers, they are also a highly traumatized group. Some 75 to 90 percent of them have been the victims of sexual or physical violence. Yet unlike men, most women in prison are not there for violent crimes. Eighty-five percent of women imprisoned in New York State, for example, are there for nonviolent crimes—drug possession, shoplifting, and fraud, to name a few. And in a 2011–12 National Inmate Survey of more than eighty thousand respondents, 42 percent of women in prison and 35.7 percent of women in jails identified as lesbian or bisexual. That is higher than the figures seen in the general U.S. population by a factor of about ten. In recent decades, women's incarceration has grown at twice the rate of men's, and a disproportionate number of them are Black and Latinx.

And yet, despite these distinctions—women coming into prison with histories of trauma, as primary caretakers, as LGBTQ+, and with convictions for nonviolent crimes—most women's facilities operate according to a model designed for violent men. Routine protocols like strip searches, supervised showers, and physical restriction can be triggering experiences. And, given that 70 percent of corrections officers are men, the inherent power dynamic itself can be highly troubling. Women are often denied necessities like tampons and bras and are forced to buy these from commissary at an inflated rate. Because there are fewer facilities for women, they lack the kind of educational and rehabilitative programming found in men's prisons. And while women's disciplinary infractions tend to be nonviolent, like talking back to an officer, they still result in the reduction of privileges that a fight among men would earn. The rule book is the same, but the population and their needs are very different.

So, for a variety of systemic and social reasons, a female prisoner is less likely to seek a pen pal than a male one is. And beyond the raw numbers and the likelihood of finding the right female pen pal, the contours of Jacques's life differentiate him from other prison wives. He's a man out in the world—well traveled, erudite, earning a healthy living in the Canadian bureaucracy. Jo and other prison wives have children to tend to. Their lives are more mired in caretaking and day-to-day responsibilities. While Jacques also has kids, he is not the sole custodian. He has a higher degree of freedom than the ladies, and more social privileges. So why write to a woman with two life sentences for her involvement in a murder? Every minute, he seems more and more the unicorn Ivié made him out to be.

But when I listen to Jacques narrate how he happened upon the site, his experience strikes a familiar chord. Like Jo and virtually every other MWI prison wife I have met, Jacques stumbled into the love of his life. He wasn't trolling pen-pal sites. Instead, as he tells it, he was conducting professional research.

IN 2011, JACQUES was living in Quebec and working in the health department, overseeing plans for all Canadian civil servants, including correctional officers. He had to visit a few Canadian prisons for his job. Around the same time, he also stumbled across the documentary TV show *Beyond Scared Straight*, in which juvenile delinquents are, well, scared straight by older, wiser offenders. Taken with the concept, he did a quick Google search for inmate-run programs to see what info he could dig up so that he might take a similar approach in Canada. That's how he came upon the website WriteAPrisoner.com. (Perhaps the algorithm has changed since, because when I do the same search eight years later, the pen-pal site does not come up, not even on the tenth page of search results.)

He clicked on the site and saw Ivié's profile on the front page. "I thought, *Oh my God, what an interesting person. My ex-wife—also a* diplomat—had been sent to India and took our kids with her, I had time, and I thought, *Why not send her a letter?*" He recalls that Ivié had a "very dramatic Shakespearean expression" and "a beauty, a grace, a sadness about her picture." He thought her profile was a nice bit of poetry. He attempted to click to send her a message electronically, but the link was broken. He'd have to send her an old-fashioned missive. He almost didn't write. But then he did.

I observe that the timing seems particularly charmed—the fact that Ivié's ad was soon to expire, the fact that he nearly decided against sending a letter but changed his mind. Jacques informs me that he usually doesn't believe in these sorts of things whatsoever. But "I think there's a strange and dynamic coordination of events, yeah," he admits.

The letter he got back from Ivié was "twenty-five pages of excitement. I thought, *Is she crazy?*"

Ivié confesses that the letter she sent back to Jacques was a bit over the top, even for someone as passionate as she is. She just couldn't believe God had answered her prayers to a T. She spent an entire night writing to him—forty pages, by her memory—sharing her accomplishments, her hobbies, her dreams, and even info on the Family Reunion Program for conjugal visits for immediate family. Like spouses. She also sent him a ten-page report from her trial, her psychological profile, and a synopsis of her life. She mailed her letter overnight priority for $25, a fortune for someone who makes less than a dollar an hour.

But the next day she felt embarrassed by how hot she had come in. She sent another letter, apologizing.

Looking back, Jacques says, "I thought it was the excitement of a child, almost. And I don't say that in a demeaning way. But I thought, *Wow, this is overboard.*" Her subsequent apology reassured him. So Jacques wrote back. In the beginning, they were exchanging a letter a day. But what did it feel like to be corresponding with a person who had charges like Ivié's?

"If you listen to the news articles," he tells me over a cheese plate at Rosemary's, "then she's the most evil thing since Attila the Hun and Adolf Hitler." He read everything that was published about her at the time in the *Daily News* and the *New York Post*, a newspaper "not known for its nuance," he concedes. "It was a shock. I knew it was murder, but to have all the details was impressive. But then, on the other side, I had her letter. It was hard to reconcile the crime with the person."

Though he makes no excuses for the heinousness of the crime, he also acknowledges the context of his wife's life then. "She grew up in a horrible neighborhood, and her crack cocaine consumption at the time was akin to that of Charlie Sheen. I believe people who are not evil can commit murder under certain circumstances." Because of Ivié's sensitive nature, Jacques maintains, she felt the pain of her childhood even more profoundly, and it had boomeranged back in an ugly way: "I believe sensitive people can become meaner monsters. When you attack them, you put them in a feeling of hurt and betrayal and it gives you a mean badass." He tells me that her boyfriend at the time was really the architect behind the plan and that she was only incidentally involved. When she heard that one of the victims had died, she was "crying, out of her mind. The portrait they had of her as an evil gang-leader dominatrix is not what happened at all."

Ivié was up front with him about the repressed trauma that had come flooding back to her. "I realized it was a complex picture of a complex situation," he says. Before the murders, "she had a good job, making good money. Then something broke in her," setting her off on the path toward drug addiction and sex work to fund her habit. So, like Jo, Jacques had put together a composite portrait of Ivié that went beyond the headlines. And they got to know each other, beyond the rap sheets. If you believe in second chances, it's an inspiring story.

JACQUES, UNLIKE IVIÉ, had a relatively stable upbringing. He was the product of a two-parent household. Born in Belgium, he grew up in Montreal before moving to Quebec City, where his father got a job as a computer engineer. His dad led the digitization of the Quebec government, designing a mainframe system for all of its business, including payroll. Jacques earned his B.A. from Laval University and an M.A. in diplomacy in Switzerland. While earning his master's in Geneva, he interned with the United Nations for six months, which turned into a job. His work took him to India, Brazil, Cameroon, and Tunisia.

In a now familiar refrain, Jacques maintains that in the beginning "there was no romantic intention whatsoever." After the furious exchange of letters over several months—which, as Ivié writes in her book, made her feel like "Cinda-Fucken-Rella"—she asked if he would ever consider being something more than pen pals. He responded that, yes, theoretically he could. "I have a very open and broad mind," he tells me. In a short note, she invited him to come visit:

> Listen,
> paper holds all the B.S. ink puts
> on it, you're going to have to come and
> deliver the ink in person and let me
> pinch you, because you're a little-teeny-
> weenie-too-good-to-be-true!

His eldest daughter was studying in Manhattan at the time, so Jacques tacked on a visit to Bedford in the spring of 2011.

Ivié tried not to let herself get too excited about the prospect of meeting Mr. Perfect. Rather than jazzing up her look with accessories, she consciously wore her state greens and no makeup. When she was called for her visit, she was shaking. She walked up behind him in the visiting room and said, "Excuse me, is this seat taken?" Her attraction was instant. In her memoir (narrated in the third person), she writes that at that first visit she "melted, as he totally stole her heart and swept her off her feet. At 44 years old, Ivié had never felt anything like it." Then she heard his French accent: "Thank God for panty liners!" she writes.

Jacques was nervous before the meeting, too. He'd been in prisons in Canada, but never in America. He was particularly nervous to meet someone convicted of such a serious crime. Of their first meeting, he recalls, "She came from behind me. When you're in a prison to meet someone who was involved in murders and she grabs you from behind, you jump!" He remembers her shaking, too. But he found it to be a "charming moment."

Like many a prison spouse, he rejects the idea that he was attracted to Ivié because of her record. "Some people would put me in the same bag as people who fantasize about serial killers. I don't think it's the same at all. I don't think I'm fascinated by dangerous people. I just fell in love with a person who committed a crime."

When Jacques talks about what he loves about his wife, near the top of the list is her attraction to him. Some people don't want to join any club that would have them as a member. Some people are repelled by those who, curiously enough, love them back. But others lap up adoration. Jacques is in the latter category.

Here is where Jacques's receptivity toward dating a prisoner begins to make more sense: "It's very infectious to have someone who is that excited . . . [She] was completely thrilled with the possibility of being with me. It was intoxicating." Ivié has found her Mr. Perfect. Jacques has found someone whose love is total, unrelenting. "I'm the best thing she has. It's something I like. It's very clear she is giving me everything. Her love is whole," he says.

After a few months of letters and nine in-person visits, Ivié proposed to Jacques on a phone call. She just blurted it out, she says. In her book she writes that Jacques responded, "My darling, that was my line, but yes of course I will marry you!"

For Jacques, the possibility of intimacy made a tremendous impact on his decision to tie the knot: "It was 90 percent the trailer visits, to be frank. We got excited by the whole romantic arrangement of it all." I ask him whether, if Ivié had been in a state without conjugal visits, he still would have married her. "I don't think I would have," he admits. "I'm a lover and a romantic. I'm not a monk."

AND HERE LIES one big difference between prison wives and prison husbands. I think back to women who are committed to men serving life sentences. They often remain monogamous to these men they may never have sex with. I just can't see many men making the same sacrifice.

According to the New York Department of Corrections, the Family Reunion Program is meant to "provide approved inmates and their families the opportunity to meet for an extended period of time in privacy. The goal of the program is to preserve, enhance, and strengthen family ties that have been disrupted as a result of incarceration." But family visits didn't start out that way.

In the United States, conjugal visits grew out of racist Jim Crow attitudes. They started in the early 1900s at Mississippi State Penitentiary, commonly known as Parchman Farm. Sex workers were used as an incentive for work, a privilege that was limited to Black inmates in the segregated prison, out of racist beliefs about their insatiable sexual appetites. Scholar Columbus B. Hopper wrote the definitive history of Parchman Farm in 1962:

> [Sex workers] arrived every Sunday afternoon on a flatbed truck driven by a pimp as lordly as any who ride city streets in pink Cadillacs. The women did a thriving business at the individual camps which were scattered over the 22,000 acres

of prison land. According to a song written by an inmate of the era, the price of a prostitute's service was 50 cents, not a small amount during the Great Depression when many people worked a 12-hour day for a dollar.

Inmates and their wives or sex workers rendezvoused in home-spun "red houses," tiny huts whose moniker was meant to echo "red light districts." White prisoners were participating in conjugals at the Farm by the 1940s. The program was officially sanctioned by the prison in 1972, when the privilege was also extended to women, though they had to be legally married.

Today, only four states offer conjugal visits. Twenty years ago, seventeen states offered such programs. California initiated its pro-gram under Governor Ronald Reagan in 1968. But in 1974, the *Lyons v. Gilligan* decision determined that prisoners have no consti-tutional rights to conjugal visits with partners during their sen-tences. The suit was brought by two men with robbery charges who wanted to be able to experience intimacy with their wives in their prison visits. The complaint stated that the inmates "felt that sex and private displays of affection . . . were an important part of their relationship and marriage." The court disagreed. By the mid-nineties, tough-on-crime policies and victims' rights advocacy groups were calling to end programs such as college courses and conjugals in prison, as they were seen as "luxuries" for criminals. Mississippi, facing a $34 million deficit in its corrections budget, shuttered its program in 2014.

The United States goes against the grain compared to prisons in other countries, which build in time and privacy for prisoners and their loved ones. In India, conjugals for procreation are considered a fundamental human right. Canadian prisons allow family members and even common law spouses (if they were together for at least six months prior to incarceration) to visit in an apartment for three days every two months. Many Latin American prisons even allow private visits for unmarried inmates. In 2007, the Mexico City prison system allowed conjugal visits for same-sex partners.

American conjugal visits are more about families spending time together than about sex. Family visits typically take place in trailers on prison property, outfitted with cooking equipment, TVs, and bunk beds for kids. Different U.S. states have different versions. In Connecticut, prisoners and their spouses can't spend the night alone; the inmate's child must be there. In Washington, if two related inmates are in the same facility, such as siblings or a mother and daughter, they can arrange a joint visit with family members. Only a third of extended visits in the state are between spouses alone. Conjugal visits today are a far cry from Parchman Farm's shipping in sex workers for the afternoon.

Family visits are offered at only twenty-two of the fifty-two correctional facilities in the state of New York, and the length of a visit is typically forty-eight hours, with longer four-day visits available once or twice a year. And of the more than 92,000 people locked up in New York State alone (which is just five thousand fewer people than the population of the state capital, Albany), only a fraction of them are eligible. Prior to meeting Jacques, Ivié used the Family Reunion Program to spend time with her mother before she passed away. "I would style her hair and do her makeup," she says. "That time was so precious."

Research shows that conjugal visits have a positive effect on prison populations, lowering sexual violence and reducing rates of recidivism. In a 2012 study in the *American Journal of Criminal Justice*, researchers found that states with conjugal visiting programs had lower rates of sexual assaults among inmates than those without. And family connections are the number-one means of ensuring success once the imprisoned person comes home. The Minnesota Department of Corrections found in 2015 that a single visit correlated with a 25 percent drop in technical violations and a 13 percent decrease in new crimes upon release. The vast majority of criminologists agree that private, extended visits are of great benefit to all involved: the prisoner, the families, the community. Conjugals are a lifeline; unfortunately, they're a politically unpopular one.

———————

IVIÉ AND JACQUES had to wait months after their prison wedding to spend the night together. The process involved petitioning officials in the state legislature for approval. While that might sound absurdly bureaucratic to most, I can just feel Jo rolling her eyes. She and Benny are still waiting to consummate their marriage. Nine months into theirs, Jacques and Ivié were approved, for four nights and five days in a special "honeymoon trailer."

Husband and wife were racked with nerves their first time alone, though for different reasons. Jacques recalls worrying about the condition of the facilities: would it be "a crappy horrible place with dirty beds?" He found it to be a modest house with two bedrooms—one with a full bed, another with bunk beds—a living room, and a kitchenette. It took about two hours to go through security, as guards examined all the groceries and luggage piece by piece, bottle by bottle. Jacques went through an x-ray machine and got patted down. He was especially antsy about that part of the process, because he was sneaking in a small gift for his wife: a negligee—which he wore himself, under his clothes. "It was a little nightdress and it was suffocating me!" Were he to be questioned by the guards for this piece of contraband, he planned to explain that he was "a cross-dresser," as he put it.

Ivié, on the other hand, had been in prison for seventeen years and had not been with a man for even longer. She was nervous about her performance. As she told a friend, "I'm scared to death. I talk a lot of shit, but I just may freeze." She got some good coaching from her fellow prisoners on how to give a blow job and do a sexy striptease.

And, per her memoir, the coaching paid off, as she quips: "*9½ Weeks* has nada on *4 Nights & 5 Days*, absolutely nothing."

Since then, their trailer visits have taken on a pleasant rhythm. Every sixish weeks, they get to convene in near privacy. Ivié still has to step outside for count throughout the day. The ease of their lives improved when Jacques moved to Connecticut after being granted his green card in 2014. He resides about an hour away from Ivié, in a bucolic corner of the state where many New Yorkers have weekend homes. He had saved enough to not have to work but opts to sell wine at a local liquor store, owing his salesmanship to his accent. He spends his leisure time reading—he tells me he's recently enjoyed books by Camille Paglia and Jordan Peterson—and following politics.

His family has not been so enthusiastic about his move and marriage. "When I told my mother," he says, "she started to cry and told me I was disgracing the family. That was hard." He tried to soften the blow by explaining that he was doing it "mostly for the green card. It doesn't serve any purpose to try to make her understand. She's too old. She will get upset." I find it interesting that Jacques would make up a cover story about a green card marriage. I hadn't thought of his citizenship as a factor. But when he brings it up, it occurs to me that perhaps this was a third party in their relationship. Then again, he already held Canadian and Belgian citizenships when they married. Beyond being in closer proximity to Ivié and the prison, how could adding American citizenship really have benefited him?

Jacques has caught flak from his children, too. One of his daughter's friends from abroad was all set to visit her at Jacques's home in Connecticut, but when the friend's parents found out Jacques was married to a prisoner, the visit was canceled. His daughter was devastated. But he tries to use his marriage as a morality tale for his daughters about being tolerant and having an open mind.

Like prison wives, he has made significant social sacrifices for his relationship: "I lost friends. Some people don't talk to me anymore. At some point you have to be strong enough to face the ridicule of society. You have to see if what you're fighting for is worth it, and in my case I think it is."

The trailers definitely make it worthwhile to Jacques. Ivié will arrive at their appointed trailer a few hours before her husband, and she always goes through the same ritual: "I change into shorts, brew a pot of coffee, blast the radio, and clean every inch of the trailer with bleach, just like you'd do on your day off." In addition to the obvious benefits of physical touch and intimacy, Ivié enjoys experiencing a sense of normal domestic tranquility. The couple will barbecue in any weather, go for walks around the prison grounds, play games on an ancient Sega Genesis. But more than anything, she loves being of service to her husband: "I pamper him, give him manicures and pedicures; I like to cook for him." Prisoners are dependent upon their loved ones on the outside for so much. In those forty-eight hours, they can finally return a few favors.

For Jacques, "the visits are the happiest moments of my month. Those two days is a time to relax, time for romance, to share, to sit down with a person and have a coffee and talk for hours about everything you want to talk about. We take walks hand in hand. It's a romantic weekend getaway! It's very pleasant, we rarely fight." Jacques seems to enjoy himself but always makes it clear who the real beneficiary is: "It's for her that I do it, too. Can you imagine having a long prison sentence like that and for two days a month to hang out and live with your partner in a bungalow?"

These visits make all the difference in the world, but they do not offset the pain of the ending, the hard smack of reality. Ivié says her heart breaks every time she reaches the end of their forty-eight hours. She cries watching Jacques's car leave through the gate. "But you have to be grateful for what you have. There are women in here who don't get trailer visits," Ivié tells me. "I'm just grateful I have that time. That's how you get through."

IN THE SPRING of 2018, things are looking up for the couple. I visit Ivié in early April, and she is her usual effervescent self. We sit at the visiting tables, her with a Diet Coke and vanilla yogurt, me with Sun Chips and water. She is very focused on working on an appeal for her case. "I'm twenty-four years tired," she confesses. She hopes sales from her memoir can help underwrite the cost of the new lawyer Jacques has hired. She's urging him to set up a GoFundMe campaign for the same goal.

Ivié is also planning on presenting new evidence to a lawyer about the triggering traumatic event of confronting the abusive family member that sent her on a downward spiral to addiction and violence. She wants to get Oprah involved and asks me to send her information on organizations that advocate for victims of domestic violence to help her plead her case. Her college graduation is coming up, and she's working on getting the right outfit for the ceremony.

With Jacques, things are good. They're corresponding and talking on the phone regularly, marking days between their trailer visits. But she makes a confession. "I sometimes wonder if he is too good to be true," she says, peeling off the label on her soda. "Sometimes I want to pool all my money and hire a PI to follow him 24/7."

I wonder what the ethical expectations are for the prison husband. The consolidated prison-wife identity is so clear to me now, summed up in an Instagram post from Strong Prison Wives & Families: "If she's willing to struggle with you just to build with you, don't mess it up bro, she's a keeper." Loyalty. Sacrifice. Chastity, even in the face of life sentences, sans conjugal visits. I ask Ivié about her expectations for Jacques, particularly in terms of his faithfulness while she is in prison.

"I know things happen," she sighs. "If he cheats on me, I'd want to know about it. I'd rather be heartbroken with the truth." She looks crestfallen, considering the possibility. "I would just hope he uses a condom so when I'm home some lady doesn't come to answer the door with a baby in her arms."

I find the poignant realism she maintains refreshing. Rather than deny the possibility of infidelity, Ivié is pragmatic. She realizes things happen in even the best of situations, and to ask the free-world partner for total monogamy would be unreasonable. But then I think about how this is also a function of Jacques's gender. He's a man, and, so the conventional wisdom goes, men have needs. The assumption that he'll cheat on her is foremost in her mind, the most obvious betrayal.

When I next talk to Jacques, he reiterates their dynamic. "Her love for me is whole," he tells me on the phone from his home in Connecticut. "She would do anything to be the best possible partner in the situation. She writes to me regularly and sends me gifts and cards." I'm already aware that one principal draw of this situation is being with someone who has a singular focus on you. I think back to my incarcerated friend Sam and all the letters, emails, and cards he has sent me over the years.

But unlike the wives, Jacques doesn't seem to revel in the free-world sacrifice. Instead, he sees his role as the partner on the outside as benevolent, big, noble, charitable. "I was inspired by the movie *Amélie*," he says, referring to the film about the French sprite who takes pleasure in doing good deeds for others. "What would it be like to be the best person for someone else? You can decide to be very generous, give money to the poor, give to charities. But you do it for a lot of anonymous folk. This is to help *one* person, as an act of civic and human kindness," he tells me. "Of course I love Ivié," he says, "but it's complex. I decided to make one other person happy."

There is a certain martyrdom in loving someone in prison. And it's not a side effect, or a bit part in the play; it's the main event. Like prison wives, Jacques has contorted himself into the role of making someone happy. I wonder if that kind of asymmetry can be the foundation for any long-term relationship, let alone marriage.

But it seems to be working. When Jacques and I had our dinner at Rosemary's in June, it was a few weeks after Ivié's graduation ceremony. He and I discuss the appeal. At this point, he says he has already spent $100,000 on legal fees. I ask how he is considering the reality of such a reversal of fortune, of Ivié being released and coming home. "I'm working under the premise that the appeal won't work," he sighs, leaning back into his chair. "The challenge isn't me living alone. I've been doing that for many years. It's how she will fare psychologically. She knows she will die in prison. That's a big blow." He pauses. "A big, big blow. And then if she's transferred to New Jersey . . ." he says, trailing off. There is still the possibility that she might have to begin another thirty-year-to-life sentence in her second victim's state. "Well, they don't have conjugals and you can't send packages. It's a lot harsher."

Jacques highlights one of the biggest surprises I am discovering. I knew that there was federal prison and there was state prison, and that there were prisons of different security levels, and private institutions and public. While being in prison anywhere is no picnic, there are degrees of awfulness. But what I hadn't realized is just how much the conditions of, say, a maximum-security women's prison, can vary from state to state, facility to facility. In New York, Ivié got to experience unsupervised visits with her mom and intimacy with her husband, receive packages of food and toiletries to soften the time. If she gets transferred just a few dozen miles away to New Jersey, for the same crime, she will have none of those small comforts. Spending time with loved ones in one state and then having that right ripped away in another is random, cruel, and arbitrary. But cruelty is always the point.

At Rosemary's, I congratulate Jacques on recently gaining his

American citizenship earlier this spring. The process took six years, all told, from their marriage to his taking the oath. I can see it both ways: Perhaps his becoming an American citizen reflects his devotion to Ivié. But on the other hand, is it possible that, as he told his mom, he married Ivié just to get his U.S. citizenship? I ask him why he decided to do it. "If I live here, I want to be a part of the community," he explains. "I'm here to stay. I love politics. I can't wait to vote!"

He laughs telling the story of his green card interview at the American consulate in Montreal a few years back. Once it clicked for the interviewer that Ivié was, in fact, the person sponsoring Jacques, he remembers him saying, "Sir, I've seen many things. I've seen people with fake IDs, people with terrorist pasts, but I've never seen this! I've never seen a former diplomat sponsored by a woman in prison!" He asked Jacques, "Is it possible you are being manipulated?"

"My response was 'I'm a man of a certain age. I think I know a little bit about the human heart. I'm convinced there's no manipulation.'"

It's hard to imagine how any such "manipulation" for citizenship could benefit Ivié. Jacques could keep sending her money from abroad. He could visit her regularly and still have trailer visits while remaining a Canadian national.

"She must be the only person in the history of the U.S. with such a criminal record who has sponsored a husband!" he says with a laugh. "I studied the law and it was very clear. There's no mention that the U.S. citizen sponsoring the immigrant should have no record and not be in prison," he observes.

Jacques's due diligence was correct. While felons cannot vote in some states, cannot obtain public housing, and must disclose their records to potential employers, incarcerated people can, in fact, sponsor foreigners on their path to citizenship.

"The right to marry is an absolute right," immigration attorney Neena Dutta tells me later. "There are no regulations precluding an incarcerated person from petitioning for a spouse's citizenship." Even if the person is in prison for a violent crime like Ivié's, they can still sponsor. The only exception falls under the Adam Walsh Act, an effort to stop sex trafficking, which says that people convicted of sex crimes against a minor cannot petition. But for a couple like Jacques and Ivié, nothing legally bars them from pursuing citizenship. Both of them will have their finances scrutinized, mainly to determine that he has enough money to refrain from collecting public benefits. They will have to go through an interview process like anyone else. "The adjudicator will set up a videoconference in the prison to interview the prisoner," Dutta says. "They can be questioned, and they will ask for visit and call logs, receipts of deposits to the commissary account, and lots of affidavits from people, stating that the union is legitimate." She says that these types of petitions from incarcerated U.S. citizens are exceedingly rare.

Jacques and I spend the rest of the dinner picking at our plates as he talks about his affection for Ivié and tells me stories of his travels. He is just as debonair as Ivié described, and I am elated to have found a success story, people with some real time on their side, and intimate experience, too. Jo and Benny have been married for two years now, but they have yet to be alone together. Sherry and Damon get to spend more private time, but it takes place within a prison. None of the women in Dallas have access to conjugal visits. It seems like Ivié and Jacques boast a substantial data set.

Jacques and I step out of Rosemary's onto the sidewalk of Greenwich Avenue, the sky over the Hudson River fading into a soft violet. We say goodbye, and I walk to the subway.

ABOUT SIX WEEKS later, on an already sweltering morning in July, I get a phone call from Ivié. Her typically buoyant voice sounds deflated. A few weeks back, she tells me, she and Jacques got into an explosive argument on the phone. She tried to call him back, but he cut off his third-party collect call account, so she had no way to access him. He canceled the trailer they had scheduled. He hadn't shown up for a visit in almost a month. In other words, her husband ghosted her.

"It's a roller-coaster kind of catastrophe," she says. Her emotions have been all over the place—anger, frustration, hurt, but most of all confusion. This is when the power dynamics do seem to be firmly in the court of the free-world partner. He can disconnect the phone. He can let her stew in her cell. He doesn't have to visit. I think about how many times I've let my imagination and ego run amok when I haven't gotten a return text from a man. What if that were my husband? And I were in prison? It seems unspeakably cruel. "I'm trying my best to take care of myself," she says softly.

I can't help but feel that the timing is suspicious. Jacques is a U.S. citizen now. He'd never acted this way before. Perhaps it's cynical to imagine, but could all this have been an elaborate, expensive, time-consuming ploy for citizenship?

I shoot Jacques an email to see what's up, and to verify that he's still breathing. He is, and he replies.

"Many things have happened. She was jealous we had a meal together," he writes, referring to our interview at Rosemary's. This seems odd, as I've just spoken to Ivié and she doesn't seem angry with me. He continues: "We won't be able to work it out. Her fixation on me getting money to get her out of jail had become unbearable. I have other challenges in my life (3 kids!) and something had to give. It's over."

It's hard to know the reality of any breakup. There's that awful saying, "his side, her side, and the truth," as if the truth is some immutable point on a continuum. The continuum *is* the truth. But so are the facts: Jacques and Ivié have broken up, mere months after his citizenship was finalized. Often we think of prisoners somehow manipulating the person on the outside, just as the green card interviewer at the consulate in Montreal had suggested. Jo and her friends occasionally fear that they are being used for money, affection, entertainment. And that does happen. What we don't think about as often is the person on the outside using the prisoner. Because with so few liberties, what could a prisoner be used for? Citizenship, it turns out.

———————

I GO TO visit Ivié in the fall, about two months after Jacques stopped talking to her. I'm seven months pregnant and I bring the pair of sweats I scored from the screen-printing store as backup in case the guards decide that the wide cloth band of my maternity jeans too much resembles the forbidden leggings. I'm let in, but only after three male guards tell me to turn around and examine my backside as I try to turn my back pockets inside out, which is, as you know, impossible. This is just one of many indignities I will witness today. Another woman is inquiring about why a package she had sent an inmate was returned. She had apparently sent a verboten brand of shampoo. "They make you pay eighteen dollars just to have it sent back," she tells me. "They make it as difficult as possible for families."

It is the day of the Brett Kavanaugh confirmation vote, and I am happy to have a break from my phone. A prisoner at another table is shaking her head about it with her companion, observing that the misogyny in this country is unbelievable. I watch the clock behind a cage above the guard's stand tick off minutes, then quarter hours, then more than an hour, as I wait for Ivié. I remember her telling me the guards had gotten in trouble for setting the clock thirty minutes ahead to cut off visiting time. I start in on the vending machine snacks, coating my teeth with sugar from off-brand Oreos.

Eventually I see Ivié's tall, loping figure in the distance. The wait was so long because on her way to meet me she got stopped by a guard who sent her back to her cell for wearing earrings, which she'd forgotten about and which are not permitted during visits. But it isn't the earrings or lack of them that stop me about Ivié that day. Her long, gray-streaked hair, which she usually wears twisted into a bun high on her head, has been shorn into a buzzcut. It seems that wanting to cut your hair after a breakup is a truth universally acknowledged, whether in prison or out. She styled it after Amber Rose and Charlize Theron, she says. But the significance runs deeper.

"I remember Jacques telling me he didn't care if I did my makeup, but that he never wanted me to cut my hair. He said, 'I don't want you coming down here looking like G.I. Jane.' But now I am G.I. Jane. Army of one."

I ask her what she thinks has been going on. She makes some speculations about the state of her husband's mental health and says she thinks that he didn't really want her out of prison. She tells me that in one of their last conversations, she fretted to him over her book sales, the proceeds of which she had hoped could secure more hours from their lawyer. He told her not to worry and asked why they couldn't just enjoy the setup as it was. She expressed excitement at Kim Kardashian's latest cause of appealing on behalf of prisoners with extreme sentences; perhaps her case might be considered. To this, she says, Jacques had replied coldly, "Why bother? You're going to be locked up for the rest of your life."

"That was probably the most hurtful thing he could say," she said.

She recently ripped up and threw out more than two hundred of his cards and letters. She took their pictures and cut out all the images of his face, stitching them together to create a Chuck Close–like composite. "I wanted the collage to say, *Who are you really?*" she says. She sent it to him in the mail.

Along with his phone calls and trailer visits, the money Jacques had been sending has run out, too. "I have nothing, not even a bar of soap," she says. The state-issued soap prisoners receive is known to bleach hair and make skin crack. I think back to my dinner with

Jacques, when he joked that Ivié has been the cheapest of all his girl-friends. Ivié makes twenty-five cents an hour from her job in the law library. She has started smoking again and has been using her earnings to buy Newports from commissary. They cost $9 a pack, cheaper than in the city, and are just about the only item that is cheaper on the in-side. (Go figure: it's the thing that will kill you.)

And yet, within such devastation, hurt, and bewilderment, Ivié conveys a stoic determination. With or without Jacques, she is not going to give up her quest. "I've fought for everything in my life, and I've always done it by myself. When I was eight years old, I had a lem-onade stand in my neighborhood. Then I was raking leaves, shoveling snow, washing cars," she says, her eyes shining with tears. "I will fight for my freedom until my dying day."

As I get up to leave, she hugs me close, despite the giant orb of my pregnant stomach in between us. She asks me what I'm going to name my son, and I tell her, even though I have been keeping it a secret from my friends and family. She thanks me for the visit several times. As I walk toward the door, she shouts my name, just so I'll turn around and she can give me a big wave. Just to say goodbye again.

JACQUES, OF COURSE, has a different account of events. "Things came to a head when I had to shift my focus away from her case," he tells me a few months after my visit with Ivié. They have now been separated for the better part of a year.

Jacques has been looking back at all the things that irritated him when they were together. He worked for hours setting up the GoFundMe campaign for her appeal, only for her to tell him to pull it when she heard that funds could be reallocated to her victims' fami-lies. He switched phones and didn't have service for one day, which sent her ballistic and she accused him of cheating. He feels she lacked empathy for the stresses he was under when his dad passed away the previous spring and throughout his custody battle to get more time with his daughters.

But the tipping point came last summer, when they were planning that trailer visit. "It's going to sound ridiculous that this was the last straw," he concedes over the phone, "but she asked me to bring an extra bag of charcoal for another inmate. When she made that request, I was floored. *Despite what's going on in my life, you ask me to bring an extra twenty-pound bag I have to carry myself for an unknown inmate?!* I said 'We're done' and I hung up and canceled my phone account." I tell him that, given the stress he was under at the time, freaking out over a seemingly small trespass is understandable. But why cancel the phone account? That part seems extreme.

"I knew because of my emotional weaknesses I'd go back to her."

Ivié also wasn't quite sold. After their breakup, she had asked him point-blank if he'd married her only to get his citizenship. He was offended, asking her how she could question his love and devotion. "Plus, to be frank," he says, "being with a convict to get citizenship is not the most obvious choice." It's true; from my scholarly research on the reality show *90 Day Fiancé*, there seem to be a great number of Americans willing to sacrifice their common sense for attractive con artists. "Her accusations hurt me," he says. "Why would I quit a job that's earning way more money than I make here, write you twenty-page letters, move? Who would spend $100,000 on somebody's case for a green card? It's an absurd thing to say. It was so wrong, it threw me a little." (Ivié disputes that he spent this amount.)

Ivié's collage threw him a little, too. When he received the multifaced portrait she created from his photographs, he found it "very creepy. Kinda *Fatal Attraction*." He has heard it's pretty easy to get a divorce if you haven't seen your spouse in over a year. So he's waiting it out.

Ultimately, I think it isn't gaining his citizenship that has ended things for the couple. Instead, it may have been Ivié shifting her focus away from doting on Jacques to improving her own future. He says she became obsessed with appealing her charges. "I tried to explain to her that her case is not a sexy case. *You were abused, but you didn't kill your abuser.* The likelihood that she gets out is very slim. She should let go of finding a scheme to get out of prison. Her future is at that facility, and she can help others, stay busy. It sounds terrible, but it's true."

He says he asked her if they could just take a break from fighting her case. "I told her, 'You are my main relationship outside of my job and children. I just need to be able to speak about silly things, politics, art, the news. I can't talk about writing to Oprah to get you out of prison every time we speak.' There was a level of delusion in her not facing the truth that was sometimes scary to me."

Scary or maybe just unpleasant. As Jacques nakedly admits, one of the things he loved most about the specific contour of this relationship was Ivié's devotion to him, her all-encompassing love, her adoration. When that shifted, he wasn't in it anymore.

When we think about delusion, we often envision the prison couple scheming on the phone about how to get the man out. How he's coming home any day now. It's the fantasy of the future that fuels the relationship through its material barriers. But Jacques refused to engage with what he sees as her delusion. His children, he says, are happy the relationship is over.

"I don't regret the experience at all," he tells me. "If there's something to take from all of this, it's that I'm still who I am. If you see something you like, go for it. If you love someone, love them with the maximum you can hold in your heart. Live your life, try stuff; you can be a bit reckless sometimes. Financially I made some decisions that were dubious, but I covered myself. Hemingway, Chanel, they took great risks to get where they are. Go with your gut and do what you think is right for yourself. My daughter asked me if I regret anything, and I said I regret nothing. I regret that I made her a little uncomfortable, but apart from that I don't regret anything. It was one of the most amazing experiences of my life. You can't imagine the closeness, the discussions we had. When you go on a trailer visit, you are taken inside the prison. I had an up-close view of that life and, frankly, it's a remote and different world. For me it was illuminating and worth it. And, of course, we had a beautiful relationship."

He pauses. Then he says something that, to me, puts him squarely in the ranks of true prison partners: that this relationship transformed him into the fiercest, strongest, most independent version of himself.

"The bottom line is: Don't be afraid to live your life. Defend your values and your inner core beliefs and try to make the best of it. I succeeded for a good chunk of time."

As for Ivié, he wishes her nothing but the best. He hopes that she can look back upon their time together with fondness: "She had six years of utter happiness and a very loving marriage. For me, it was great. I hope it was the same for her."

———

AS FOR IVIÉ, she is at work on a sequel to *25 to Love*. The new installment is entitled *25 to Lies*. She recently sent me a poem she wrote, called "Seeking Arrangements:"

Why did God give you life?
Maybe to help save the rest of mine?
Maybe.
I know some will read this and gather doubts, but
"Faith can move mountains, Doubt can create them"
Within time.
"I walk in faith knowing the good I seek is already mine."

Be that so, I still need help in trying to save the rest of my life
I have spent 26 years now in prison
And still with another thirty in line
I'm an artist, author, designer and musician
And a poet if you're nasty, but a lady at all times
I am a business woman, self-supportive
An extreme-individual, playful but firm
If you're in the position to help me
Priceless would be the return.
If indeed my journey ends with taking my last breath in prison
That last breath will be followed with a legacy
Of a true G.I. Jane, Army of One.

SIX

NEW YORK

IN THE FALL of 2018, I receive a screener of the documentary *Met While Incarcerated*, directed by Catherine Legge, whom I had first met when she filmed Benny and Jo's wedding. I don't watch it immediately, as I'm eight months pregnant and having a hard time focusing on much of anything beyond my aching feet. When my baby is three months old, I find it while dusting off my notebooks and files. I cue up the documentary as a way to ease myself back into the prison-wife saddle.

Catherine's film, which played on cable and the Canadian Broadcasting Corporation and at festivals, is a beautiful triptych of Jo and Benny and two other prison couples. One of the other men is on death row in Louisiana. The second, in prison for thirty years for a violent sexual assault, comes home to the woman who has been waiting for him.

We meet Jo back in that hotel room in Oregon the day before her nuptials. We see footage from their wedding in prison. And off to the right, there I am, bearing witness to the blessed event, almost three years ago. I look blonder and thinner. We all look happy. We all exude the stubborn optimism of someone on their wedding day, the cheery determination it takes to make promises, when potential storms ahead seem far off the radar, brewing in another hemisphere. At the time, I had been dating Scott for a few months. Things were going well. I had no idea then that we'd soon have a baby, that we'd get married and make these promises, too.

But beyond the Proustian swirl of reverie over the happy day, the documentary also revisits the pasts of all the men and the crimes for which they are currently imprisoned. This is information that I know about Benny—that he is in prison for trying to murder his girlfriend—but that I haven't dwelled on. Jo and Benny, the first prison couple I met, have imprinted on me a model for viewing the phenomenon. They speak about how the entirety of a person's character should not be based on the worst night of their life. Their relationship is refreshing because it seems so positive, their gazes set toward the future as they strive to be the best people they can be today. I have been focused on tracing the crest of the couple's relationship as the clock ticks closer to homecoming. How are they getting ready? What are they afraid of? What are they looking forward to? Like Jo and Benny themselves, I've had my eyes trained on the future. But now here is a slap from the past.

Catherine's voice-over reminds us that Benny is currently doing ten years for the attempted murder of the last woman he was with. She includes local news footage from the time he was arrested. His mug shot flashes on the screen. He looks terrifying: pinprick eyes; mouth agape, revealing a chipped tooth; scratches and bruises across his face and head; chin jutting upward stubbornly toward the camera. The news anchor, with his shiny voice, says:

> Ben Reed was booked on one million dollars' bond. They say he kidnapped a woman and her daughter from Portland. Troopers say the woman stopped the SUV and took off on foot down the freeway. Reed got out and chased her. He is said to have sexually assaulted the woman at a truck stop a short time

later. She was able to escape at one point and flagged down a truck driver for help. Police discovered the accident a little further down the road.

Benny's initial charges, on top of attempted murder, were kidnapping, sodomy, and rape. Those last three charges were dropped when the victim did not show up in court.

I watch him explain himself onscreen: "I was really just trying to scare her more than anything, because I was so fucking pissed. I tried to swerve at her. She was standing maybe five feet in front of the car, so I step on the gas. Her daughter was in the car and she had some bruising from the seat belt. That gave me assault, too."

I feel nauseated. But the weirdest part is that I know most of this. I know Benny's charges. I remember pulling up his mug shot and rap sheet from the Oregon Offender Search system in the motel room before I met him on his wedding day. I didn't know, however, that the woman's daughter was in the car when he tried to run over her mother. I feel ashamed of my ignorance, willful or subconscious.

I've heard explanations before, from both Jo and Benny—he was wasted, he was angry, he wasn't *really* trying to harm her, those rape charges aren't true because they were dropped. There is some part of my brain that is able to accommodate this context. But something Benny says later in the documentary gives me pause: "I've had domestic violence with my ex-wife, with the stripper girlfriend I had in Arizona. Pretty much every relationship I had been in with a girl over the past fifteen years I usually hit, or beat, or something along those lines."

It strikes me that Jo is the only woman he has been romantically involved with whom he has not hit. And, with all of their interactions occurring through fiber-optic cables or under the scrutiny of prison guards, he has never had the chance. I watch him say these words on film matter-of-factly, as if rattling off the names of cities he's lived in.

It's just a part of his biography, one that he has apparently grappled with. Perhaps his nonchalance comes from his healing and the transformation he has undergone inside. Who he was then feels very far away from who he is today. That's the charitable interpretation Jo seems to take.

And in a way, I get it. It has been much more pleasant for me, too, to focus on his turnaround and his potential for his post-release life. But I can't get past these facts. Jo may forgive him—perhaps her heart is bigger than mine—but I find the attitudes and actions toward women that he expresses in the documentary unconscionable. Maybe when more time is on his side in the free world, when he and Jo have logged years of domestic tranquility and seen Davin and Elijah off to college in eleven years . . . then, maybe, I can think about forgiveness. (Not that anyone asked for my forgiveness in the first place.) At the same time, I do believe he deserves the opportunity to prove himself.

What puzzles me most is how willing I've been to overlook Benny's rap sheet, to file it under the annals of "everyone has a past," words I've heard in Oregon, in Dallas, every day in online forums, the prison-wife ethos I've absorbed. Early on, Benny himself had told me point-blank about his old ways: "I started going to county jail at eighteen, I went to prison at twenty-three, and all I wanted to do was sell drugs, bang strippers, and rob people." But somehow I have been able to gloss over these glaring facts. I would think about his traumatic childhood—being on his own from a young age, his early drug use, the violence he was steeped in—and how hard he has worked to get beyond that chapter.

In confronting these black-and-white facts, animated in news footage and interviews, I have to reconsider just how much I have skirted the issue of Benny's past, how invested I've been in squinting to see the man Jo sees. Part of the problem is that I find the free-world counterparts in these relationships more fascinating—the Jos, the Jacqueses. They wax poetic over their significant others to me. I have centered my attention more on parsing why and where they find love rather than on who these beloved men and women are, or what they have done.

I decide to listen back at an interview I did with Benny via video visit shortly after my trip to Maryland. I reach the part of the tape where I ask him a question about how he and Jo communicate, a seemingly benign question. He contrasts his current method to how he used to be:

BENNY: That isn't the way I should communicate with a girl, by calling her bitch or hooker or something like that. Ever since meeting Jo—we've been together three years—I've never once called her one of those things, and I won't let anybody else call her one, because I don't get to. I respect her, I love her.

ME: Had you done that before in your previous relationships?

BENNY: You know what I mean, figure her name was Bitch.

ME: Wow.

BENNY: Well, I mean, like on my phone to call my wife, my voice activation would be like "Call my bitch," and it would call her.

ME: Wow, wow, yeah, that's different.

Listening back to any interview can be cringey. *Why am I interrupting this person? Why am I not asking that obvious follow-up question?* But this, in my more than a decade of reporting, takes the cake. "That's different"?! Understatement of the millennium! Benny had told me exactly who he was.

I don't write about people to judge them. I'm drawn to studying people to try to understand how what seems outlandish at first is really on a continuum of self-deception that we all practice. I've interviewed people who have done illegal things and who have done extreme things, like fake their deaths. *I've* done illegal things—taken drugs, used a fake ID when I was underage, obtained my own death certificate for research for my previous book—and immoral things, like cheating on a boyfriend and lying about it. I understand none of us is perfect. But looking back at this interview, I am shocked at just how clearly upsetting I found this exchange, how obvious it is that I didn't know what to do.

Rewatching the footage, I still don't know what to do. I slam my laptop shut and walk to the kitchen for a glass of water. I feel angry. Angry at Benny for hurting people, angry at Jo for . . . . for what? For misplacing her empathy? For walking back into harm's way after working so hard to extricate herself from violent relationships? With a little distance from the couple and their story, I see things differently. I don't think either necessarily wants to overlook the past, but they are eager to move on from it. I was apparently eager to move on from it, too.

Now, I have amassed more observational data from other prison couples. I've seen so many breakups; Ivié and Jacques were just one. Lauren, whom I met in Dallas, broke off her engagement with Spencer when he cheated on her upon his release. Breakups due to infidelity. Breakups due to incompatibility. Breakups due to reoffending. I've seen too many examples that contradict the hopeful platitudes. Fresh off maternity leave, I can see now how I had drunk the Kool-Aid.

STRICKEN, I DECIDE to ask Benny to tell me about the night of. I've been dwelling on this information for months now, but I know I have to come to terms with this episode. Plus, I found the chronology presented in the news somewhat confusing, and I wanted to hear Benny's account in his own words. Even if Benny and Jo have found a way to domesticate this terrifying behavior into their story, I need to examine it more directly.

The outline of the news story remains the same, but he fills in more details. It was December 31, 2009. His girlfriend had left to buy heroin, and he was left behind with her infant daughter. He passed the time by drinking Four Lokos and growing more paranoid and infuriated.

"So was the baby sleeping or were you, like, drunk babysitting?" I ask.

"Drunk babysitting," he says over the phone. "I am not a role model. I was a terrible person." He laughs, but a weary shame peeks through.

When his girlfriend didn't return for several hours, he believed that she was out cheating on him. By the time she returned, he was enraged. A neighbor overheard their domestic dispute and came out to see if anything was wrong. Benny punched him several times and, fearing the cops' imminent arrival, grabbed his girlfriend by her hair and told her that they were leaving. With her daughter in a car seat in the back, he forced her to drive, as he was too drunk. Just past midnight, they got on I-84, a scenic highway leading out to waterfalls and gorges. As they drove farther out of the city, her tone changed. Benny says she started apologizing, wanting to make things right.

"Now, after taking classes," Benny says, "I think she thought I was going to kill her out there."

They pulled over at a rest area, where Benny says he used the bathroom and they had sex in the car. Afterward, they got back on the highway. At some point he realized he didn't have his glasses and wanted to pull over to find them. When they stopped, she asked to use his phone and stepped out of the car. He was pawing around for his glasses. With the window open, he swears he heard her say, "I'll be right there, baby." Thinking she was talking on the phone to another man, he grew enraged.

"That's when I jumped in the driver's seat," he says. He slammed on the gas and peeled off, swerving at her first, then leaving her on the side of the road, her daughter still in the back seat. A few minutes later, he decided he should go back for her. He was speeding, drunk, and caused a pileup of several cars that were trying to avoid hitting him. There were no fatalities. His car rolled over three or four times. When the cops came, the car was upside down, the baby crying, still strapped in her car seat.

"Pretty horrific stuff," Benny says quietly.

I ask him how he makes sense of it today.

"I know I could never say I was sorry," he says. "That would never be enough. No words could ever express what I put her through, what I put her daughter through that night. But I will never be that person again. I haven't had a drink since that night, and I will probably never have a drink again. I know the person I turn into. It destroys my life in every way and the lives of people I love."

I hope that he's right, that he's resolute in vowing to make some good come from the hurt he inflicted. But I still feel angry. Angry that this ever happened, and angry at myself for straining so hard to see redemption in what could easily be a pattern of repeated trauma and dysfunction.

Yet that can't be the whole story, either. To me, it seems as if making a marriage with Benny work could heal Jo's pain of relationships past, particularly the abusive ones. In both of their tellings, Jo is the one who changed Benny, because she demanded a certain level of respect—respect that perhaps she had not demanded in the past. So instead of Benny being the one seeking redemption in the most obvious of ways, perhaps it is Jo who seeks absolution, who hopes that, by transforming an abuser into a partner, she can alchemically morph from victim to survivor to healer to healed.

I think about what Jo has said, time and again: "I'm not worried about who he used to be, because that man doesn't exist anymore." I hope she's right, too.

SEVEN

CRYSTAL AND FERNANDO

CRYSTAL WAS EIGHTEEN years old when she first learned of him. It was a night like any other in her devout Oklahoma home. Then a heaviness descended upon her when she saw the man on TV. He was on the national news, declaring his son Fernando's innocence in the New York City murder in which he was implicated. The father was pleading for the public's help in delivering justice. Crystal rested her head in her mother's lap. At that age, Crystal wasn't especially interested in the news. It just happened to be what was on when she glanced over, saw the anguish in the man's face, and felt her heart pierced. Something about the story possessed her in a way that she didn't quite understand but that felt overwhelming.

"I said, 'Mommy, I feel terrible,'" Crystal recalls, her Oklahoma accent making "terrible" sound like "turrible." Her mom registered her pain as a kind of message from God. "Honey, that's called a burden," she told her. "Let's pray and you'll feel better in the morning."

The next morning came, but Crystal didn't feel any better. She still felt sick, physically unable to shake off her feeling of this man and his son's predicament. Her mom acknowledged the heaviness of such a burden that wouldn't lift with prayer alone. She encouraged her daughter to write the imprisoned young man and tell him about the Lord.

Before she could write him, she needed an address. At the time, Crystal was working at the call center of a Christian company in Oklahoma City. She was also going to college and working toward her dream of becoming a lawyer. The year was 1991, and she had access to phone books from all over the country—the Google of that time. She sat in her cubicle, writing out in a notebook versions of the unusual last name she had heard on the news, trying to pinpoint the correct one. Bermuda? Burdez? She looked up the phone numbers to local jails in the New York area where the man might be held. Time was of the essence, because the company where Crystal worked had just been outed as a massive pyramid scheme, and everyone was getting fired. That day. She had but hours—maybe minutes—to remember the correct name and find the right jail. She said a prayer: *In the name of Jesus, please release me, help me find him. I don't want to have any more of these feelings.*

She picked up the phone and dialed the number for Rikers Island, and the name Fernando Bermudez came tumbling out of her mouth.

"Lady, what do you want?" The corrections officer on the other end of the line shouted.

"I just want to tell him about *Jesus!*" she pleaded into the phone.

The officer laughed and relinquished the inmate's information and the address of the jail. Crystal sent the letter. And her burden was released—or maybe just transformed.

———————

TODAY, CRYSTAL TELLS the story with a weary laugh, hardly believing anyone was ever so young. We are sitting in the late-afternoon sun on a custom-built pagoda in the backyard of the 8,300-square-foot home she shares with her husband of twenty-seven years and their two teenage children. The house is the largest in a neighborhood of stately homes on a winding private drive in an affluent suburb in North Carolina. A Mercedes, an Audi, a Jaguar, and a Maserati are parked in the driveway, all of them blinding white. There's a kidney-shaped swimming pool in the backyard, along with an outdoor kitchen and a massive trampoline. The yard decor is like a miniature menagerie out of Xanadu, with statues of dinosaurs, flamingos, penguins, toucans, a giant iguana, a saguaro cactus, cherubs, and an Easter Island head.

Inside, there's a screening room with rows of recliners and framed posters of popular movies, including *The Shawshank Redemption*. A pantry overflows with boxes of organic soup, flavored water, and bulk cereals. The multiple living rooms are filled with wide couches and blankets, capacious and comfortable. Each room spills over with air fresheners, essential oils, candles, and silk flowers. Studio portraits of the family cover the walls, along with paintings bought on vacations to Rio and Santo Domingo. A glass display case holds several dozen mugs from some of the three hundred universities where Crystal's husband has lectured.

He is often mistaken for a professional athlete by neighbors and deliverymen. His broad shoulders and tall, proud stature do suggest the NFL, to say nothing of the sports cars and the palatial estate, like something out of *MTV Cribs*. He maintains his physique with a regimen of jujitsu, running, and weight training. He speaks with inflections of his New York upbringing, in the Dominican neighborhood of Washington Heights. His light brown eyes and tan skin are striking, and he dresses with a casual confidence, in baggy shorts and T-shirts that stretch over his toned back.

Crystal is equally attractive. On this day in May, her unlined face is delicately accented with pink eye shadow and lipstick to match her sundress. Her eyes turn up at the corners, an inheritance she credits to her mix of Japanese, Cherokee, and African ancestry. She laughs easily and talks rapidly and digressively. She describes herself as "country" and disarms everyone with her warmth, making her a close confidante to many.

The couple teases each other, responding to the little tics of personality and preference the way you do with someone you know as well as yourself. When they welcomed me into their home, a bouquet of flowers bought from Sam's Club especially for the occasion had been meticulously arranged and placed on the table in the foyer. Their thirteen-year-old son, Fernando Jr., whom they call Nando, was working on algebra with his homeschool tutor. They showed me pictures from the junior prom their sixteen-year-old daughter, Carissa, attended last week. Their older daughter, Chayla, lives in Ohio with her two children. Somehow, this impossibly youthful pair are grandparents. They discussed the business of daily life: what to do for dinner later, how to monitor Nando's screen time on the new computer game he is obsessed with, last-minute adjustments to the twenty-three-day European vacation they will take this summer, touring Monaco, Italy, Spain, and Portugal.

By any measure, this is a portrait of a successful marriage, a vibrant family living the dream in suburban America. But it is also true that inside this gigantic house, the windows are sealed tightly, the curtains are always drawn. Not much light gets in and the air feels thick. Most of their day is spent inside, withdrawn from neighbors and the outside world. And the home, the cars, the vacations have been hard-earned. They were bought with eighteen years of Fernando's life.

CRYSTAL AND FERNANDO met in 1991, after she wrote him that fated letter while he was on Rikers Island, awaiting trial for murder. They are a classic MWI story—she wasn't looking for anything romantic; she only wanted to tell him about the Lord. In contrast to the demographics of middle-aged white women who met their partners during incarceration, Crystal, who is Black, was just eighteen when she wrote to Fernando. He was only twenty-one himself. But something spoke to him. They struck up a correspondence, and she visited him in jail. They married shortly thereafter. Crystal held him down, supporting him and their three kids through a twenty-three-years-to-life sentence and ten lost appeals. She has all the self-sacrifice of a loyal prison wife. And he has the thoughtful erudition of a man who has spent a great deal of time contemplating life, justice, and fate.

But there's one big difference in this MWI story. Fernando did the time, but he didn't do the crime. With the help of the Innocence Project, he was exonerated in 2009 after serving eighteen years in maximum-security prison. He sued the State of New York for $30 million and was eventually awarded a settlement of $4.75 million.

Fernando, even though he spent an excruciating amount of time in prison, was not guilty of anything illegal. But he still came home with all the trauma of anyone who has spent almost half his life behind bars. He has stomachaches and explosions of anger. And Crystal is traumatized, too: she endures chronic migraines and has trouble staying focused. Yet despite the obstacles of imprisonment, exoneration, and homecoming, Crystal and Fernando have achieved what few MWI couples have: a successful, time-tested marriage, post-release, in society, on the outside. So is the secret of their success the fact that, unlike every other inmate I've met thus far, Fernando is not guilty of any crime?

FERNANDO BERMUDEZ WAS born in New York City in 1969, the first of five children of immigrant parents from the Dominican Republic. They left the island in the midst of a civil war and came to the States chasing the American Dream. Fernando's father earned a healthy living working in a parking garage, and his mother was a housewife. It was a stable two-parent household, where everyone worked hard and stayed on the right side of the law. He calls his family the Brady Bunch of Washington Heights. He attended Catholic school, graduating from St. Nicholas of Tolentine High in 1988. Then he went into the parking business with his father and was enjoying the life of a young man, working on bodybuilding and chasing girls in his spare time.

In the summer of 1991, he was gearing up to begin studying nursing at Bronx Community College, with hopes of eventually becoming a physician's assistant. That summer was to be his last hurrah of youth before he hunkered down and got serious with his studies. On August 6, he was celebrating with a few friends and their dates, driving around in his father's BMW. As the night wore on, Fernando suggested the group go back to his house, as the streets weren't safe late at night. They parked the car by the entrance of his apartment building, but they couldn't get out—a swarm of cops had suddenly surrounded them.

"The next thing I knew, the cops descended on us with their guns drawn," Fernando says. An officer pressed a gun to his temple, and plainclothes detectives whisked him away. He remembers his mom screaming from the apartment window. The police never informed him what he was being arrested for. Fernando was eventually told that his name had come up in relation to the fatal nightclub shooting of sixteen-year-old Raymond Blount near Union Square two days earlier. Fernando was six miles north in Washington Heights at the time. But the words of his friends, who became his alibi witnesses, weren't enough to convince the police.

A few months before, Fernando had been arrested on a marijuana possession charge. He had stayed out of trouble since then, but his face had been photographed and put into a mug-shot book. When police were investigating Blount's murder, they showed witnesses these books—thick volumes of young Latino men with arrest records, not even necessarily for violent crimes but, like Fernando, for various charges in the past few years. In the Blount investigation, police broke protocol, failing to separate the witnesses as they leafed through the mug shots in an attempt to identify the shooter. One young woman selected Fernando's face. "Who's this cutie?" she asked, according to court records. Together, the group of witnesses decided that this man resembled the murderer they had seen in the club. (False identifications are a top cause of wrongful convictions.)

On the night he was taken into the Sixth Precinct, the police interrogated Fernando for ten hours. They denied him a phone call, saying that if he was innocent he wouldn't need help from a lawyer. He was forced to participate in a lineup, which he thought would clear things up. Oddly, he was told to sit down. He would later come to learn that the police had made him sit because the gunman had been described as five feet ten and 165 pounds. Fernando is six-two and at the time weighed 220 pounds.

"I believed in the American criminal justice system," he says. "All my life, I believed that if you're charged with a crime, if anything bad happens, just tell the truth and it will be resolved."

Five teenage witnesses fingered him in the lineup. Fernando was charged with murder. He was held at Rikers Island as he awaited trial. It didn't matter that the state could not present any physical or forensic evidence linking him to the crime. It didn't matter that three friends of Blount's had told the prosecutor that Fernando was not the one who shot their friend. It didn't matter that all the witnesses would later recant their testimony identifying him as the shooter. Fernando was given the maximum sentence: twenty-three years to life.

———————

DURING ALL OF this, Crystal was living at home in Oklahoma, working and going to college. She, too, came from a stable, two-parent household with high expectations for their youngest daughter. She had older siblings who were already grown and out of the house during her childhood, so she was raised as a sheltered only child. Her father was in the military and a pastor at their church. Her mother was a kindergarten teacher and also deeply religious. Crystal didn't have many friends, and her communication with them was limited to talking on the phone. While Fernando was out in the streets, Crystal was under lock and key. But their meeting, to hear them tell it, was divinely ordained.

Not long before seeing Fernando's father on television and feeling the burden come upon her, Crystal had an experience that would haunt her for years to come. She had gone out on a blind date with a friend of a friend. She thought the guy was okay, because he was a local football star and had opened up his own security business. He was older, but they knew many of the same people. When he dropped her off at home after the date, he asked to come inside. Her parents were away at a church revival, and letting him in late at night was not allowed. He persisted. She tried to keep him on the couch, but he came into her bedroom. "He took advantage of me," Crystal remembers. "I said no, but I was scared for my life. He was bigger than Fernando. I knew no one would believe my word against his, because he had credentials, being a football star and having a good job." She was terrified of her father finding out that she had been raped. She didn't tell anyone for many years. This was the backdrop of her life when she made the fateful decision to write Fernando.

At this point in my prison-wife journey, the shape of this story is familiar to me: she wasn't seeking out a prisoner but found him by some cosmic intervention; she wasn't looking for anything romantic; she had a traumatic past, particularly in her romantic relationships. The lay diagnosis is obvious: she sought out a companion who was safe because he was in many ways unavailable—out of state, behind bars. I run the theory by her.

"I think some of that is true," she concedes. But to her, that isn't the entire story. "Some of it was also God's plan," she says. "I had just met three people in a row who were from New York," a significant co-incidence, given where she grew up. "I always had a heart for prison, too." Her mom was involved in prison ministry, and Crystal had an older brother serving time in California. I think back to the conversations I had with Dr. Major about how people who are more enmeshed in the world of prisons typically don't seek to meet prisoners romantically. But in Crystal's telling, none of that mattered. Her burden was meant to be.

———————

FERNANDO RECEIVED A lot of mail from supporters, perhaps because of the obvious miscarriage of justice, perhaps because of his movie star good looks. But Crystal's message of the Lord's good news struck him. Words of hope from a total stranger were what he needed to hear. It was a respite for him, because he had been putting on a front of toughness while in prison to protect himself. "Warning coloration," he calls it—like with animals in the wild whose brilliant coats send up caution signs to predators. He was a young kid who had never been in serious trouble and now found himself among dangerous people and actual murderers. He'd drop down and do push-ups, shadowbox in the yard—anything to project hardness from a young man who didn't know the first thing about lockup.

He replied to Crystal's letter with a list of his past transgressions—dabbling in drugs and alcohol, womanizing. Being in jail, though he was innocent of what he'd been accused of, had given him time to reflect on who he was and who he'd like to be. He had even stopped cursing. He told her he had lost his faith but that he was looking to regain it.

One can see why this letter did Crystal in. This kind of rehabilitated bad boy is an alluring prospect: he is neither a manchild clinging to his mother's apron strings nor a practicing player. He's the perfect hybrid of danger and safety, a lout who has seen the light, a rebel reformed. When Crystal describes how inspired she felt reading about the ways in which he had repented, I see shades of Benny, Sherry, Damon, even Ivié.

"I'm a church girl, and I wanted to be in a committed relationship," Crystal says, reflecting on the teenager she was. "He was saying all these things, about the man he used to be and who he is now, and that said *security*. And he was innocent! It sounded like he was going to be coming home any moment now."

The couple exchanged letters for a few months, and the moment came for Crystal to make the pilgrimage to meet him. The plan was for her to stay with Fernando's parents in Washington Heights and they would all visit him at Rikers together. Crystal was terrified. She'd never left home and had never spent a night away, not even at a friend's for a sleepover. Before she got on a bus to Texas to catch a plane to New York, her mother sat her down and laid out the rules. "When you stay at that lady's house," she recalls her mother telling her, "make your bed every morning. Be respectful. Don't eat anyone's food. Keep your money in different pockets, in case you get robbed. Don't make eye contact with people on the street."

Crystal felt scared entering the jail but melted upon seeing Fernando. "He was just as intelligent in person as in his letters," she says. She found him handsome but was completely taken with his sensitivity. He cried upon seeing her for the first time. Fernando thought Crystal was beautiful, and she renewed a sense of faith in him. "She opened me up," he says.

THE COUPLE MARRIED after several more months of visits, calls, and letters. At first, Crystal continued to live in Oklahoma, but she dutifully visited him at Sing Sing Correctional Facility, in Westchester County, whenever she could. Being legally wed, and with the small silver lining of the wrongful conviction occurring in New York State, the couple was eligible for conjugal visits. The decision to have children was a no-brainer. "We felt as if so much had been robbed from us, we weren't going to let them take this away, too," Fernando says. Crystal concurs. "I didn't want to miss the opportunity to have children. And it's not that I wanted a family so bad," she says, "it's that I wanted *our* family so bad." She got pregnant with Chayla right away.

Being a mom to a young child while your husband is in prison is no joke. But both parents found innovative ways to make it work. During Fernando's eighteen-year captivity, Crystal moved to the Northeast and took jobs with the phone company, with the electric company, in customer service, in the advertising department of a newspaper, as an office assistant, and as a caseworker. She also charged a fare to shuttle women and family members to Sing Sing, a kind of proto–Uber service.

Even from prison, Fernando found ways to contribute. He worked in the prison kitchen for thirty-eight cents an hour, up to twelve hours a day. "I'd read books for the majority of the time I could get away with," he says. He did such a good job in the kitchen that he got a salary bump up to forty-five cents an hour. "That was executive pay!" he laughs. He worked as much as was humanly possible. When the prison did an internal audit of employees to crack down on excessive overtime among staff, Fernando's name ended up on that list, alongside corrections officers.

He also had a healthy side hustle going. In New York, prisoners are allowed to accentuate their uniform of state greens with other clothing. Crystal would scour end-of-season clearances at department stores and send packages of name-brand sweatpants, gym shorts, and T-shirts to Fernando. She would purchase items for five or six dollars each, and Fernando would resell them to inmates, doubling or sometimes quadrupling the initial investment. They would pay him in packs of cigarettes or stamps, the principal currencies of prison, or with other commissary items, and some customers would have family members send cash directly to Crystal. The clothing business wasn't exactly legal, but Fernando wasn't a troublemaker, and COs looked the other way.

It was such a lucrative business that Fernando managed to save all his legit prison kitchen income for the duration of his sentence, which totaled several thousand dollars by the end. Crystal never needed to add any money to his commissary account. That account—which covers food and hygiene products—can cost prison wives hundreds of dollars a month, causing many to go into debt. Fernando would even send home to Crystal commissary items like laundry detergent and toothpaste that he knew would help her out. He often reinvested the packs of cigarettes with which he was paid by loaning them to gamblers at the prison poker table—with interest, of course.

Fernando credits this kind of industry as one of the keys to not losing his mind. Even though he wasn't physically with his family, he felt as if he could still support them. The trailer visits in the Family Reunion Program were also crucial to providing a sense of normalcy. "Those visits were part of the cement," Fernando says. "We got three days together every few months. That kept us going." Fernando recalls barbecuing and playing with the kids outside on a jungle gym in the late-afternoon sun, when he otherwise would have already been locked in his cell. In eighteen years, Crystal never canceled a single trailer visit. "I went there sick, pregnant, all kinds of ways." Like Jacques, Crystal brought tons of groceries to cook lavish meals. "I'd tell him, 'We're taking a trip around the world. Where do you want to go?'" And she would prepare cuisine from his chosen country.

Having the children around brought a sense of humanity not just to Fernando but to the whole prison community. Crystal calls Chayla, her firstborn, "the trick baby," as she was so well behaved that she lulled her parents into having another. "Everybody loved her; the guards would pass her around. She had all these godparents," Crystal says. It look longer to get pregnant with Carissa. (The Department of Corrections isn't terribly concerned with prison-wife ovulation cycles.) By the time their second daughter was born, Fernando had developed a circle of friends among Latino prisoners who respected his business and how he comported himself. On her birthday, "the guys announced that they had had a little fundraiser among them and all pledged money they had sent to Crystal. Some gave $15, some $50, but it added up to more than $500. That was an inmate love gift from some of the toughest guys in there," Fernando recalls. He says receiving the gift felt like being knighted by fellow crusaders. On the family's first trailer visit with Carissa, Fernando cut a lock of her hair to keep with him in his cell as a source of inspiration as he fought for his freedom. Fernando Jr. was born four years later.

In addition to his work in the kitchen and selling clothes, Fernando took college classes while he was inside. He read thousands of books and listened to audiobooks to learn how to pronounce words. He taught English to non-native speakers and gave impromptu lectures on Latin American history to friends, earning him the nickname "the Professor." All the while, he worked on his case, whether petitioning his lawyers or reading in the legal library. He filed one appeal after another. He lost them all.

———

LIFE FOR CRYSTAL was arduous. She worked several jobs at any given time. Her dream of becoming a lawyer was put on hold. One year, when the children were still small, she was cutting the Thanksgiving turkey and the knife slid down her hand, severing tendons. The accident resulted in three surgeries and a permanent numbness that caused her to almost completely lose the use of her hand. By that point she was living in Danbury, Connecticut, far from her parents in Oklahoma, and felt that Fernando's family did not support her and the children the way they ought to. At the age of fifteen, Chayla was hit by a car in an accident that was nearly fatal and required a long hospitalization. Crystal found herself and her children living in public housing. Her heat and air-conditioning were often cut off out of neglect from the management. She came from a middle-class background and had never imagined she'd find herself in such a scenario.

The lowest point was Fernando Jr.'s second birthday, which co-incided with Fernando's tenth appeal, after serving seventeen years in prison. He lost. The couple had a visit shortly after the devastating blow. Fernando told his wife he felt there was no hope left for him at all.

Crystal, though it seems beyond the scope of imagination, refused to give up. "I said to him, 'Okay, I've got your kids; we'll be your escape. You've got your son, your Junior, your namesake. We'll just do this thing.'" She pauses dramatically. "'But guess what? You *are* coming home.' I said, 'Look at me! You *are* coming home!'" To reenact the scene, she starts pacing and waving her hands like a minister at a revival. She is a tiny powerhouse in a pink sundress. I feel swept up in her fervor.

Fernando looked around the visiting room and fixed his gaze on a fellow inmate who was getting released. "That guy is a sinner and he's going home. Why him and not me?" he asked her.

"When God releases you, he is going to release you differently from any other man," Crystal prophesied. "He is going to show you favor and you will understand why. You're going to walk out of here like the president!"

A few weeks later, the couple had a trailer visit. They were watching TV when "he said, 'Crys.' He's the only one who gets away with calling me Crys," she editorializes. "He said, 'Crys, I'm going home.' I said, 'That's all God wanted to hear. You are going home.'"

They had decided he was going home. But how? He had by then assembled a dream team of lawyers working pro bono and had captured the attention of the Innocence Project. The state had offered him a plea bargain. This could get him out but would be tantamount to admitting to a crime he didn't commit. One of his lawyers advised him to take the plea deal. The others told him not to. They could still appeal on grounds of procedural errors. And by 2014 he would have been eligible for parole. But in the eyes of the law, receiving parole would also be equivalent to having done the crime. He'd be forever marked as having taken a life.

At the last trailer visit the couple would ever have, Fernando gave Crystal his answer. He would not take the plea. He would never live a lie. He would go to court again. Crystal says she knew he was coming home but also prepared herself for the worst. She remembers telling him, "I'll just raise your kids and we'll visit and we'll be together forever. I'm a strong woman and that's it. I'm here to stay."

On his eleventh try, he won his appeal. On November 12, 2009, Fernando was declared innocent and his conviction was vacated by Justice John Cataldo of the State Supreme Court in Manhattan. In his seventy-nine-page decision, Justice Cataldo wrote that Fernando's rights had been violated because the witnesses had not been separated and had influenced one another. "I find no credible evidence connects Fernando Bermudez to the homicide of Mr. Blount," the judge wrote. "All the people's trial evidence has been discredited: the false testimony of Efraim Lopez and the recanted identifications of strangers. I find, by clear and convincing evidence, that Fernando Bermudez has demonstrated he is innocent of this crime." Before leaving the courtroom, Justice Cataldo apologized to Fernando. "I felt a wave of relief to be acknowledged," he tells me. "It felt vindicating to me as a human being. That I mattered."

The appeal made case history in New York as the first exoneration in the state that did not rely on DNA evidence. The officer who questioned Fernando on that fateful summer night in 1991, Detective Daniel Massanova, stayed on the force long after Fernando's wrongful conviction. In 2004, he seriously injured two Staten Island women while driving drunk. In an interview with *The New York Times* in 2007, Massanova said, "Bermudez is in jail because a number of people said he was the shooter. I can't use a lie detector test on everybody who comes in."

On November 20, 2009, Fernando Bermudez walked out of

prison, a free man. He was given $40, garnished from his wages working in the kitchen. Yet, unlike all other prisoners, who are routinely released from the side door, he walked out the front door. He was greeted by a mob of reporters and camera crews. His kids tackled him in an embrace and he gave a speech to the media assembled there. Just as Crystal had prophesied, he walked out of the prison like the president.

But they could barely get off the property. The car was so weighed down with Fernando's books that it stalled out at the top of the hill.

His first meal was at McDonald's. "To walk into a place on solid ground without being shackled, for somebody to say 'Hi, may I take your order?' and then to pay with your own money . . . that's freedom," Crystal says.

His homecoming in Washington Heights was momentous. "I began sensing the electricity as soon as we got off the Major Deegan Expressway and crossed the bridge into Manhattan from the Bronx. I received a hero's welcome," he says. Neighbors were blasting music, hanging out of windows banging pots and pans. "My car transformed into a float," Crystal remembers.

He was ushered upstairs into his parents' apartment. Every inch felt familiar, even though he hadn't been there in years. Friends and family filled every room. "We were finally reunited, and the battle had been won. It was a really happy moment," he says.

Fernando and Crystal relive this story, each telling me their parts as we sit together on their back patio by the pool. Their emotions still swell recounting this day—the payoff, the gratification. When we hear the story of the innocent man walking free, we think of that moment as the ending. But it is the opposite; exoneration is just the beginning. Fernando looks down at his hands. "I didn't see then the difficulties that lay ahead."

"WHEN THEY COME home," Crystal says, "they become men again."
By this she means that they lose their sheen of conscientious perfection. "When they are inside, they remember everyone's birthday, every
little holiday. Out here they're like, *What?*" The sparkle of creativity
that comes when the rest of the world is shut out—of devising ways to
create intimacy across distances, of innovating connection, of dream-
ing about the future together—begins to fizzle. Life happens.

Crystal experienced more than a decade of the suspended reality
of trailer visits, the excitement of seeing your partner only every so
often. "You may have been married for twenty-seven years or something," she says, which also happens to be the number of years she
and Fernando have been married, "but you have to remember you
have not been *together* for that long. You have the years, but at the
same time, you don't. I used to say that's nonsense. But it's the truth.
You get kind of a false impression. When you're on a trailer, you're so
happy to be together. When someone spills something on the floor,
you both rush to clean it up. That's not daily life."

This doesn't feel terribly surprising, but it is resonant in a way I
hadn't yet heard in the words of the prison wives and girlfriends I'd
been interviewing. These couples had not yet experienced a shared
day-to-day, with all of its mundane grievances. Crystal's description is
not as rosy as being carried by piggyback to the kitchen to eat pancakes, as Jo had joked, but it feels undeniably true. It's the grim reality
I fear may be waiting for Jo, Sherry, and Damon.

That reality came as a shock to Crystal. "Nobody teaches couples
that there's going to be institutionalization." She's referring to the
common phenomenon of the formerly incarcerated being unable to
shake the habits of prison. When Fernando came home, he would
wash out his underwear in the shower, as he had at Sing Sing. He
paced in his bedroom, as if still in a prison cell. He can be hypervigi-
lant, on guard for danger at all times.

"Nobody tells you there's going to be PTSD. And the men refuse to believe they are going through it," she says. She describes briefly the ways she has seen Fernando's PTSD manifest: walking into the grocery store and becoming completely overwhelmed, getting triggered by the jangle of keys, fits of anger that seem to come out of nowhere.

PTSD is an insidious beast. The most common symptom is experiencing flashbacks of a traumatic incident. Those aftershocks can then lead to a host of other unpleasantries: despair, depression, irritation, guilt, isolation, confusion, insomnia. PTSD interrupts daily life often and without warning. Prisoners have a higher rate of PTSD than the general population. A comprehensive literature review from 2002 that analyzed sixty-two studies and a total sample of twenty-three thousand prisoners found that rate to be higher by orders of magnitude, with some estimates as high as 21 percent in prisoners, as compared with 3 percent in the general population. The prison environment itself is triggering for people who, like Sherry and Damon, enter already traumatized by violence and disruption. If you wanted to design an environment specifically to tap into those fears, prison would be it.

But if, like Fernando, you enter prison without trauma, there's a good chance that you will leave with it. A 2013 study in *The International Journal of Law and Psychiatry* found a "post-incarceration syndrome" in a sample of twenty-five released inmates who had served an average of nineteen years in a correctional facility. In addition to PTSD symptoms, released prisoners also experienced institutionalization, social-sensory disorientation, and alienation from friends, family, and community. Researchers contend that this is "a discrete sub-type of PTSD that results from long-term imprisonment." Formerly incarcerated people reported recurrent distressing dreams, sleep disturbances aligned with the schedules of prison, persistent avoidance of crowded spaces, panic attacks, and emotional numbing—"wearing the prison mask," or showing no emotion, which may have helped inside but on the outside is maladaptive. Crystal mentions this last symptom in connection with the fact that Fernando doesn't like to celebrate his birthday. "When I was inside," he explains, "I ignored that day because it brought too much up." Since being out, he still has trouble getting excited each year, which has left his family hurt and confused.

Teaching family members about the specific challenges released prisoners face can help them reintegrate into life on the outside. Giving prison wives a sense of what to expect and how to support them— whether in the form of a pamphlet, classes, or support groups—can also help the transition home. But as of now, nothing official exists to facilitate learning about this. Prison wives are the untapped resource when it comes to reintegrating into society. They are hungry for information, motivated for action, and caring to a fault. If there were any kind of game plan that prison wives could get their hands on, they would be the first to implement it.

Crystal and Fernando's story feels so far from where I had started. I think back to Samantha Spiegel, whose schoolgirlish letter writing and crushes were literal child's play compared with the work of building a life and a family in the wake of injustice, trauma, and uncertainty. Both of these women wrote letters to prisoners, yet the outcomes were so different. Samantha was, by her description, making these pen-pal relationships with high-profile murderers into a kind of game: could she tangentially feel and understand these men's depravity, and then pull back to safety when it got too real? Crystal, by contrast, wrote to a man who she knew in her heart was an innocent victim of a racist system. The couple went on to make a family and a life from the foundation of that injustice. From it, they had found freedom, but they also live with prison's scars every day.

ON A GLARINGLY bright afternoon, I slide into the back seat of Crystal and Fernando's white Maserati convertible to head to lunch at the

Golden Corral. Fernando bought all his cars in white to reflect the color of innocence. The interior is a red leather, the shade of a candy apple's shell. He turns the satellite radio to an oldies station and sings along in spasmodic joy to "Boogie Shoes" and "Tainted Love." With the top down, he guns the engine to showcase the car's horsepower. He drives with his left wrist dangling over the top of the wheel, wearing aviator sunglasses. Crystal is in another pretty sundress. She teases her husband that he is the only Dominican man in the world who can't dance. With the wind blowing through their hair, it's almost impossible to see the trauma that lives inside them.

On the winding country roads to the strip mall, Crystal points out a Confederate flag. She tells me that there was to be a Ku Klux Klan rally at a Walmart nearby, but it ended up getting canceled. "We asked our white friends [who live here] about moving to North Carolina from up north. They all said it was great. We should've asked our Black friends," she deadpans.

They relocated after the money from Fernando's lawsuit came through. It took six years of legal battles. In that time, Fernando was retraumatized, having to constantly relive the nightmare of his wrongful conviction by repeating and retelling the story in court appearances again and again. A good portion of the $4.75 million settlement he eventually received went to paying off the debt they had accumulated in the time they were waiting, along with legal bills. They needed to leave the expensive Northeast to find a place where they could stretch their money. "When we learned what the property taxes are down here, we did the cabbage patch dance," Crystal says. But given the troubles they've had with their neighbors, that savings comes at a price.

The stigma the family has experienced is not due solely to being Black and Latino in a white area. Nosy neighbors have taken to googling them and learning their story. Nando was bullied and beaten up on the bus, which is why he is now homeschooled. A classmate of

Carissa's asked a pointed question about her dad's past in front of the entire class in an effort to humiliate her, as no one yet knew their story. "She drives an Audi to school, so they all thought she's just another rich girl," Crystal explains. Even if you're innocent of the crime, the stigma of prison still sticks.

It's hard to put a real figure on how many innocent people are imprisoned in this country at a given time. But both data and common sense suggest the figure is far too high. Each year, the number of exonerations in the United States climbs. According to the National Registry of Exonerations, in 2016 a total of 166 wrongly convicted people were exonerated, some with crimes dating back to 1964. Also in 2016, there were on average three exonerations per week, more than double the rate in 2011. The increase can be credited to prosecutors' offices taking more accountability. Twenty-nine counties around the country, including in Chicago and New York City, have adopted special review units to scrutinize questionable convictions.

The rate of newly exonerated people has created a subculture unto itself. Crystal tells me that exonerees in particular face their own challenges: a specific kind of PTSD that comes from being innocent of any crime and having your life taken away. And there's the unique phenomenon of competition among exonerees themselves. In a curious way, she contends, exonerees are reaching for a slice of the attention pie—in the form of book deals, documentaries, podcasts. They want to get their stories out, but there are only so many platforms and appetites for such stories of injustice.

Then there's the question of the money. Not all exonerees receive a settlement. If you are wrongly imprisoned in Alaska, Arizona, Arkansas, Delaware, Georgia, Idaho, Kentucky, New Mexico, North Dakota, Oregon, Pennsylvania, Rhode Island, South Carolina, South Dakota, or Wyoming, you are entitled to nothing. Wisconsin caps the amount of compensation one can sue for at a paltry $5,000 per year, with a ceiling at $25,000, the lowest in the country. (The Wisconsin State

Assembly passed a bill that would raise the amount to $50,000 per year of wrongful imprisonment with a cap at $1 million, but the bill failed in the state senate.) Florida caps compensation at $2 million, no matter how much wrongful time you did.

Fernando, in some sick sense, was "lucky" enough to seal his fate in New York, where exonerees are entitled to sue the state for some form of compensation. But when it comes to the amount of damages he was due, he was at the mercy of the state attorney general and the city comptroller. In Texas, for example, wrongful convictions pay out at $80,000 per year served, plus an annuity for the same amount, as well as a tuition waiver for college classes, a case manager, reentry services, and assistance in obtaining healthcare, both physical and mental. In 2004, President George W. Bush endorsed a bill that paid $50,000 per year of imprisonment to those wrongly convicted in federal court, and doubled that to $100,000 per year for time spent on death row.

When we get to Golden Corral, Crystal examines her fork to make sure it's clean enough. She decides it is, and we pile our plates high with an ungodly combination of chicken, tuna salad, macaroni casserole, olives, bacon, and whatever else we want. Fernando tells me about the European vacation he is planning for the family this summer. He's creating the itinerary himself this year, without the help of the travel agent he used in the past, when they went to Australia and Japan. After all his deprivations, it seems only fair that Fernando should be able to travel the world and drive his Maserati to a giant lunch buffet. We hit the dessert section hard.

Lunches like this, surprisingly, have become a part of daily life coping with trauma for the family. The logistics that go into meal planning, grocery shopping, and food prep have felt too out of reach lately. Crystal hasn't been driving because of her anxiety, and the tasks, appointments, and work of the day often pile up before she and Fernando can organize breakfast, lunch, and dinner. Last night we ordered takeout from Applebee's, and earlier in the day we had lunch at a Mexican restaurant. Fernando doesn't like it, as he's very conscientious about protecting money from the settlement. Feeding a family of four on restaurant fare at every meal adds up.

The settlement weighs heavily and perpetually on Fernando's mind. We talk about this late in the evening in one of their many living rooms. Fernando is in comfortable athletic wear, and Crystal in a waffle robe from the Peabody hotel. She wears a chain around her neck that Fernando gave her on their first meeting, when he was in jail. She never takes it off. They are night owls, often staying up until one or two in the morning, watching movies and TV shows like *The Real Housewives of Atlanta*. I have a five-month-old at home and have fallen into his schedule of rising and falling with the sun. I try to suppress my yawns as they tease me about having kept me up past my bedtime.

"The lawsuit wasn't on the level it should've been, and it will never compensate me for those lost years," Fernando says. He refers to the fact that he was awarded a mere fraction of the $30 million he sued for. "But you get the money and whoa! Suddenly you're in a different category. It's a little intoxicating. The money isn't endless, but there's a little more to play with. So that's what we did. We got the cars. I had a personal shopper at Saks for a while. But now, as the song goes, the thrill is gone," he says, his feet up on the coffee table.

Whenever anyone says money doesn't buy happiness, I think about how I'd like to test that theory. Fernando has, and if anyone deserved to, it was him and his family. But you can't go wild, or else you end up like MC Hammer or any of the professional athletes who go from balling to bankrupt in a matter of years. Fernando has employed a team of financial advisors to help with investments and budgets. He's currently reading a book about boundaries, personal and financial, to protect his assets. Many family members have asked for large sums, and he feels sheepish trying to explain that even a big sticker price diminishes quickly when it comes to buying property, paying for a kid's education, floating the family through early retirement. Neither he nor Crystal are working, and they pay $2,200 a month for the family's health insurance alone. When I ask what we as a society can ever do to pay back wrongfully convicted people, Crystal says lifelong Medicaid would be the very least.

"I have a lot of anxiety around maintaining the compensation," Fernando says. "And I think about those eighteen years. And then it becomes a feeling of angst. But if I could stretch those thirty-eight or forty-five cents an hour, surely I can stretch this." Fernando has a mind that perseverates, no matter the object. Lately it has been the family finances. He checks the markets and their accounts constantly, pores over spreadsheets. "I'm a brooder," he admits.

"He's OCD," Crystal says. "He's a perfectionist. Whether it's jujitsu or the settlement, he's not going to be happy about it until he can work it through in his mind. If he takes a break, he thinks he's cheating, he feels guilty—"

"My interpreter!" Fernando interjects. "My ventriloquist! Look, I think about the markets, we live on a fixed income, those are real things."

Crystal starts to give me an example of Fernando's frugality, a story about wanting to redo the kitchen, and he cuts her off. They erupt into one of the confrontations I've witnessed over the past few days.

"Why are you interrupting me so I can get mad and she can see what mad looks like?" Crystal yells.

"I see that every day . . ." he grumbles.

"Your temper can be really bad and scary! When I interrupted you, I apologized," she hisses.

Fernando says he is sorry. Like she has told me, they are quick to anger and quick to apologize. Their eruptions don't seem to be freighted with significant meaning. But they feel erratic, a minefield of emotion.

They both look back to the six-year period when they were waiting on the settlement as a happier time. "Danbury," they sigh with nostalgia about the town in Connecticut that they moved to after he was released. Fernando picks up a self-help book about boundaries and says, "Danbury was to create a boundary of safety from New York." He refers to this on a level of physical safety: New York was the place where bad things happened, so he could never feel safe there again. When he had just gotten out of prison, they were more conscientious about using therapeutic tools. They did a morning reflection on any conflicts that had arisen in the previous day and what they could do better. They were part of a vibrant church congregation.

Perhaps the biggest difference was that Fernando was traveling all over the world giving lectures. He landed these engagements by cold-calling institutions like the Harvard and Columbia law schools and offering to tell his story. Crystal would chauffeur him, since he didn't have his driver's license back yet, and he would earn up to several thousand dollars per gig. It went a long way in helping him to build his self-esteem: being able to support his family while making something positive out of the hell he'd experienced. And it was exciting. "When you're lecturing, let's face it, you're the star of the show. People pack into a room to hear you. And you feel like you did something good to prevent wrongful convictions," he says.

In those six years, both Crystal and Fernando were engaged with the world, meeting people from universities, staying busy. And they had the shared goal of Fernando's last fight: getting his compensation. Once the settlement came through and they moved down south, that momentum came to a grinding halt.

"We've atrophied since moving here," Fernando admits wearily. "We haven't been using our minds." Their bad experiences with nosy neighbors have caused them to retreat socially, and their church here isn't as great a fit. Being in retirement has meant a lack of structure in their lives, which has allowed depression and anxiety to fester. He has a memoir he's been working on, but it's been on the back burner for a while. "I've got to get the mental stability to devote the energy to the project," he says. "I have got to get my head right."

They had both thought that the money would be the solution: the well-deserved, hard-earned payoff. But for Crystal, it's been a kind of compounded disappointment. Once they got to North Carolina, she crashed. Hard. She turns to Fernando to speak directly to him for the first time in our conversations. She often refers to her husband as "he" and "him," even when he's sitting just a few inches from her.

"I had a nervous breakdown doing all this courageous stuff you didn't know I had to do when you were in there," she tells him.

Earlier today she told me, as many prison wives have told me, that she strived to remain stoic while Fernando did time. The men have enough to worry about in prison, so their women shield them from the unrelenting realities of their lives. She told me she never once cried during a visit with him in those eighteen years but would often bawl her eyes out in the parking lot. She had shouldered so much. "I went through all this stuff of finding a job," she continued, "Carissa's speech delay, Nando's impulsive behavior, Chayla getting hit by the car. I had to keep these secrets from my own family because I didn't want them to worry." I think back to the saddest thing she told me when we were alone together, the thing I worry about the most for all of the women I've met: "I thought when he got out," she said, "that he'd be able to take care of me."

I think of Jo and her fantasies of playful retribution when Benny gets out. The women expect there to be adjustments for the men coming home to the world after so many years in exile, but they know that they did their time, too. They are ready for their payback. Now the men will be home to lighten the load. It's like abnegating the self on earth in exchange for eternal delights in heaven.

But this hasn't been the case for Crystal, even though, in some ways, they have the best of all possible post-carceral worlds: Fernando didn't come out on any kind of probation, where the state can still threaten you with an imminent return to prison. They have been celebrated in articles and documentaries for their fight. They have a degree of financial security that many do not. And yet. Fernando came home to her with severe PTSD, fits of anger, behavior she can't understand. Those eighteen years wore her down, too.

Now, in our late-evening chat, I ask her if there's anything she can do specifically for herself, like a hobby or some kind of self-care ritual. She says she doesn't get her nails or hair done, even now that they can afford it. She's so used to going without.

"No one else is going to love me the way I love myself, and I don't even love myself right, because I've been loving everybody else. I need to find myself. I used to sing, but I don't even sing anymore. I used to be shy and quiet, but now I talk way too much, to try to defend myself. I have nervous energy from being in the house too long. All these different aspects changed my personality. I need to find my own self," she says. Fernando looks at his lap while she speaks.

I ask her how she might get there.

"I want to get back to cooking," she says. "I stopped cooking because I'd let the food burn. My mind would wander off. I'd like to start driving again. I used to love to drive, but then I started to feel like I was going to go off a cliff. That's not safe. I really want to make sure my mind is healthy for my family."

I can tell Fernando wants this, too, for himself and for his wife. I believe they can get there. But in this moment, they both seem stuck. The kind of stuck that comes from finally exhaling, finally letting the pieces fall after having carried them for so long—and not knowing quite how to pick them back up again.

IT'S MIDMORNING BY the time the couple rises. The house is silent and dark. They had meant to listen to their morning sermon on the radio to get centered for the day but slept through it. We take our coffee cups to the back patio. The sun is shining through the tall pine trees in the backyard, and a scrim of humidity coats everything. Their dog, Mishka, a husky-Pomeranian mix who looks like a little fox, with two different-colored eyes, jumps up and down in excitement. Fernando wants to plot the day, figure out our meals and what needs to get done, but Crystal has something she needs to unload.

"You know what annoys me?" she asks me, sitting in her robe, a bit of sleep still in her eyes, but skin as smooth as if it's been ironed. "And I don't mean any offense to you."

Uh-oh, I think.

"I really can't stand when people ask me about years, specific dates, what happened when," she says. Guilty as charged. Yesterday we talked for hours, her stories ricocheting from one set of characters and circumstances to the next. I kept trying to arrange the fragments of her memories into a timeline I could follow.

She urged me to ask Fernando instead. He is the one who became good at marking time inside.

"I get lost in years," she says. "It all blended together. It was like this—"

She stands up from the glass table and starts marching in place, her gaze fixed ahead on a horizon point. The ends of her bathrobe belt skim the patio tiles. "I could only focus on the day ahead of me. I couldn't concentrate on the years." She marches for a few moments, like a windup toy soldier.

I think back to one of the first things Jo ever told me about the way she and Benny make it work, about what is so beautiful about prison relationships. She called it the twenty-four-hour rule. *What can I do in the next twenty-four hours to be the best possible version of myself? To fulfill my needs so I can meet my partner's? How can we get through this day gracefully and meaningfully?* In the face of a prison sentence, twenty-four hours is often as much as you can afford to let in. When I look at Crystal marching down her imaginary road, I see how that rule benefited her at the time, kept her and her family alive. Those twenty-four hours were a coat of armor, protection from thoughts and fears spiraling out of control. I also see how living in such a state of immediacy changed her.

"I just kept going and going," she says, her march winding down to a stop. She sits down next to her husband. "When we came here, I crashed.

"We *both* suffer from PTSD," she follows up.

She felt triggered just last weekend, when the couple went into Durham to see *Beautiful: The Carole King Musical.* Security guards asked to look inside her bag, and she had to walk through a small metal detector. All of a sudden, memories of all the times she had to clear security at the prison came flooding back, of the guards making her take off her bra because it was setting off the metal detector, of how humiliating it was to walk by a half dozen COs, of feeling vulnerable and exposed. She felt her breath get short and spilled her purse all over the floor.

She says to Fernando, "I don't think you even noticed." She is gently chiding him, but highlighting the small ways she still carries her trauma. She has it controlled to a degree that it can go undetected. Just as there is a post-incarceration syndrome in former prisoners, I wonder if there isn't an equivalent condition in prison wives.

Her voice begins to tremble. "My husband suffered a lot. He has been mentally injured, and it is not his fault. And I will always have to be stronger than him."

She begins to cry for the first time since we met. She hadn't cried when she listed one horrific experience after another, the relentless onslaught of disappointment mingled with unyielding responsibilities that were those eighteen years. But she cries when she tells this simple truth: that even though Fernando came home, and even though they now live in a beautiful place, her work will never be done. She will still be in the position of holding him down, even on the outside.

Fernando is quiet while Crystal speaks. He takes in her pain. Then he says, "You asked me about how we ameliorate all of this. Part of that is being grateful."

"That's right," Crystal concurs, wiping her eyes. "That's how I didn't fall off the road."

They both come back to gratitude often, as the key to staying intact, especially during the prison years.

"And now if something happens, we stop and try to figure out what went wrong, what was the trigger," he says.

And as quickly as the wave of emotion swept over both of them, it dissipates and they are back to interrupting each other to tell a story about a time on their trip to Australia when Fernando got triggered in a souvenir store and the whole family was yelling at one another. They can laugh now at the scene they caused: they've named Fernando's PTSD "Jimmy," as in "Jimmy was there that day." Now that the mood is playful again, Crystal says to me with a sly smile, "Did you notice I didn't answer your question last night? About how I take care of myself? I don't even know where to begin."

———————

IT IS LATE afternoon by the time Fernando and I are back on the patio with bottles of Bud Light Lemon Tea. He had to eat several times— hunger is triggering for him, and Crystal always has snacks on hand. Then he had to nap, then he had to go for a run to exorcise his anxiety. Several times in our morning conversation, he got up and did jujitsu moves with an invisible opponent. His mind seems to always be going, and his ambient anxiety requires a physical outlet. But now he's fresh from the shower, his equilibrium restored.

Witnessing his dynamic with Crystal has been fascinating. They are like a single organism in some ways, finishing each other's sentences, not liking to be apart from the other for very long. But together, it is hard to keep focused on the matter at hand, as the conversation often devolves into domestic spats or each fact-checking the other's story. I have been dying to hear from Fernando himself about his experience.

I want to understand the way Fernando thinks about the strange equation of his life. He was victimized by the justice system. But this is also the way he met his wife, and eventually had his family. In that respect, the worst thing that ever happened to him is also the best thing. The lavish home he lives in today is a payoff, however fractional, but it also traps him within a web of anxiety about how to maintain it. The retirement is well deserved, yet, as he said, it has atrophied him as a person. How does he make sense of these paradoxes?

"When I think about my life, I have been blessed," he says, a bottle of beer sweating in his hand. "My skill set has evolved in ways I never expected, whether that's academically or in the martial arts or just accomplishing a family. My family has been the stability of my life."

At many points in prison, he tells me, he felt despair. Suicide entered his mind. It was the obligation to his wife and kids that pulled him back from the edge. Having to be accountable to a cause greater than himself is what kept him going in the darkest of hours. "To make relationships work," he says, "you have to die to yourself. You can't be so concerned about yourself. 'I' is too ego-based." He credits a faith-based life for the ability to surrender to the family and to shut out the temptations of the world.

As I have become immersed in the world of prison relationships, I've grown preoccupied with the power dynamics in these arrangements. Outside observers often say that the person on the outside, usually the woman in heterosexual relationships, is the one wielding the power. She can decide to pick up his phone calls, whether to add money to his commissary account, whether or not to visit. But this has never quite added up to me. I have seen the way prison wives are shackled to their phones, constantly paranoid about missing that precious call. It seems inherently unbalanced.

"In terms of power, it depends on who is more infatuated with who," Fernando observes. Just like outside, it seems. The person who needs more is always at a loss. So, too, in prison relationships. Perhaps that universal truth is a great equalizer. But still, he thinks, the person in the free world is the person with the more material power. She has adjusted to living by the norms of society. "The guy can't act as he normally would when he's free, and the guy is not seeing how the lady lives. I mean, she may be—what's that noise?"

He stops midsentence. He jumps up at a vague buzzing sound that is undetectable to me amid the low insect swarm and the trees rustling in the yard. Fernando is clearly unnerved. He darts around the patio. "I think it might be a bullfrog?" I offer. After pacing the perimeter, he sits back down. He takes a deep breath and continues. "Okay . . . when he's in prison, the woman knows where the man is. That already becomes a level of control, right? You can know where he is, unless he's doing some down-low stuff."

He echoes Crystal's sentiments about prison being a time of suspended reality. "When you get married in prison, you don't know a person. You don't even get to go on a date, and that's what happened to us. We love each other, but you just don't know."

What he means, I think, is that the love in prison relationships is real: you can fall in love with a piece of someone, and that piece becomes amplified. The limited access you have to your person makes it possible to gloss over the differences that might cause friction, and the other million mitigating factors are easier to overlook within the confines of visits and phone calls. But at the same time, you never know, do you? Any relationship can stay superficial or live in a suspended animation, if both parties are willing. The contours of prison just highlight that fact.

Beyond the incredible work it takes to make a marriage and a family function in the wake of PTSD and a gross miscarriage of justice, I'm curious to know how Fernando makes sense of having done another man's time.

The murder of Raymond Blount was eventually connected to Luis Muñoz, known on the streets as "Wool Lou." The "wool" in his alias is a reference to the crack vials he dealt. Muñoz has remained at large since the time of the murder. Some believe he fled the country. This man's actions set off a ripple effect. The full spectrum of consequences could not have been known to him at the time. One man would die, one man would go to prison, one woman would be the bearer of a great burden. Children would be born. A family would be made. Love and strife and struggle would happen, and one man's justice would finally be realized. But it would be a messy justice. Healing would come, as would much pain. So I have to ask Fernando Bermudez: "What would you say to Luis Muñoz?"

Fernando exhales sharply. He looks at the ground and says, "I would just say to him, 'You're an asshole, man, for letting me stay in prison so long, man!'"

This seems indisputable.

He pauses and laughs. "I would say that. But I would also say this: God had a plan. I know my life had a purpose based on where I am today. I went through a rough conviction that took over eighteen years of my life, for a crime I didn't commit. I stood up to the challenge and I did the best I could to educate myself under negative conditions. I want people to know that if you fight and have hope and have faith, anything is possible. I really believe that. I've sought to live by my principles. I've been consistent. I invented myself. You have the power within you to choose."

You have the power to choose whether you send the letter to the prisoner. To choose whether you write back. You can choose to open yourself up to love. You can choose to use the time wisely. You can choose to leave. You can choose to get your head right. You can choose to make a family when everything else has been taken from you. You can choose to go on.

"The power to choose is the ultimate freedom," he says.

———

LATER THAT NIGHT, Crystal cooks dinner. We eat while watching an episode of *Dateline* that features a friend of theirs who says he was wrongly convicted. The story is about how his mother defended his innocence even after his conviction, by stalking and entrapping a juror she believed to be corrupt. It is yet another story of a woman going to great lengths to support a man in prison.

Crystal serves us fried chicken, asparagus, mashed potatoes that are a buttery velvet heaven. Everything is delicious. To an outside observer, it may not look like much, but the energy and focus required to make a list, go shopping, organize the ingredients, and prepare the food has been out of reach for Crystal for a long time. She is serving her family a home-cooked meal, sure, but she is also doing what she's been yearning to do: getting back to herself. Getting back to cooking. To feeling in control. Maybe this is how healing happens, in these small ways. I compliment her on the dinner. "It's just a simple country meal," Crystal says and smiles, as she takes a seat on the couch next to her husband.

EIGHT

GEORGIA

A FEW MONTHS AFTER my crisis of conscience over Benny, in the dead of the winter of 2019, I log on to Facebook to discover a lengthy post from Jo. She posts prolifically. But this one, on February 15, stops me:

> Ok. Time for the "big announcement."
>
> I know there will probably be a few of y'all who will really have a hard time not saying "I told you so" and frankly, with all the love of Jesus in my heart . . . FUCK y'all. You're ignorant and self-righteous and you don't know nearly as much as you think you do. This isn't for you.
>
> For the rest of you, without going into detail, Benny and I didn't make it. Things have been rough for the past few months; there was also some stuff brewing on his end I was unaware of before that, apparently. I've been quiet while I tried to work things through and did a lot of praying and kind of waited to see how this would shake out. I'm not going to disrespect him OR discuss it but what it boils down to is that his fears over homecoming and a couple of other situations got the best of him and caused some behavior I can forgive but just can't live with. He's not in a place, at least right

now, where he wants to fix it and so I'm letting it go. I don't know everything the future might hold but for now we're definitely done. As in "papers and a new plan" done. It is what it is. I'm HURTING but I'm OK too because I know it's the right move. I love you guys. If I'm quiet, I'm just kind of getting myself together. Just wanted y'all to know, so there it is. Keep BOTH OF US in your thoughts and prayers, please, especially him. Thanks, gang.

I can't believe it. There, in black-and-white, is the dissolution of Jo and Benny's marriage. The news is shocking, but it is still Jo through and through, the woman who can say "with all the love of Jesus in my heart" and "FUCK y'all" in the same breath. We haven't spoken in several months. I have a newborn and have been on my own planet of nighttime feedings and endless diaper changes. I scroll down her page and it becomes evident that she hasn't been posting about her beloved for a while anyway. I pick up my phone to shoot her a text. She responds with "I'm not mad. I'm not bitter. But I am done." I call. On the phone, Jo's voice sounds tired, but grounded, determined.

Their troubles had been percolating for a while but came to a head two months ago, in December. His main gripe, she tells me, was that she did not send him a calendar of sexy photos of herself, a Christmas gift they'd discussed for a long time and that he had been eagerly anticipating. I think she can hear the disgust in my voice as I react to this as the inciting event. When she let him know it wasn't happening, he threw "a tantrum," by her description, and they got into an ugly fight. She is quick to empathize with his side of it, explaining that these photos are the way he feels intimacy with her, his wife. But she has always felt awkward styling herself this way. I remember her telling me as much in Dallas nearly three years ago.

"I own that," she says, referring to the vaunted calendar. "I didn't do it." The reasons she didn't do it, aside from a general discomfort with posing in her underwear for photos that many a corrections officer would see before it made its way into her husband's hands, are numerous. One of her dogs died unexpectedly in early December. She had vet bills, her kids' grief, her own grief. Her parents were coming to town for the holidays. In triage, pulling together an expensive photo shoot did not take priority.

Then January 1 rolled around. For the past five years she had been depositing $100 into Benny's commissary account on the first of the month. But in multiple conversations they had about preparations she was making for his homecoming, they'd agreed that the monthly commissary allowance would be better saved. He seemed to have forgotten this. This angered him further.

"He basically told me that he could get other women to fulfill his needs. I told him that's not how adult relationships work. He was acting like his old self, very narcissistic and sarcastic," she says. He sent her dozens of attacking messages. She told him to stop and that she would talk to him when he was ready to be respectful. This was the old Benny, the one she had told me so many times was dead and gone.

On Valentine's Day, she logged on to GettingOut, the messaging system his facility uses. Prisoners can use the email and text applications, as well as post photo albums on their page. Jo saw a new album, one she'd never seen before, all of the pictures showing Benny smiling into the camera. She surmised it was not intended for her, as he had captioned his portraits "How does this thing work?" and "What's your name?" She asked him about it in an email. He didn't respond, but the next time she visited the site, the album had been taken down. She told him that if there were other women he was talking to, she'd send him divorce papers. And he said he'd sign them.

"Now the papers are in an envelope on my desk," she tells me.

I think back to her presentation at the conference, coaching women to recognize the signs of manipulation. My mind clicks through the conversation we had in Maryland, at her neighbor's baby shower. She had walked me through the ins and outs of her prison-wife life, with streamers and balloons surrounding us, and as we nibbled on cookies, she had laid out her fears. She wasn't afraid of being cheated on, she had said, so much as she was terrified of being used for money. Given the order of events, it sounds as if her biggest fear has been realized.

She is sitting on those divorce papers, though. It seems as if Benny is making overtures, however feeble. He had seen a mutual friend of theirs, another Oregon State Penitentiary wife, at a prison event. He told her to tell Jo to get in touch. He has been hitting up all their mutual friends to urge Jo to speak to him, without contacting her directly. This incenses her. "I don't think someone who has been in prison for almost ten years has forgotten about the U.S. Postal Service," she says. Even in the midst of sadness, she's still cracking jokes.

She is hoping a letter will arrive soon. More waiting, more anticipation. She's thought about sending the divorce papers, but his birthday is coming up in early March and she doesn't want to ruin it. Excuses? Hope? It feels like both.

I ask her how she feels. "I feel both devastated and relieved," she says. "The blessing is that this is happening now, and not ten months from now, when he comes home."

I feel relieved, too. After revisiting Benny's past, this breakup before he arrives in her life full-time seems like an act of divine protection. Jo chalks up his behavior to classic self-sabotage. As his out date draws near, he is trying to alienate the one person he knows can help him. She hopes they can work it out, though. He has a long road before he can earn her trust back, should he choose to. "He has six months to get back into my good graces," she says. "Then he may sleep on the couch."

Fortunately, she has a strong community around her. She, Kyle, and the kids have relocated to Georgia, where Kyle is stationed. Right after the breakup, a group of friends from her church took her roller skating to get her mind off things. She is getting sensible counsel from her pastor, who has advised her to leave him be and to let him show her who he is.

I wonder how the breakup will position her in the prison-wife community. So much of Jo's identity and time over the past five years has been tied up in being the poster wife of an MWI couple. She is Mama Jo, shepherding newbies through their fears and anxieties, giving tough love to women who are letting themselves be treated by their men as less than. Who will she be now?

"Prison was a big part of my work," she says. "But it was always more about the relationships generally than prison anyway."

This is what I've always believed, too: I've seen the women bonding in a way that makes the men secondary. Prison is the gateway, but the friendships and self-actualization are the real gifts. Jo says the breakup has brought her and Ro even closer. And her work as Mama Jo has doubled her accountability to herself: "I can't tell women all day long to know their worth and then not do the same myself."

There are layers of shame within the prison-wife community. She and others have told me that they feel enormous pressure to make their relationships flawless, because they are already so stigmatized from society. But Jo hopes that her transparency will allow other women to become more honest, to not hide behind facades of Instagram perfection.

She sounds circumspect, centered in her uncertain moment. She says she is just trying to sit in the storm for now. "But don't get me wrong," she says. "I've cried so hard, I've had to stop crying to go throw up and come back and cry some more." Right now she is waiting, which she's used to. But this is a very different kind of waiting: waiting to see what moves this person will make in a place where he can move very little. How he will exercise his power.

"Either way, I'm going to be fine," she says. "He may not be. But I will be."

NINE

SHEILA AND JOE

SHEILA RULE'S TWO-BEDROOM West Village apartment is in a prewar co-op with the building's name in cursive script on a green awning. African sculptures and family photos adorn shelves and end tables. With original moldings, a working fireplace, built-in bookcases, and hardwood floors, it is the spacious apartment of New York real estate fantasy.

She bought her place during her tenure at *The New York Times*. She began in 1977, at twenty-seven years old, as a metro reporter, later writing national stories and eventually moving up to foreign correspondent. After traipsing the globe for the paper of record, she wanted a place to call her own.

When I arrive at Sheila's apartment on a humid evening in August after a downpour, just a few blocks south of where I dined with Jacques two years ago, she greets me at the door with a wide smile that flaunts the charming gap between her teeth. Her thin dreadlocks are piled high into a bun at the crown of her head, and she's wearing red cat-eye glasses. Even in the comfort of her own home, she has a regal bearing. A pot of Brazilian shrimp simmers on the stove. She offers me a glass of pinot grigio and I sit in the living room with her husband, Joe, who is sipping Malbec and watching MSNBC. He's reclining in an easy chair, his red Air Jordans up, unwinding after a day's work at a law firm. Joe is soft-spoken and mild, with a neatly trimmed goatee and a shaved head. He has a disarming ease and a soft warmth.

This is the apartment Joe had seen in pictures before he ever set foot over the threshold. This is the apartment he came home to after serving twenty-five years in prison—more than half his life—for taking the life of another man. Like the crime Fernando was wrongly convicted of, it was also a bar shooting in New York State in 1991. They were roughly the same age, young men in the first flush of freedom. They were locked up in some of the same facilities. The big difference is that, while they both did the time, Joe really did the crime.

Joe and Sheila have been married for fifteen years. Joe has been home for the past three. Twelve years of their relationship were in prison. They have pushed through the barriers of the system, homecoming, the inevitable bouts of PTSD and adjustment, and the capriciousness of parole—both of receiving it and of living within its parameters, which Joe is set to be done with in two months. After that, he will be completely free, or "off paper." Sheila and Joe live a quiet, comfortable life. Their marriage is happy, familiar, pleasantly worn in, "like an old shoe," Sheila likes to say.

They did it. They came out on the other side. So how do they make it work?

I'M THRILLED TO find a happy marriage at this point, after witnessing the breakups of Jo and Benny and Jacques and Ivié. I need to prove to myself what I intuitively sense—that it *is* possible for MWI couples to thrive on the outside—despite mounting evidence to the contrary. I had heard so much about these audacious love affairs from so many prison wives, and the big payoff of togetherness they're waiting for at the end of the sentence. And yet I have found that many couples are unable to get there. Without that happy ending, I fear that the harsh stereotypes about "these deluded women" and the men who sit in cells making empty promises might edge too close to true.

Joe committed a horrible crime, which resulted in a hefty sentence, so he likely has experienced serious post-incarceration trauma and institutionalization. Yet, from what I know so far, they seem to be devoted to the daily work of making a marriage. Given the challenges they've faced, I desperately want to know how their success came to be.

The first thing that strikes me about Sheila and Joe is that they have good time on their side. Joe has been home for three years. And Sheila is financially stable in a city where being middle-class equates to being wealthy anywhere else. She has a close relationship with her thirty-year-old son, Sean. She has had one of the most competitive jobs in the field of journalism and a rich inner life filled with culture, connection, service.

Like many of the other free-world members of the MWI couples I have met, Sheila had never experienced any personal contact with the criminal justice system. She didn't have a friend or family member in prison, so for her the whole world was new. As with other prison wives, Joe was not her first marriage. And, like the vast majority of free-world partners I've come to know, she wasn't looking for anything romantic at the start.

SHEILA GREW UP in St. Louis. Her mother was a nurse, and her father held a range of jobs, from working as a cook at a hospital to becoming a high school custodian to odd jobs. Though from their address in "the ghetto," as Sheila calls it, they may have been considered poor, "we never went without," she says. "My mother drilled into her daughters two things: *Life is hard* and *Be able to take care of yourself.* So, as a result, she raised three independent daughters. I'm the middle."

She was always a reader and a writer. "Every summer I wrote 'novels' in little stationery books." Sheila was always emulating her elder sister, so when that sister came home from school one day and said she wanted to be a journalist, Sheila decided that was the career she would have, too. After graduating high school, she attended the University of Missouri's journalism program, the best in the country at the time. She and her sisters were the first in their immediate family to attend college.

At the end of her junior year, Sheila landed an internship at her hometown newspaper, the *St. Louis Post-Dispatch*. They gave her a full-time job when she graduated. She started out writing for the Women's Page, where she would turn up in her Afro to cover upscale Junior League and society events. "People were just not expecting me," she laughs. "Not even Black people. When I interviewed the poet Nikki Giovanni, I was wearing my gele, and even she said, 'I didn't know they had people like you at the paper!' It felt great."

After a fortuitous move to the city desk, where she got to write more rigorous stories for four years, she applied to several big-league papers and ended up at *The New York Times*. In the eighties, she worked as a foreign correspondent in Nairobi and London. When she made her way back to the States, she worked as a culture reporter through the nineties. "I wasn't very good at it," she says. "I knew my days were numbered when I'd get an invitation to a Grammy party and I'd say, 'It starts at 11 p.m.?!' My friend told me, 'You're too old to be covering somebody named Snoop Doggy Dogg!' "

When Sheila and Joe first connected, she was stepping into an era of serene settledness. No longer frequenting Grammy parties, she had moved into management at the newspaper, running the internship program and scouting for reporters. She was in her fifties, and Sean, the son she had adopted when he was three years old, was now entering his adolescence. She had planted deep roots, created a robust support system. She wasn't in a relationship, but that didn't bother her. She had been married twice before, the first time to Gerald Boyd, who would later become the first Black managing editor of *The New*

York Times. The two met as cub reporters in St. Louis. She met her next husband when she was living in London. They were still legally married, but had no relationship and little contact, when she met Joe. (She had to track him down in South Africa to get him to sign divorce papers.) She had crafted a family of her own, a stellar career. It was a life of "hard-won satisfaction," she says.

As a practice of gratitude for her life's blessings, Sheila felt compelled to be of service. She'd done volunteer work before and was committed to progressive causes and social justice. Like Jo, she was drawn to a prison ministry table at a volunteer fair. But unlike Jo, she was motivated to work with a prison because of the disproportionate numbers of Black people behind bars. Soon Sheila was given some letters to respond to. She was corresponding with more than a dozen inmates, exchanging facts and anecdotes about their lives, when a letter from Joe Robinson, in Five Points Correctional Facility, came across her desk in August of 2002.

Sheila was struck by the letter. While she was feeling settled in her life, Joe was not. "It's impossible to feel settled in prison," he later tells me. But he was feeling confident, comfortable in his own skin. He had grappled with the person he once was, the drug dealer with a baby to feed who had taken the life of another young Black man. Joe made no excuses or rationalizations for his past. But his portrait of who he had become was compelling. He told her about his upbringing in the East New York neighborhood of Brooklyn, his childhood dreams. He said that although he was in prison, "my soul is free." Upon reading Joe's letter, Sheila recalls, "I said, 'Wow.'"

He had done ten years, inching toward the halfway mark of his twenty-five-year sentence, when a friend told him about the church pen-pal program. So he decided to give it a whirl. He said he was interested in corresponding with a "young lady." In her return letter, Sheila let him down gently, saying that there were no *young* ladies working in the prison ministry.

In the time between sending his letter and Sheila answering him at the end of the summer of 2002, Joe had been transferred to Sullivan Correctional Facility. In a stroke of humanity, whoever was working prison mail that day forwarded Sheila's letter on. A small kindness like that is never guaranteed. Joe thought it was funny that Sheila had taken his desire to hear from a "young" lady so literally and explained in his reply that he was using the term colloquially. With that semantic confusion out of the way, the pair struck up a robust correspondence.

She told him flat out that she was twenty years his senior and couldn't be his companion, but that she could be his friend. Even though the trajectory of their lives could not have been more different, Sheila saw someone of deep intellect and feeling. "I will respond in kind," she wrote. She told him about her life, her work, her son. For Joe, the exchange was therapeutic. He found a place in Sheila's letters where he could be vulnerable, something he wasn't used to doing after years behind bars. And Sheila reciprocated with the same kind of emotional honesty Joe poured out on the page. "After we began exchanging letters, my life went from black-and-white to Technicolor," he says.

Joe spent most of his childhood in East New York, with a stint in Harlem from 1984 to 1985—to outsiders, places synonymous with crime, poverty, and peril. Joe was the eldest of five, and his father, a pilot, was mostly out of the picture. Joe bounced around with his mom and siblings, from his grandmother's, in the projects, to shelters, to an apartment when his mom found a place of her own. His mom worked odd jobs and in factories, all unsteady work that would place her on public assistance when she was unemployed. When Joe was fourteen, the family landed in another homeless shelter. Joe hated it— the stigma, the danger.

The family was eventually placed in an apartment in Harlem when Joe was fifteen. It was the eighties. He'd walk over crack vials on his way to school; women would proposition him for sex for money on his walk to the subway. He was attending Park West High School, in midtown Manhattan, getting good grades, with dreams of becoming a pilot one day, like his father. He was in a special program to take flying lessons at Farmingdale State College. Joe's aspirations were specific, and he was on his way to achieving them.

Joe was often put in charge of his younger siblings. His mom would say she was going out and sometimes not return until a day or two later. "We'd have to get creative with our food," Joe recalls. "We'd stretch cold cuts between the five of us for a couple days." His world was shattered one afternoon when he was babysitting for the kids. He was in his mom's bedroom watching his favorite movie, *An Officer and a Gentleman*, about a Navy pilot hopeful, for the tenth time. As he was rewinding the tape in the VCR on her dresser, he bumped it and several empty vials of crack rolled out of a drawer. He recognized them from his walk to school.

"When I first discovered the paraphernalia, I thought, *Wow, she's one of them. A crackhead.* I remember feeling scared, like, *What does this mean for our world? She's the leader of our family*," he says. Joe tried to keep evidence of her drug use hidden from his younger siblings. But a few weeks later, his seven-year-old brother came out of the room holding the same vials. Joe's heart broke.

A year later, the family moved back in with his grandmother in the Louis H. Pink Houses project, in Brooklyn. "The eighties were about fashion and money. As a kid, I didn't realize how powerful those forces are," he says, and he got caught up in the pressure to conform to the values of the day. "When I look back at it now, it was based on poverty. Whether you're poor or not, you want what everybody else has. I just went about it the wrong way." He began committing petty robberies with older friends in the neighborhood. They would buy food and clothes—Guess jeans, Nike sneakers, sheepskin coats, leather bombers. Soon he ended up at Rikers. At sixteen, he spent four months in the jail, as his family could not cobble together the $1,000 bail. In his time there, he witnessed stabbings and slashings. His grandmother came to visit him, but his mother, still in the grip of addiction, never did. He left with his GED and probation.

Joe dreamt of getting out of New York and going to Embry-Riddle Aeronautical University in Florida, but no one in his family had ever gone to college and he didn't know how to go about securing financial aid. In January 1989, he began school at Mohawk Valley Community College, in Utica, New York. The college had an airframe program, and more than anything, he wanted to be near airplanes.

The first summer he was home from college, his girlfriend got pregnant. Reluctantly, he dropped out. He had a job as a messenger, but that was hardly enough to cover the expenses for a new family. Desperate, he got a credit card and a cash advance to buy maternity clothes and necessities for the baby. He also used the cash to buy drugs to sell. It turned out he had a head for numbers and business. He started selling crack, the same drug that had taken hold of his mother.

Joe wasn't using, but he was hooked. On a good day, he could make $4,000 or more. He was thinking about providing for his son, but he also enjoyed the adrenaline rush of making a deal, the thrill of cash in his pocket. The feeling of having enough.

The summer after his son, Joseph, was born, he went back up to Utica to sell more. There, he ran into Nolan Woods, another dealer up from the city, just six months older than Joe. Both were twenty-one years old. Nolan had been robbed a few weeks earlier, and he confronted Joe because he thought he might have been involved. He hadn't been. Joe told his girlfriend about the confrontation. Things were getting dangerous. She told him he should just come home. But he didn't. He was addicted to the lifestyle. "All I had to do was just go home," Joe says today.

The young men ran into each other at a bar a few weeks later.

Nolan stepped up to Joe, asked if they had beef. Joe felt a gun in Nolan's waistband. He himself wasn't carrying a weapon. In a split second, Joe thought, *It's him or me.* He grabbed Nolan's gun and shot him three times, fatally. He dropped the gun and ran out into the night. Joe was on the lam for five and a half months, in a fever of anxiety, guilt, and paranoia. When he was finally arrested for the murder, he says he felt a wave of relief.

———————

SHEILA AND JOE spent a year telling each other their stories through letters. It didn't get flirtatious, but there was a growing understanding that their relationship was developing into something that had great depth. Sheila would confide in her best friend, Rose. She told her that this was a special relationship and she was sure that Joe was going to be in her life forever, maybe as something of a surrogate younger brother. Rose wondered why it couldn't be more.

It wasn't because Joe was incarcerated. Perhaps owing to her training in interviewing people of all stripes, Sheila easily saw beyond his crime and his current address. "I never had qualms about being with someone in prison," she says, "but I had qualms about dating someone so much younger. For other people I'm like, *You go, girl!* But for me, it was weird."

After a few months of letter writing, Joe asked to meet his pen pal. Sheila initially said yes, then rescinded. She didn't want to risk jeopardizing such a great friendship. Then she had to have a surprise medical procedure. "It made me think, *Nothing is promised.* That's what spurred me."

Even though Joe had sent her a picture of himself, she didn't feel comfortable doing the same. She told him she had dreads. He told her he was looking forward to giving her a big hug and a kiss. She told him she was looking forward to collecting.

The couple met in person on October 3, 2003. Because of her

years as a journalist, Sheila wasn't nervous about entering a prison; as a reporter for the *Times*, she had written a story on the nursery at the Bedford Hills prison. Out of habit, she took in all the details—the vending machines, the guards, the clusters of couples playing cards—with a curious open eye. Joe found the woman with dreadlocks right away and scooped her up in an embrace. They spent several hours chatting, gazing into each other's eyes, getting to know one another, the air buzzing with the same electricity you feel on a good first date. When visiting hours were over, though, Sheila felt relieved. The whole experience had been so intense, and she needed some air to breathe.

Her fears about this in-person meeting had been realized. Their relationship had changed. When she got back to the city, she wrote him a letter.

Joe:
If I do not say this, I will explode . . .
I love you. I love you. I love you. I am in love with you. I am
in love with you. I am in love with you.

She put it in the mail and spent the next few days feeling like a fool. A few days later, she got Joe's response. On the outside of the envelope, so she wouldn't even have to wait to open it, he wrote:

I love you, too.

The couple married fifteen months later.

AS HAD HAPPENED with many of her prison-wife peers, Sheila's friends and family were surprised at the turn of events. That response caught her off-guard, because she felt so confident in Joe. She hadn't given much thought to mentioning her new love. She remembers telling one friend, a dyed-in-the-wool progressive, of her new relationship. "She said, 'How can you do that? Date someone in prison?!' I can't tell you how stunned I was." Another friend echoed the sentiment, asking how she could be with someone with charges like Joe's. Sheila informed her she wasn't marrying Joe's past. She was marrying the person he had become. Weary of the pushback, the couple reverted to telling "one right person at a time." At work, she kept her relationship quiet, as she did with most of her personal life.

Despite the negative reaction, "I didn't have second thoughts," she says. "I never had misgivings about dating someone who was incarcerated."

Her mother wasn't thrilled. She asked Sheila what her father would have thought. "And for that, I had an answer," Sheila says. "Daddy would have cared about the content of his character. And this is a man of great character." Her sisters pushed back, too, worrying that she was being used. But just before Sheila and Joe were to be married, on January 25, 2005, they called and told her, "We are here for you. We want you to have a happy marriage. We have your back." Later, her family became fully invested in Joe. Her eldest sister, Marsha, came to visit from Seattle and, sitting at the visiting table in prison, she said to Sheila, "Just think of what I would've missed. He's so sweet."

The ceremony, in the visiting room of Sullivan, was attended by their teenage sons, Sean and Joseph, along with Joe's mother, and Rose, who had pushed Sheila to take the leap. When Rose asked Joe how he felt, he said he was the happiest man in the world. When Rose asked Sheila the same question, she said she felt honored. In their vows to each other, they promised to live the spirit of their letters: the passion, their honesty, their respect for each other.

Because Joe was incarcerated in New York State, the decision to marry was sweetened by the possibility of conjugals. The couple was approved for a forty-four-hour trailer visit after six months. Sheila made the drive up to Sullivan, her car packed with groceries from

Trader Joe's for the weekend, and she remembers thinking on the highway, *Please, God, don't let me get hit by a bus on the way to be alone with my husband for the first time!*

Typically an erratic sleeper, Sheila slept soundly that first night together. Being in the arms of her husband made her feel secure, relaxed. Joe, on the other hand, couldn't fall asleep. He hadn't spent a night out of a cell in thirteen years. He stayed up, taking it all in: the comfort of the bed, the softness of the pillow. It was surreal to be lying next to his wife.

His world had gone from black-and-white to Technicolor, just as he described, and now that he was able to have visits with Sheila, her care created a veil of protection around him. Guards would notice and comment on the packages of Trader Joe's food Sheila would send him. If they see you are loved, that you have someone going out of their way for you, then they don't mess with you. "Or at least not as much," Joe qualifies. "They will abuse you, but they'll think twice." This is one of the powers of being in a relationship when you're in prison—the level of respect from staff and other inmates that it can engender. Hearing your name at mail call and for visiting hours means that someone on the outside cares. It means that someone on the outside has your back.

Sheila and Joe teamed up to work on a number of prison-related projects. Joe, a born entrepreneur, read every business book he could get his hands on. He traded cigarettes to build his personal library and taught finance classes to men inside. Compiling his knowledge, in 2007 he published *Think Outside the Cell: An Entrepreneur's Guide for the Incarcerated and Formerly Incarcerated.* To celebrate the release, he and Sheila had a mock publication ceremony on a conjugal, using the fake leather couch as a dais for Sheila to introduce him before Joe addressed an audience of invisible fans.

From there, they worked on several more books and events for the incarcerated and their families. Collaborating energized their sense of shared purpose; their teamwork extended beyond their marriage to helping others in their position. But it also surfaced their divergent styles. Sheila liked to complete one task at a time, while Joe preferred bouncing among several projects. Sheila was more introverted than Joe, who was eager to network and market their ideas. He began to feel frustrated because of his reliance on Sheila to execute his ideas on the outside. She feared they were becoming more focused on their business than on their relationship.

"It was horrible!" she laughs today. "He'd say, 'Look for conferences for budding entrepreneurs.' That's just not my world. I don't know anything about business, and I don't really *want* to know anything about business! I was trying to be whatever he needed me to be. I think it's a dynamic a lot of prison couples fall into. It can almost feel like the person in prison is an invalid. That person's mind is active, but it's as if the body doesn't work. You can begin to feel like the eyes, the ears, the legs. You're doing as much as you can, and you're doing it out of love, but you're doing things that are really beyond your capacity."

On a trailer visit in their second year of marriage, they caught a segment on *Oprah* that helped to clarify their particular challenges. It was an episode focused on describing your marriage in five words. In their first year of marriage, both of them chose positive adjectives like *healthy, focused, working, growing, enriching*. But in 2008, after having logged years of marriage within the prison system, blending families and work projects, they were at their lowest: *complicated, heavy, serious,* and *frustrating* were the words they were using.

As they waited out the eleven years until Joe was up for parole, they encountered family challenges, too. Joseph's mother died from HIV-related illness when he was four years old. Joe had been in prison for two years at that point, so Joseph's maternal grandmother stepped in to raise him under her roof in Connecticut. Being incarcerated never stopped Joe from being an engaged father. Joseph would visit him often with his grandmother or aunts, and then with Sheila. At visits they would play games of Monopoly and catch up on life. Joseph was able to join the new couple on conjugal visits. Joe recalled one of the visits that included his then seventeen-year-old son. In the middle of the night, Joe got up to use the bathroom and glimpsed Joseph thumbing through photo albums from when he was a baby, with pictures of himself, Joe, and his mother all together. Joe kept these albums in his cell, and Joseph had never seen them. Being able to spend the night together as a family enabled him to see those photographs.

In his teen years, Joseph fought with his grandmother, stopped going to school, and would sometimes run away. Whenever he was picked up by the police, he would give them Sheila's name. She traveled all over New York City, and once to New Jersey, to retrieve him. Another time, an assistant at work interrupted a meeting Sheila was leading to inform her that the police were on the line for her, as Joseph was in trouble again. As Joe wrote in an essay, Sheila "was taken for a loop by his chaotic life. It was just the opposite of the quiet, comfortably predictable life she'd led with Sean for the past twelve years. For me, the chaos underscored how I could not be present in my life as I longed to be." Phone calls from Sheila now almost always brought bad news, and Joe found himself shutting down, making it difficult for Sheila to know how to help.

But the time apart from each other also meant time to process and think about how to tackle their problems. Through reflection and conversation, Joe realized he had been trying to live through Sheila. And Sheila realized she was trying to save Joe. This is a phenomenon I'd come to see in many couples, yet these two were the first I'd met who identified and named it. Ivié wanted Jacques to access resources to help her work on her appeal. Jo badly wanted Benny to be free of his old ways, perhaps more than he did. Crystal kept hope alive for Fernando, even when it came at a depleting cost to her.

After having this epiphany, the couple shifted their focus. Joe stopped nagging her about the business, and they went back to concentrating on their marriage. As Sheila describes it, "Our marriage is the engine that makes everything else happen. With whatever we do—whether it's a criminal justice project or dealing with our family—it starts from the base of our marriage." Two years later, they were back to describing their union as *sturdy, resilient, promising.*

They found ways to work through challenges in their marriage, even at a distance. But they were always dealing with the random caprices of the system. Package items would sometimes get sent back without reason. Once, when Sheila brought Joseph and Sean to visit, the guards tried to reject their IDs as invalid, even though they had been approved on prior visits. And of course, there was the looming question of Joe's parole. His sentence was twenty-five to life, so eleven years from the time they married was the earliest Joe could hope to come home. I ask Sheila if she ever thought about the possibility of his never coming home. The answer she gives astounds me.

"I just didn't let myself go there," she tells me over dinner in her apartment. We're soaking up the last bits of curry sauce off our plates. Even beyond the question of Joe's release date, Sheila applied strategic blotting out to get through. "I told Joe the other day that I don't think I let myself realize how hard it was." Thinking back to the blinders she applied, she connects to another overwhelming uphill climb:

"It reminds me of the early days of my career, when African American journalists were just integrating newsrooms. I was in the second or third wave. I'll never forget a copy editor at my first paper saying he saw Shirley Chisholm on TV and how surprised he was because, one, she's Black and, two, she's a woman, and, *Wow, she was really articulate!* That's what we walked into," she says. "At *The New York Times,* Black journalists typically did the night rewrite." This was the thankless, invisible work of waiting for something newsworthy to occur in the small hours, writing briefs, chasing down stories that had already appeared in tabloids. It was not a stepping-stone toward a successful career but rather a place to be kept apart. "We fought it, we sued, we won. But I think we didn't really let ourselves let it all in, because we probably wouldn't have gone back. It's a good thing we didn't know the depth of it. My God, it was hard. But you just kept moving."

Sheila and Joe kept moving, too, inching closer and closer to the parole hearing in 2016. I ask Joe if he would read to me the letter he submitted to the board. He returns from the bedroom with a thick three-ring binder, containing the letter along with other proof of his rehabilitation. Among those papers, I notice a document from the Parole Preparation Project.

Joe let me know that Nolan Woods's girlfriend was pregnant when Joe shot him. She had a daughter who never met her father. In 2015 that daughter, now a young woman, requested a meeting with the man who killed her father. With the help of a mediator, Joe came face-to-face with his victim's daughter. In discussing this sit-down, Joe gets quiet. "That was really, really tough," he says. "I can't even describe it." He pulls out the letter to the board and begins to read.

"Nearly twenty-five years ago, I took a life." He stops, swallows. "This is going to be really hard. I can feel it already." He pauses. "I shot and killed Nolan Woods. I am profoundly remorseful for taking Nolan's life, and I have made a firm commitment to use my life to purposefully honor his. Toward that end, I was instrumental in organizing the first-ever New York State prisoners gun buyback program. I have facilitated a fourteen-week manhood responsibility course for more than ten years. And I have personally mentored dozens of young men.

"In 2002 my life would be enhanced in ways I could not imagine. In August of that year, I wrote a letter to the Riverside Church Prison Ministry seeking a pen pal." He stops and chuckles to himself. I look over at Sheila, who has a small smile on her face. Her eyes are misty.

"My hope was that I might also find a companion, someone with whom I could share my pain and my dreams, someone with whom I could engage in stimulating conversation that could help me stay in touch with my humanity. I received a response from Sheila Rule, the prison ministry volunteer responsible for responding to incarcerated people. We began exchanging letters regularly, and I was more engaged with the world. I had hope, a greater sense of purpose. As months went by, I fell in love with Sheila's heart, compassion, sharp intellect, and genuineness. She fell in love with me, too, and we were married on January 25, 2005.

"Today I am a mature forty-six-year-old man who is happily married to a loving and supportive wife. I have a deep sense of responsibility to my family, my community, and the larger society. And I have the stability I have been unconsciously seeking since my youth . . . I reached a place in my journey here where I can say with great certainty: I am not my past, I am not my mistakes, I take full responsibility for my actions, I am prepared to lead a life I can be proud of. After you review the balance of my packet and letters of recommendation, I ask you grant me parole."

He puts the letter back on the table and wipes his eyes. We are all crying.

"When I was inside," Joe says, "I thought a lot about the capacity of human beings to do good work and also to do things that are really harmful. The same person can do both. Prison brought out the best and the worst in me, and so did my neighborhood. I've made a good impact, but there's also the capacity to take a life."

A paradox like this would seem to suggest a choice: Will you be good or bad? Will you turn to darkness or to the light? But Joe is saying that the human condition is not either/or. It is both/and. These conflicting desires and impulses are all mingled and mediated within a single person.

The same goes in prison relationships. While I initially approached the subject with binary questions like *Are these women out of their minds? Are these relationships real? Can they ever work?* I've seen that they transcend these tidy boxes. Prison relationships are sometimes a bubble of heaven against a backdrop of hell. They can be deluded with great expectations yet anchored by the day-to-day pragmatism of figuring out the most essential components of connection: *How will we speak to each other when we are separated? How will we express love when we are barred from physical touch?* They are both safe for women who have been hurt, emotionally or physically, and also the most naked ledge to stand on.

As I've spent these years reporting on prison relationships, I've occasionally told people what I'm writing about, and they'll offer their (unsolicited) read on what's really at play. *Those women are afraid of true intimacy,* they'll say. *They are the ones with the power, who can pick up the phone when he calls, go to visit, or not,* they'll say. I'm sure in many cases this is true. And I'm also sure that's something people who have never experienced the corrections system would believe. Everyone—both the prison wife and the person in prison—feels utterly powerless.

When I ask Sheila if she ever felt she wielded more power than Joe in the relationship, she says, "On any given day when you walk into a facility, you don't know what you're going to get. It's the CO who has the power and who determines how your day is going to go. I never felt I had any power. What attracted me to Joe is that he knows who he is. He has no problem being wrong. This is a person who is so comfortable with himself, and that is what I want."

Joe was granted parole on his first shot. In 2016, he got a second chance at life on the outside.

———

ONCE THEY HAD a release date, they had three months to get ready. They were consumed with making lists. Sheila googled a list of men's wardrobe essentials. They brainstormed all the things they wanted to do when Joe got home—go dancing at SOB's, catch a stand-up show, and more risqué items. Sheila wrote them down on strips of paper and kept them in a basket, waiting to be drawn from. They joked that when Joe got home, Sheila could finally kick back and be taken care of, that Joe would feed her grapes.

On October 3, 2016, thirteen years to the day after their first visit, after twenty-five years behind bars, Joe walked out of Fishkill Correctional Facility and into the arms of his wife. They got into the car and onto the highway to hit the outlet mall on their way back down to the city. It was the first time Joe had been in the passenger seat of a car in two and a half decades and felt the speed underneath him. "Sugar, slow down," he pleaded on the road that took them away from the prison.

Back in the city, they dropped the rental car at Avis. Sheila had planned their walk home to cross Washington Square Park, in Greenwich Village, with its iconic arch, a place she had often described to him. Dusk was settling over the trees and the fountain. The sprinklers were spitting. A man was playing piano. Students were gathered on benches. Dogs tackled each other. Kids were drawing on the cement with chalk. A juggler tossed beanbags into the air. As they rounded the corner and took in the scene, Joe gasped. He stood at the lip of the park, astonished by the beauty of a regular moment in New York City, of people going about their lives. "I'll never forget that gasp," Sheila says.

In his first months home, Joe would experience that feeling often. They'd be out on a walk, running errands, and he would feel the layers of grief and defense he'd been carrying fall away from him. Shedding prison, he calls it. It would come over him like a wave, and he'd feel something peel back and depart. For Sheila, the homecoming felt surreal. For the first year, when they'd be talking, eating dinner, it would hit her: *Oh, Joe's home!* "The first few months were filled with gratitude, joy, wonderment," Joe says. "But also tension."

That tension surfaced in surprising ways. If Sheila tried to slide past Joe in their narrow kitchen, he would tense up. If someone bumped him walking down the sidewalk, he'd get frustrated. Once, after seeing a movie with a friend of theirs, they walked down Waverly Place and a drunk student stumbled into a friend and knocked her glasses off. Joe grabbed him and asked him what he was doing. That reaction surprised even him.

Personal space is a huge boundary in prison. "Space is my autonomy, my barrier between me and the rest of the world," Joe explains. That barrier is one of the few things within your control, and when someone encroaches upon it, it feels disrespectful. "People just shouldn't be up on you," Joe says.

Joe and Sheila were also navigating the parole system. Joe would be on state supervision for three years. This meant meeting with his parole officer every few weeks when he first got home, then every four months. Parolees are required to be in school or working, and he chose to do both. He enrolled at Borough of Manhattan Community College and works at a law firm helping the formerly incarcerated readjust to life on the outside.

Joe couldn't leave the city without permission; he had random drug testing and a 9 p.m. curfew. Fortunately, he didn't have to do drug counseling, as substance abuse was never an issue for him. The absence of addiction, plus Sheila's savvy and economic stability in offering a comfortable place to live, put him at a great advantage during this period of adjustment.

Beyond those obvious advantages, Sheila provided a safe harbor. "He had a place where things would be handled, taken care of," she says. "He knew everything was going to be okay. He didn't have to go back to the old neighborhood. After the trauma he had been through, he could rest easy for a while. He didn't have to go directly into the next trauma, like so many people have to."

But even with almost everything working in their favor, they were not immune to the continued disruptions of the system. Parole officers can check in on you anytime, twenty-four hours a day. Sometimes, when the couple was sound asleep in bed, they'd get a rude awakening. "It happened a couple times past eleven at night. The officer would ring the doorbell insistently, look inside the bedroom while I was still in bed. It was totally destabilizing," Sheila says. For her, those unscheduled pop-ins were the hardest part of Joe still being a number in the system. The randomness, the intrusion into the privacy of her home, her bedroom, was nothing short of traumatizing. "I'd wake up in the middle of the night, worried someone had come and we'd missed them. I'd go to the door to see if there was a note, saying we slept through the visit. There was always this sense that something could happen, that someone could show up, that there could be some misunderstanding."

That feeling of violation was nothing new to Joe, but it served to remind him that he still wasn't entirely free. And the couple had disagreements that also brought back his time in prison. Anytime he felt Sheila was talking down to him or telling him what to do, Joe would get terse. "Sheila would be trying to be helpful with technical stuff or the computer," he recalls, "and I'd get very short. The underlying rationale is because in prison they infantilize you. That's the way it's set up." Once, when Joe mentioned that he was going to pop in on a friend without warning, Sheila said she wouldn't do that. She was met with stony silence.

Back in prison, when he got activated, Joe would take the space he needed, and he took it through quiet disengagement. He was accustomed to dealing with problems by retreating to his cell, processing his emotions privately, sleeping it off. He'd wake up refreshed. But now, while he recharged, Sheila stewed in her own feelings of sadness and confusion. She took his retreat personally, as passive aggression. They now look back on this phase of disconnection during the first year as "the silences." They realized they needed help.

They started therapy at the Ackerman Institute, in a program tailored to the needs of families who have experienced incarceration. Once a week for a year, Sheila and Joe sat with three therapists to break down the dynamic at play and to get tools for how to work through these conflicts. It was far from easy. "I'm not a crier," Sheila says, "but I cried more in therapy than maybe I ever have." It was work, and it was uncomfortable. That year of sessions was instrumental in helping them get through to the other side, where there would be no silences. Or at least shorter ones. "To be able to name things made all the difference," Joe says.

They realized that even little misunderstandings could contain multitudes. Like who would carry the grocery bags, for example. At the checkout, Sheila would grab a few, out of habit. Joe would insist on carrying all of them. For him, seeing her grab the grocery bags reminded him of all those years she had spent hauling things around on his behalf: "On every conjugal, she brought in the maximum thirty-five pounds at a time. She carried books, magazines, food for over a decade. She did all that schlepping. So, what, now I'm out and you're going to carry the bags, or go half and half?! No! I got it. I work out! Bask in it, take the little bag," he laughs. "This is your grapes!"

As for Sheila, she began to see how her expectations for Joe were harming them both. Unlike Crystal, Sheila hadn't assumed that Joe would be her caretaker upon his return. She was ready for the challenges he'd be walking into and the deficits he'd come home with after spending more than half his life in a prison cell. Still, it was hard for her to watch him fumble to remember a login password, or get frustrated with his cell phone. "I've always considered Joe to be the most fully formed person I've ever met in my life," she says. "So it was surprising to me to see him struggle."

"Those are high standards," Joe sighs.

Sheila realized that her great admiration for Joe was actually eliminating the wiggle room he needed to be human and make mistakes. "It could be suffocating," Joe admits. "Therapy helped her see what it was like for me."

In addition to getting insight into the other's perspective, they came away with actual tools to help them through their conflicts. One tool was naming the intention behind bringing something up and verbalizing fears about how the other might receive it. Joe gives an example: "Sugar, I've noticed you've been down the past few days. I hope you're okay. Rather than assume anything or shrug it off as 'you're just feeling blue,' my intention is to explore what's causing you to feel down and find out if there's anything I can do to help you feel better."

Therapy, for Sheila and Joe, was crucial in his homecoming transition, and in deepening their marriage and relationship. They'd always been committed to doing the work themselves but found they had exhausted their own wells. Joe is now a therapy evangelist. "I especially recommend therapy for people who have done time," he says. "It's not enough for your loved ones to say, *Welcome home*. That stuff wears out. People get tired of you. They don't understand you. There's a lot more you need."

———

ON A COOL Saturday evening in October, with the first nip of fall in the air, friends, family, and colleagues gather in Sheila and Joe's apartment. They have set up a buffet of pasta, salad, wings, and plenty of champagne. Of all the occasions one goes out for on a Saturday night to toast—birthdays, engagements, weddings—this one truly feels worthy of celebration: Joe is off parole.

"We can finally exhale," Sheila tells us. "We checked the Department of Corrections website this morning and it says he is off, so it's official!" Joe's final parole visit took place three days ago, but they've still been waiting with bated breath to see his status change online.

Earlier this month, Joe's parole officer had banged on their door at 11:30 at night. A final send-off, just a reminder that, at least then, he still could. Sheila had been waking up throughout the nights since, scared to miss a pop-in that could jeopardize Joe's parole in the homestretch. "Those visits are the part I will miss the least," she tells us.

The couple wanted to do something to celebrate on Thursday night, the date the entirety of his sentence concluded. But it was rainy, and nothing sounded quite right. They ended up taking a walk through Washington Square Park, the place where Joe had gasped three years earlier, on his first day out of prison. Now he was walking through the mist like any other citizen, sharing an umbrella with his wife. The couple is looking forward to staying out past 9 p.m. on occasion and to crossing state lines freely. Joe is going to Connecticut to see Joseph in a few days, now that he can do so without having to get his officer's permission. They are planning trips to New Orleans to visit friends, and to Seattle to visit Sheila's sister.

At the celebration, Sheila's son Sean kicks off the toasts to Joe. He is warm and gregarious. "They kept you in, but they didn't keep you down," he says. "Now here's to smiles, travel, seeing people you couldn't see before—to a new chapter."

A friend of Joe's whom he met in prison, who did thirty-two years and recently got off parole, takes the floor: "There was a lot of bad, but there was a lot of good, too. I feel so lucky to have met Joe, who had upstanding morals and values, even though in the face of society we were criminals. Seeing you and Sheila stand here today reinforces the union. This wasn't just a prison marriage. This was a beautiful thing that took a lot of work."

Sheila stands up to give her toast. Even among close friends, it's obvious that public speaking isn't her favorite activity. She thanks everyone for being here, for supporting Joe and her through it all. Here, in this moment, is the culmination of what is simple but never guaranteed: a home, a marriage, freedom. She shifts from foot to foot, cradling her plastic cup of red wine. Everyone is gazing at her with love and something like awe. "I heard a saying," she says. The room grows hushed. "Go where the love is." She looks around at all of us. She looks at Joe. "And that's what I did."

TEN

A RECKONING AND A REUNION

W HEN JO AND Benny broke up, she said it was better to have this freak-out happen now than when he came home, when he'd be around the kids. I believed in Jo's capacity to be completely, unequivocally okay. I had spoken to her and heard the strength in her voice. I had seen the stream of jokes she posted on Instagram daily. (My favorite: "I've heard a lot of ladies talk about bleaching their ass-hole, so do you like dump it over his head or do you make him drink it?") I knew her personal history of resilience after abuse, addiction, war—far worse circumstances than a breakup.

Then, on April 26, 2019, their third wedding anniversary, I logged on to Facebook to see a new post:

"Too many people say 'I do' when they really only mean 'I'll try.'"
—Unknown

There have been a handful of days in my life I've known I was EXACTLY where I was meant to be. 3 years ago was one of them. Sometimes love feels joyful and effortless. Other times, you have to fight and believe with everything in you while you choose it, no matter HOW you feel, because at the end of the day, it's worth it. 🖤

1,940 days together (that's 5.3 years for those of you who just grabbed your calculators)

1,095 of those we've been married.

251 days until you're home.

All the rest of them after that.

I SUPPOSE I still "do" 😊

Happy Anniversary, babe. 💕

Jo and I talk later that morning. She switches rooms, away from Davin and Elijah, to tell me she is taking them on a surprise spring break trip to Legoland tomorrow. She has packed their bags surreptitiously. Then she tells me about Benny.

She ended up sending him that birthday card back in March during their breakup, but sans divorce papers. That led to them messaging back and forth, reestablishing their playful rapport before diving into the root causes of the blowup.

"Here we are," she says, exhaling deeply. "It was a big wake-up call for him and me on some things. He had a need that wasn't getting met—our sexual connection. He had been stewing over it and it had been building up for him. He wasn't communicating it in a way for me to understand how frustrated he was. I promised him the calendar and he was really looking forward to it. Then the dog died, and I had that unexpected expense and couldn't pull it off. But by then he had already been frustrated for months. We were both very burnt out at the end of the year. Then January first came and I started saving money. All of that combined to make a perfect storm for him to say, *You know what? Fuck it, I'm done.*"

None of this is news since the last time we spoke, when she was in the throes of fresh heartbreak. "He helped me see that he tried to tell me about his needs and I wasn't listening. Without meaning to, I made him feel like he wasn't important. We kinda see each other's point now." It sounds like she has had more time to process the information within the context of their relationship. That and to shoulder a bit more of the blame. Sure, she didn't make a boudoir calendar. She also didn't resort to passive aggression.

Benny tells me his side of the story over the phone, and it matches up with what Jo is saying. "I felt like she wasn't putting me number one anymore," he admits. And by number one he means number three: "For Journey, it goes *Jesus, kids, me.* I know that. But she had stopped doing the things that I felt like I had become accustomed to." He did grow enraged about the calendar, which he thought would be easy for her to do. He got pissed about the money, because "I'm not going to need help when I get out. Then I'll be able to do for myself. But I need help when I'm in prison." I am slightly in disbelief that it is actually as simple as Jo had described to me: sex and money.

In the interim of their breakup, he set up another pen-pal profile. It featured a shirtless photo of himself and said:

My name is Benny and I am about to finish up a 9 year sentence for attempted murder and Assault II, had too much to drink on New Years eve 2010. I have about 11 months left as of Feb 2nd before I am able to go back to my home town of Portland, Oregon . . . I am looking to connect with someone who likes to laugh, is confident, doesn't mind giving me some attention, and is photogenic. I am not looking for anything serious right now, just something super simple and involves a lot of harmless flirting.

Benny says the ad got a lot of responses. "Fish were jumping in the boat, so to speak." It was the validation he felt he had been missing from his wife. "I'm pretty needy. I can be self-absorbed at times. I didn't feel reciprocated, and it bothered me."

But that time away from Jo was hard. And when he reflects on their separation, I hear him express his admiration for his wife: "She gives me something to strive for," he says. "She has incredible values and morals. The thing that really attracted me to her was that she was this honest, good person, and eventually one day I want to be like that. I knew that if I didn't have her in my life, it wasn't going to be shit. It wouldn't be what I had worked so hard for. That's kind of a selfish reason, but I missed her."

"He knows he has to earn my trust back," Jo says. "He's not making excuses."

I wonder, though, is she?

"You have to believe with every fiber in you that you didn't make a mistake and have enough faith to hang on to that," she says. "This is a time I am choosing to love, choosing to be kind, choosing not to fight with him. Choosing not to give in to my own self-protection instincts. My faith plays into it. I've spent so much time seeking counsel, praying, pouring out my emotions to God. I'm on the other side of this now. I'm okay with him coming home. I wouldn't say our marriage is 100 percent as strong as it was in the past, but I think it will make us stronger. It will help us be more mindful of each other and love each other a little better. It was a hard thing, but I don't think it was a bad thing, necessarily."

I find myself conflicted by her explanation. On the one hand, I could not agree with her more. Love can be hard. Marriage is a choice you make every day. You choose to stay. On the other, I think of stories like *Dirty John*, stories of women so motivated by forgiveness and a commitment to Christian values that they can't see the harm in their midst and end up getting seriously hurt as a result. I want Jo and Benny to work, with safety and second chances. Or not to work, to each go their separate ways and be fine and better for having had the relationship. But in either case—just as I would want for any friend or family member who outlined a similar scenario to me—I don't want her to slog through a relationship that isn't worthy of her. Yet, as with any relationship, since time immemorial, the true test is: *Are you happy?* Jo tells me she is happy.

In eight months, Benny will be out of prison. In September, 120 days before his release date, Jo will file his interstate transfer application. This document essentially asks the State of Georgia if it will take a former prisoner from the State of Oregon into its probation system. Jo is optimistic it will go through. So many prison wives say that the last year of the sentence is the hardest. The days become longer, the countdown more glacial. Jo hasn't been feeling this way, though.

"It's a little surreal, because I'm not anxious about it," she says. "I'm excited about him coming home, but it also feels very unreal. We've been doing this for so long. We've been telling ourselves *someday*, so it's a little weird for it to happen. I'm a little resistant to losing my independence. In the back of my head I'm like, *Are we really fixing to live together for the first time?* Like I've said before, every couple that's been together makes a big transition at some point, whether it's from engaged to married, or learning to live together. I think we're actually in a better position than most couples."

I ask her if she still thinks so after seeing the old Benny rear his head.

"I'd never seen that side directed at me," she admits. "That's what threw me for a loop. I know there's a lot of stuff my husband is carrying and dealing with. A lot of damage and pain. All of us, when we get shook hard enough, have the capacity to have that top pop off. All of the damage and the wounds can come out. I'm not condoning it, but I think that's what happened. All of that unhealed junk manifested. We were actually laughing about it the other night. He's starting to see the ridiculousness of it. He didn't think I would actually get divorce papers together. Well, I did. I take you at your word. What did you think the outcome would be? He said, 'You're right, I was completely caught up in my emotions.' But we all say things we don't mean."

———————

SO THEY'RE BACK together. I've been wanting to discuss some of the material that I've gone back to—namely Benny laying out his past violence toward women—but it feels rude to bring that up on her wedding anniversary. The truth is, I've been very much on the fence about bringing this up with Jo at all anyway. Why would my opinion on her husband matter in the slightest? She has crafted an identity around not giving a flying fuck what others think about her marriage. She didn't come to me seeking my approval, nor do I really have approval to give, not in any meaningful way.

I find myself beginning to feel a bit Janus-faced in our conversations. Jo has told me the most intimate details of her history, her relationship with Benny, her hopes and fears for the future. She's opened up her private life to me. I've seen her bedroom covered in pictures of him. I've hung out with her kids, attended her wedding. Hell, she even gave up her bed for me when I stayed with her in Maryland. And we've been talking in depth about her personal life for more than three years.

Over the years, and the phone calls and emoji-filled text messages and comments on each other's Facebook posts, our relationship has come to resemble a friendship. I've always recorded our conversations, and she's always given me permission. I've always had my notebook and pen out when we were talking. But, whether tacitly or explicitly, I have registered my support for her relationship. Simply by checking in with her every few months or liking pictures of her and Benny on social media, I've been saying I hope she and Benny make it. And I do. Yet I can't shake my queasiness over Benny's charges and the violent attitudes and actions toward women he has expressed. I know that by bringing it up I won't be showing Jo anything new. She knows it all, far more than I do. But it is beginning to feel dishonest to me to dodge these troubling facts.

WE CATCH UP over the phone in early summer. Jo is beginning to put together their interstate compact packet, in the hope that Benny will get to live with her in Georgia upon his release. I ask what will happen if they get denied. She says she hasn't even begun to consider a plan B.

Benny was recently transferred to a pre-release facility in Portland. He was informed that very day by prison staff that he was being moved, without any time to say goodbye to any of the men he had lived alongside for the past nine and a half years. Jo has been fielding messages from his friends at OSP, sending him their love and support.

"Doing that with no warning just seems unnecessarily cruel," I say.

"It makes perfect sense from a security standpoint," Jo corrects me.

"Ah, this is CO Jo speaking now." I marvel at how she can take on so many sides of this experience at once.

"When we would move people at county, we would get them up in the morning and take them to holding, but the phones would be shut off so they didn't have any way of letting anyone know they were about to be on the road. You'd be driving sometimes for long stretches when there would be no one around. You could easily call a family member or a gang member and say, *Hey, they're fixing to ship me out, and you know the route, so come bring your buddies and your automatic weapons.* Now you've got a prison break on your hands."

That I hadn't considered.

The savings that Benny had slowly accumulated were decimated upon his transfer. Prisoners are not allowed to bring their commissary or hygiene items to the new facility, so he had to drain his account to purchase these necessities all over again. Feeling the squeeze financially, they're kicking it old school, writing almost daily letters again, the cheapest (and slowest) way to maintain communication.

"He's busting his butt to get me comfortable again," she tells me.

"We'd spent a lot of money on messaging, since he can't get to the phone a lot right now. I've been putting fifty dollars a month on the phone, which is the most I can do. We've been doing workbooks again, writing our thoughts out. He told me he'd do whatever he has to do to earn my trust back. And he really has."

Looking back on it, the outburst that temporarily broke them up seems like a classic form of self-sabotage, or, as Jo said, an attempt to alienate the one person who can truly help him. I ask Jo if this has been the case for her. "Uh, yeah, it is, on a couple different fronts. We went through four months of hell where I really didn't think we were going to make it. Fear got the better of us. Now I just feel like I'm in the third trimester of pregnancy. It's not quite time to have the baby, but you've gotten through the morning sickness, the hemorrhoids, the energy drain. And you've had the fun times with the baby shower and buying the little outfits and decorating the nursery. Now you're ready, but you've still got quite a few hurdles in front of you. You're hot, fat, and mad at the world."

She also feels resonances of her time in the military in facing down these final months. "It's a lot like being in combat. There's a certain level of adrenaline that you get used to operating at. But at the same time, there are plenty of times where nothing is happening. Honestly, you're just bored. You're restocking cabinets, cleaning your rifle, throwing rocks at bunkers. But that could change any second. Prison is like that. Your whole world can be upended in a minute with a phone call. You just never know. Yet you can't dwell on it, because you'll lose your mind. But you learn to always have your phone charged and handy. You'll always listen with one ear for the ringtone. You always stay ready," Jo says.

I think back to Crystal and how the PTSD of prison-wife life continues to haunt her. Given Jo's time in combat and PTSD, she is no stranger to an intense experience lingering past its shelf date.

"I don't think I'll ever exhale again," she says. "Going into this, I had no idea it could be like that. I was super naive."

We talk about how she and her ex-husband Kyle are planning for Benny's homecoming. As of now, they are going to take it as it comes. Kyle isn't planning on moving out. He told her he doesn't see anything wrong with their current arrangement. "I was like, 'Well, then you two need to talk about it and decide if you can handle it as men. Because I am not going to live in the middle of a constant dick-measuring contest,'" she says. He and Benny had a phone call, but Jo doesn't know what was said, because she stepped out of the room. The house is a five-bedroom, and, given their schedules, Jo and Kyle are now like ships passing. She is confident they can make it work in their current arrangement.

As the conversation winds down, having covered current events, I now face the sticky task of broaching the subject of Benny's charges. Which seems outrageous, given that Jo and I have been talking like this for years. No time like the present.

"So, obviously, this isn't about me," I say by way of preface. (I always have trouble saying the difficult words that need to be said.) "I've known you and Benny for years now. I've interviewed Benny, I've written to Benny, I know his whole rap sheet. But hearing him say that he abused every woman he was ever with prior to you was really hard. It was hard in a way that I hadn't experienced with Benny, because, either willfully or subconsciously, I hadn't gone that deep with him in terms of violence to his partners. I was thinking about you, and it made me nervous."

I exhale.

Without hesitation, Jo owns it all, on his behalf:

"Yeah, he did. I mean it was (a) how he grew up and (b) that was the culture of the people he was hanging out with. It was just kind of expected. These women. He was as good as they got. They were just as thug, too. And (c) he was coked out of his head most of the time," she tells me.

Sometimes it's hard to differentiate context from excuses. Maybe, in Benny's case, both are true.

"I asked him point blank one night, 'Did you try to kill her? Did you try to run her over?'" she continues, referring to the attempted-murder charge that put Benny in prison this go-around. "He said, 'Babe, I don't even know. I don't even remember. I was too high. I was too drunk. And so I was probably trying to get her out of there and she was standing in front of the truck.' And I was like, *Oh, well makes sense.* I understand who he used to be."

I ask what she means.

"I guess for me it's a little bit easier, because I'm around these peo-ple all day long, every day, by virtue of the kind of work I do." She has been working as a lay pastor and addiction counselor at her church. "I let felons babysit my cats. I'm letting a former IV drug user housesit for me. I know my people."

For Jo, it all comes down to trust. "I'm not going to hand you my trust because you've got a sob story. I know plenty of people like that. They were assholes then and they're assholes now. I'm from Missouri, and I'm a Missouri girl. You better show me you've changed," she says. (Missouri is "the Show-Me State.")

I ask whether any part of her fears that he may hurt her when he comes home.

"I know my husband," she says. "When he's clean and sober, he is not the person he was back then. I'm not worried about it. I'll never tell you, *Oh, he'll never lose his temper, or cuss, or get angry, or put his fist through drywall.* If he gets worked up enough, he may do those things," she says. Then she pauses. "But I can guarantee you he'll never lay a hand on me."

I feel the relief of offloading my guilty conscience. I wish I had brought up this unsavory business sooner. And I feel the relief of how thoughtful Jo is, and how thoughtful prison wives in general are. There's nothing I can say to them that they haven't already turned over in their minds millions of times. I find no such relief, however, in her guarantee. I hear hope, but no certainty.

———————

JANUARY 2, 2020. The date is a bull's-eye. Exactly six years from the day Jo sent her first message to Benny, the final day in her countdown app has arrived. Slowly, the minutes tick down to the moment when Benny will walk out of prison and into the arms of his wife.

The date has loomed large in my consciousness as I've gotten to know the couple over the past four years. When it finally arrives, I'm in Argentina, having recently married my baby's father and sworn off all modes of screen for the trip. But, at the end of the day, I log on to the hotel's WiFi and on to Facebook, to check the status update.

In the photo from the post, I see the couple standing cheek to cheek, grinning ear to ear, mugging for the camera in some kind of parking lot. "He snuck up on me!" Jo posted at 10:17 a.m.

I've seen entire albums' worth of pictures of the couple together over the years, arms entwined in embrace against prison visiting-room backdrops. But never have I so beheld the closeness—and necessity—of a selfie. For the first time, there is no one else around to take the picture. For the first time, Jo is alone with her husband.

———————

"I WAS AFRAID I was going to accidentally sign the visitors' log when I picked him up," Jo says, recounting her final visit to Oregon State Penitentiary. She didn't, and she even managed to eke out a few hours of sleep the night before, after having traveled since three in the morning from St. Louis, where she had dropped off Davin and Elijah with her parents for the momentous occasion. I think of the nerves she must have felt, so much more than before a wedding night. Because, even though their wedding night occurred almost four years ago, they hadn't yet experienced physical intimacy with each other.

They called their prison visits "the bus station," because it felt like they were in a crowded public place, waiting for a bus that was taking far too long to arrive. Plus, they hadn't even seen each other in eighteen months. Jo had skipped her regularly scheduled visit the previous year, when they were broken up. But the day had finally come. These two middle-aged people had the nerves of two kids ready to lose their virginity on prom night.

The couple had a frank conversation about their reunion on the phone the night before, and about the greatest of expectations weighing upon it. Benny asked her if she would mind if they didn't go to the hotel room to get busy immediately. They needed to take some time to reconnect. "I was so relieved when he said that," Jo admits.

After she picked Benny up from the prison, they got a big breakfast at a diner, then went back to the motel to gather Jo's things before checkout. He got into the shower, and Jo sat on the bed and looked at the clock, which told her they had about thirty minutes before they had to be out. "I thought to myself, *It's now or never*." She took off her clothes and slipped into the shower with him.

Jo was especially nervous about him seeing her naked body for the first time. Even though he had seen most of her in the various boudoir photos she had sent over the years, as she says, "I don't send him pictures of the cellulite on my ass." He was very complimentary, in awe of his wife's body, which he found perfect. Their sexual congress was brief yet satisfying.

With the main event out of the way, Jo could focus on getting Benny set up. Though she was picking him up, he would not be coming to Georgia, as she had learned a month before. At first, their interstate compact, for Benny to be transferred from Oregon to the probation system of Georgia, had been provisionally approved by both states. The couple was elated. Then, two days later, Jo got a call saying that the compact had effectively been denied. They could appeal, but for now, Benny would have to stay in Oregon. The news was devastating. While the nightmare of prison was over, there was still more long-distance, more uncertainty, more breath holding.

Jo had told both her sons and her ex-husband that Benny would be coming to Georgia. Now she had to walk it back. Kyle took the news with little emotion. The boys were a bit disappointed, but not shattered. Jo has made it a point throughout her relationship to make Benny a positive figure in their lives, but an auxiliary one. The boys spoke with him on the phone occasionally and exchanged a few letters. "They already have a father," she says.

And then, in the last stretch of Benny's sentence, he ended up in the hole. He had failed a drug test, the results of which showed he had ingested heroin. "I always told him if he ever goes to the hole for foolishness that could've been avoided, you are going to do every day of that time yourself," Jo says. For those forty-five days, they did not speak a word or exchange a letter. "He thought he was going to get served divorce papers when he got out." Instead, Jo laid out a plan he had to follow to the letter: "He has to live at a treatment facility for ninety days, get a sponsor, work a program, and take his sobriety seriously. He agreed to everything. If he ever relapses or drinks again, I'm gone. There will be no more second chances. That was his one get-out-of-jail-free card."

Benny unpacks the heroin incident for me later on. He had mere months left "to the gate," yet he had no idea what his life was going to be. Would he be going to Georgia? Would Jo stay with him if he had to remain in Oregon? Would he fall back into his old ways?

"I'd already been smoking a little weed and dabbling in Suboxone," he tells me over the phone.

"I didn't realize you could get high off of Suboxone," I say. The drug is used to treat heroin addiction, using a low dose of opioid to reduce cravings.

"You can if you do it right," he says.

A guy in the prison, also named Ben, had a stash of meth and heroin and was going out of his mind with paranoia. He asked Benny to hold on to it for him and said he could do some as payment.

"So what was your thought process in choosing to do heroin so close to being released?" I ask.

He pauses and laughs. "My thought process was *Oh, cool, I can do heroin and I don't have to pay for it. I can just veg out and watch TV.*"

As Benny once told me, any illicit behavior in prison comes with an expiration date, as someone will rat you out eventually. Another man told a CO that Benny was doing drugs, and both he and the dealer were given a urinalysis, which came back positive. He was ashamed to tell Jo, so much so that his counselor ended up telling his wife for him. "She sent me one email saying, *Don't fucking talk to me, you're an idiot* . . . I wrote her back, but she wasn't responding to me. We were just starting to mend fences, and now I'm telling her I'm getting high on heroin."

To my surprise, his drug use didn't result in any time being added to his sentence. His convictions fell under what is known in Oregon as Measure 11, meaning a mandatory sentence for certain classifications of crimes. He had no opportunity to earn good time or a sentence reduction, nor to have time added on, unless it was for something serious, like assaulting a CO.

With the uncertainty of his fate still hanging in the balance, Benny smoked weed and used Suboxone for the duration of his sentence. Being drug-free was a precondition for Jo to feel safe in their relationship. He began his journey to sobriety the day Jo picked him up from prison.

––––––––

WITH MILITARY PRECISION, Jo organized Benny's first days out to get him everything he needed to live as a contributing member of society in a sober-living transitional house. They had to buy him a wardrobe of basics, since he walked out of prison with literally the clothes on his back (which Jo provided). They had to get him food stamps, ID, a cell phone, a mass transit card, toiletries, healthcare, an eye exam. They had to meet with his probation officer and start the process of finding Benny a job. The list was daunting.

Things went pretty smoothly, but there were moments when it was too much. On the first day, they went to buy jeans. "He got overwhelmed," Jo says. "He hadn't had to make a choice in nine years, because the prison chooses for you." She stood outside the dressing room, giving him space but remaining nearby as he tried on options. At a certain point, the choices became too much and they left. Jo asked him to be clear in his communication with her about how he was feeling moment to moment so that she would know what to do.

"But I get it," Jo says. Having been on several deployments and reintegrating into civilian life with PTSD, Jo knows firsthand what being overwhelmed feels like. "When I came home from my first long deployment," she tells me, "I went out to eat with my parents at a Culver's. I remember standing in front of the soda fountain slack-jawed for like twenty minutes. I didn't have to make a choice the whole time I was deployed. Now I did, and I didn't know what to do."

That insight into what Benny was going through allowed her to buffer him through his first days out. When they went to a restaurant, she allowed him to take the seat facing the door. She walked on the left-hand side of him. They were able to laugh a bit about some of the tics he had brought home. At one point she saw him standing in front of a door, waiting for it to open. In prison, COs usually buzz doors open. "I was like, 'Babe, doors don't open on their own on the outside, remember?'"

Their first days together were a whirlwind of activity. Jo posted on Facebook: "Chillin' at the DMV and various staffing agencies today, teasing the husband that he really needs to take me on better dates."

They went out for food that Benny had been craving, like Popeye's, Mexican, and Chinese.

But amid checking off the to-do list and all the emotions, Jo was experiencing her own stress. "On the second night, I broke down," she says. "We'd been running around all day and he was feeling emasculated, following me around like a kid with his hand in my pocket. We got back to the hotel room and he was too tired to have sex. I freaked out. I said, 'What kind of man doesn't want to have sex his second day out of prison?!' But really what I was afraid of is that he wasn't actually attracted to me and that this isn't going to work. I cried and cried, so hard I almost threw up. He just held me. It all hit me— the past six years—in that moment."

On top of six years of frustration and fear, she felt like her work helping him reintegrate into society was going to backfire. "I felt like I was setting him up to leave me," she says.

Functionally, she was. After all the running around, she would be getting on a plane and leaving him in Oregon, just as she had every time since she met him. In some ways, though, she was trying to be grateful for the space that would once again be placed between them.

"I know it sounds cynical, but in some ways it's good that we have this probationary period. If he's going to fuck up, he's going to do it there and not blow up my entire life and my family," she says. She is tentative as she says this, as if she's afraid to admit this might be a bit of grace. As if speaking such things might deliver them into existence.

I SPEAK WITH Benny on February 1. He has been out of prison for almost a month, and just earned his thirty-day sobriety chip. He is readjusting to the world, though he has gotten lost on his way back to his sober-living house several times. "I haven't lived in this area before," he says, "and I'm used to being in prison, where I know where everything is at!" He laughs. On his way to a job interview at a call center, he had a panic attack on the bus. "I have my backpack and I look like a hobo, I'm simultaneously trying to upload my résumé to this guy, the flashlight of my phone is on and it's draining the battery and I have no idea how to turn it off, my phone is dying, and I start crying! I had to take twenty-seven deep breaths." He ended up arriving on time—and getting the job.

The week he had with his wife was wonderful, he says. "Over the past six years together, my mind has been focused on her and our life together. So that week we got to spend together was how I had been picturing my life. Even though we were in a hotel room, Journey made it feel like home. I was on the computer, she'd be doing her own thing . . . it felt normal."

I ask him how he feels still being separated from his wife, for now. "A thing prison taught me is that they are always going to say no to you the first time," he says, and I hear him pull hard on a cigarette. "I have to figure out what I can fix to turn that no into a yes, or at least a maybe. So long as I have the goal of getting to Georgia, I feel okay. My goal might seem far away, but as long as I'm doing something toward it every day, whether it's ten minutes or three hours of work, I'm going to get there."

He learned these lessons from earning his college degree in prison. Sometimes he would have to study a tough concept for hours at a time, sometimes he could review for a quiz in ten minutes, but he mastered the consistency of hard work. Still, Benny sometimes feels discouraged that not everyone sees how far he has come. "Most people still judge me on the worst night of my life, on the worst night of my victim's life, and assume I'm the same person. People don't see the whole timeline. They just see the little data points. I struggle with that a bit." But he's optimistic. "Before, I was a hammer, so everything was a nail. Now I have more tools. I've got a screwdriver, a wire cutter. But I've still got the hammer if I need it."

Even though Benny is out of prison, the couple faces uncertainty.

But they are handling it the way they always have: twenty-four hours at a time. Because that is how life, regardless of any relationship, happens.

"I'd be lying if I said I wasn't a little scared," Jo says. "He has to do all of it—stay clean, stay faithful, not reoffend, work a job—all without me. I told him, 'I can't be your personal Jesus, your higher power, your moral compass. You have to figure all that stuff out on your own now.' And that's hard to do if you're forty years old and have never done it before."

Benny staying faithful to his wife at a distance of 2,700 miles after not having had sex for nine years is another challenge the couple faces. "We've had discussions about hall passes," Jo says. "And he understands that he doesn't have any." Even in the few short days after Benny's release, Jo found herself roiling in jealousy in a way she'd never experienced before. She saw lots of women she didn't know posting on his Facebook page, welcoming him home.

"I didn't like it," she says. "I logged in to his account and read all his messages. I have all his passwords. I copped to it, like, *Babe, I had that crazy bitch moment.* I really had to check myself, because I don't want to live like that." She is worried about him cheating, as she knows getting a confidence boost from women is a big trigger for him. But she's philosophical about it. "I've been cheated on by men who slept next to me in my bed every night. If a man is going to cheat, he's going to cheat. It doesn't matter whether he's living under the same roof or on the other side of the country. I just can't drive myself crazy with every single what-if."

But what if he goes back to prison?

"Then I'm done. And he knows it. That's just not the kind of life I want for myself," she says.

I've heard her say things like this before. If he talks to other women, she's done. (He did, when he set up the second pen-pal account.) If he ever uses again, she's done. (He did, just a month before he was supposed to come home.) And here we are now, at yet another crossroads, and the direction Benny will take, only time will determine.

BEFORE JO GOT back on the plane to Georgia to her kids, to her life on the other side of the country, married but still without her husband, the couple took a trip to the Oregon coast. It was the first time Jo had had any kind of leisure time on these trips, a chance to see the sights. They spent the night in a nice hotel, walked on the beach, breathed in the openness of the fresh salt air. They both posted photos of the trip on their Facebook pages, the couple in an embrace, waves crashing against the rugged coastline in the background. They are pressed up against each other, beaming.

On his post, Benny wrote: "You read about the ocean in books but you never truly know how beautiful it is until you see it for yourself." And in that moment, with the past six years behind them and the ocean before them, Benny and Jo look happy.

EPILOGUE

T HEY MADE IT. Jo and Benny fell in love within a system designed to keep people separate. Jo weathered judgments from those closest to her. Her friends and family eventually came around. Even her mother, who harbored perhaps the harshest assessment of her husband, now has a friendly relationship with him. It just took time. Benny fought to stay clean and manage his emotions, to prove to his beloved and to the world that he is, in fact, the person that Jo sees. They were apart for some time, yes, both when they broke up and when he went to the hole. They decided they like their lives better together.

What Benny and Jo experienced together forever changed them both, in ways that seem inexorably good. They are still navigating probation, yet another leg in their long-distance, transcontinental marathon. Through necessity, they are innovating what a marriage looks like.

The couples I met did not find love in spite of prison; they found love in the midst of it. Jo and Benny shared the happiest day of their lives when they exchanged wedding vows in the visiting room. Sherry and Damon found in each other the truest stability and most steadfast love they have ever known. Jacques and Ivié shared a bubble of bliss on their conjugal visits. Crystal and Fernando made a family and shared the victory of his exoneration. Sheila and Joe live a peaceful existence of work and service after Joe spent more than half his life in prison.

These couples knew struggle, obstacle, and having their fate in the hands of a force far greater than themselves—the prison system. And they shared a bond just as fierce: the emotional connection that comes from learning a person through letters, from across a table, from across the country. Each couple reached levels of intimacy they had never known before. And yet the question persists: Why do some people find that with strangers in prison?

Relationships are the stage upon which we all play out our baggage—our family systems, our trauma, our self-belief or lack thereof. A relationship manifests in whom you choose as a partner and in whom you reject. Many advance the theory that a woman who chooses a partner who's incarcerated must be highly traumatized and that dating a prisoner creates a "safe" environment for her. She doesn't have to be in close proximity to him; she can decide when to visit and when to pick up the phone. I have learned that there is some truth in that, but it is also an incomplete diagnosis.

We live in a society that still makes women feel they must be validated by a man in order to matter. It's one reason why women stay in relationships with violent men. And it may be why a woman might look to prison rather than stay single. Better to have somebody to love you than nobody, they may feel.

Many of the relationships I saw were healthy and loving, and prison and people's naysaying made the wives even more determined to make them so. But it doesn't always happen that way.

On Christmas Eve 2019, Melinda Sprague, a member of Strong Prison Wives & Families, went missing in Wichita, Kansas. Two days later, her body was found in a car. She had been murdered by her boyfriend, whom she had met on a pen-pal site seven years earlier.

She was a mother of three. Melinda had voiced concerns about her boyfriend to the group. Members urged her to reconsider her relationship.

"We all knew he was trash," Jo said. "She wouldn't leave." In a post to the group, Jo wrote, "I hate everything about this—for her, for those who loved her AND for the rest of us. Domestic violence doesn't just suddenly appear out of nowhere. This is why we do what we do, and it has nothing to do with prison. I despise this not only because it never should have happened but also because it's going to be 'woman murdered by prison pen pal' instead of 'woman who had huge red flags in her relationship and stayed anyway, murdered by guy she happened to meet this way.'"

Jo and I spoke about the tragedy a few days later. She was frustrated that even some group members lacked compassion. "Instead of *What can we do to help people in prison heal* and *make sure women everywhere are safe from abuse*, some say, *Well, this is why everybody who goes to prison is no good, and I don't know what the dumb bitch thought would happen.*" Jo was sickened by the murder, and it made her even more determined to help women gather their strength to leave such awful situations. "This isn't good on any front. And yet it's the reality. Which is exactly why we spend so much time helping women figure out what's healthy and what's not."

But the idea that prison wives are desperate and willing to accept abuse is also incomplete. Every time I thought I had an answer as to who the MWI prison wife really was, it got turned on its head. At first I thought it might have something to do with race and privilege. When I was in Dallas, the demographic I saw suggested that meeting while incarcerated might be a very white experience. But then I met Sheila. At another point, I was convinced that this had to be an exclusively female trope, and then I met Jacques. I thought maybe it had to do with never having had a loved one in prison— perhaps not knowing the horror of it might make it alluring to dip a toe into this parallel universe (as, admittedly, it had been for me at the beginning). Then I met Crystal, whose brother was incarcerated. The love stories I had heard from free-world partners, of the deepest intimacy and connection they had ever known, led me to believe this might be a strict inside/outside dynamic. Then I met Sherry and Damon.

In relationships lies everything. Yes, your trauma, but also your past, your preferences, your aperture toward life, the story you tell about yourself and about the world. It is easy to behold the prison wife and her long-distance love affair and say she's delusional. But all relationships, in their very essence, are acts of delusion. We choose to overlook unpleasant aspects of our partners in favor of their better sides. We pick our battles. We commit to marriages on untested premises that we will remain compatible in an ever-changing world, body, mind. In every marriage, there are rooms with doors we dare not open. Are we not all delusional, on some level? Prison relationships are the funhouse mirror to the mutual delusions we must all engage in to be in any kind of romantic partnership.

We all engage in the delusion, and yet not all of us log on to the pen-pal site. Not all of us feel thrust in the direction of fate I heard so many describe. It is to a certain degree a matter of self-selection. It's the willingness to send the letter, the openness to visit, to believe in love in hopeless places. I do believe that most people end up where they are because they want to be there on some level. Something about the arrangement works for them.

I stayed in touch with many of the women I met in Dallas. At the time, Lauren was engaged to Spencer, whom she met through a friend when he was in federal prison in Texas. He got out and ended up cheating on her. They broke off the engagement. But before long she was with another incarcerated man, whom she also met through another mutual friend with a husband in prison. "I work a lot and my kids are still young," she explained. "I like having someone to ask about my day. I like having someone to write with and visit. It's just a setup that works for me," she said.

I first got interested in this subject because of my friendship with Sam Israel, which grew out of reporting my first book. Sam is in Butner Federal Prison for fraud. I jokingly suggested he do some first-person muckraking and find a girlfriend while I conducted my research. He did just that: he met Paige in 2016, while I was writing this book. They fell in love through a year of emailing, phone calls, and letter writing. They got engaged on their first in-person visit. It's a setup that works for them, too.

There are 2.3 million people incarcerated in the United States. These are just a few love stories. There are countless more experiencing the tolls and trauma of incarceration. It doesn't have to be this way. Right now, in the wake of George Floyd and Breonna Taylor's murders, conversations are taking place about policing and the way we spend resources, and what a society might look like that puts the $182 billion a year we spend on prisons into communities, education, healthcare, and social services. The way we do prisons in this country is not normal, from a human rights standpoint or in comparison with prisons in developed countries around the world. It doesn't have to be this way.

Conversations about prison abolition never came up organically in the interviews I conducted—most of the people I spoke with were too mired in living the day-to-day realities of prison to make large-scale activism their focus. Rather, they advocate for the individuals they love, in the microcosm of where the horrors of prison play out. Ro never gave up hope fighting Adam's 213-year federal sentence. Back in Dallas, neither Ro nor her fellow prison wives were sure the couple would ever get to pursue the life they dreamt of together in the free world. Her determination paid off. Adam was granted a compassionate release based on "extraordinary and compelling" reasons. After serving twenty years for armed robbery, on August 13, 2020, Adam walked out of FCI McKean and into the arms of his fiancée. They will get the chance to live out the promise of "kids, dogs, beach" from the index cards they both kept tucked away in their pockets. Ro got pregnant shortly after Adam's release, and the couple is expecting a baby boy in the summer of 2021.

Beyond finding love and advocating for individuals, prison relationships have real systemic implications. Prison wives are resourceful and conscientious. They are committed to supporting their partners, both on the inside and when they get out. They research every angle of protocol and every corner of the vast bureaucracy. They come in as neophytes and become experts in navigating the system. They are a crucial source of strength in riding out a sentence and in homecoming.

If there were a resource for what to expect when someone is released and the kind of support he might need, prison wives would be the first to read it cover to cover. Wives and families are already engaging in this kind of resource-sharing through their own networks. But the partners of incarcerated people are a group that the Bureau of Prisons would be well served to recognize as key to reentry. They want their people to succeed more than anybody.

Family visits are a crucial element in building toward that success, and three of the couples I followed were fortunate enough to have them. That proportion is outside the norm for most incarcerated people in the United States. For the vast majority of people in prison, their relationship's reality is more like Benny and Jo's. Family visits provide a vital lifeline, not just for the prisoner but also for the families and communities they will come home to. Getting just a small taste of the normalcy of sharing a meal and watching a movie together incentivizes positive behavior and provides space to feel human.

Every piece of data shows that the resources spent providing these opportunities for the incarcerated and their loved ones have ripple effects, from the remainder of the sentence all the way to homecoming.

Facilities with conjugal visits report fewer sexual assaults. By strengthening family ties, conjugal visits can reduce rates of recidivism in the long term, thus saving money over time. More states and the federal system would be wise to invest in these kinds of visits. Yet with the COVID-19 pandemic, all in-person visiting was cancelled at prisons for months on end. Many loved ones on the outside just hope to get back to regular visiting.

Just as people who come home from prison experience post-incarceration syndrome, so, too, do prison wives. Crystal is dealing with PTSD from supporting Fernando through his eighteen-year sentence and their ten lost appeals, as she still decompresses from nearly two decades of walking through metal detectors and being scrutinized by prison staff. Even though Benny is out, he is still in the limbo of probation, and time will tell if he will be able to uphold its conditions for three years. That sense of insecurity, of randomness, of powerlessness, has permeated Jo's existence. "I don't think there will ever be a time when I'm not holding my breath," she said.

For so many couples, homecoming is the finish line in the distance. But when they cross it, they find a new set of challenges. Those challenges become insurmountable for many because they come as a surprise. Being able to anticipate some of the trauma wives themselves might experience would be one step toward normalizing it.

The very act of writing to prisoners is a simple harm reduction tool. Black & Pink started so more queer prisoners would hear their names at mail call. Not only does that connection with the outside world feed the incarcerated person, it fortifies them with a sense of protection. It shows they are loved, that someone cares. Someone is looking out. If you're a person on the outside who cares about mass incarceration in this country, send a letter. It is simple, cheap, and incredibly effective. You never know. You might just fall in love.

I WANTED TO quit this project many times. In my previous reporting, I spoke with people who had made great messes of their lives by faking their deaths, so I had conducted interviews in correctional facilities. But I was nowhere near equipped to immerse myself in the agony of the American prison system, and to meet people whose lives were so determined by it. Once you see that horror up close—of people being transferred and their families not knowing where they are for weeks or months, of not receiving basic medical care, of abuse and humiliation— you can never unsee it.

Even though I thought I understood, I was not ready for the degree of pain and intimacy people would share with me. For years, I sent and received letters to facilities all over the country, to high-profile serial killers, to people with numbers after their names. (My mail carrier definitely has theories about me.) Plus, I didn't anticipate when setting out just how damn long a project set inside prisons would take. People in prisons sometimes wouldn't receive my correspondence for months. Visits would be set and then postponed at the last minute on account of lockdowns or visiting hours randomly being canceled. As my childhood friend Cedric, who is currently on his second federal bid, put it, "Prisons don't really specialize in customer service."

Beyond the routine frustrations of reporting from prisons, familiar to so many who support an incarcerated loved one, the heaviness of these stories would linger with me long after we had spoken. I'd return from reporting trips to people's homes and prison visiting rooms with an exhaustion that was hard to shake. I'd feel the tremendous weight of responsibility to get these stories right, to show that they are more than the familiar stereotypes.

I often struggled to determine the right boundaries. Was it right to like Jo's Facebook photos when I was afraid for her? Was it appropriate to let people into my life because they let me into theirs? I bought one prison wife in Colorado groceries because she had nothing to feed her kids. I put money into Sherry and Damon's commissary account over the holidays so they could eat something special. Experts in journalistic ethics might look askance at these decisions, but I believe there are higher laws governing these transactions. When people are struggling, it's unethical not to give a little. Yet I often questioned the right balance of neutrality and care.

If I had known at the outset how difficult all of this would be, I likely would not have done it. I'm grateful I didn't know. Being a straight, white, middle-class, educated woman, I embarked on this project (and indeed my life) with a great deal of privilege. I have friends who have been or are incarcerated, but no close family members, nor a romantic partner. While I was aware of my social capital in the obvious ways, what I did not realize was just how privileged I am in subtler instances. My challenges are nothing compared with the burdens of the people I spoke with, and the millions of people out there going through something similar. My privilege allowed me to go into these places, and the same privilege allowed me to leave. I took for granted the ability to love someone, to hang out with them, even to be annoyed by them, up close. And I will never look at the simple pleasures of loving someone the same way.

I often thought back to what Regina observed at Pappasito's in Dallas. She noticed a couple at dinner, each on their phones, each in their own worlds, and expressed frustration at how easy it is to take your partner for granted when you have access to them all the time. It is no small thing to be able to share time and space with the person you love. That daily togetherness is not guaranteed. Shutting my laptop and stashing my phone in the other room when I hang out with my husband at the end of the day has become a sacrament. The simple act of just being together feels nothing short of radical.

The couples I met showed me what love can look like. But mostly it was the wives, the ones who sacrificed, strategized, and improvised, who revealed what you're capable of if you press against the confines of preconceived notions about love. Choosing an unconventional relationship can be a gateway for women to make more choices that previously felt out of reach. Jo completed her B.A. at age forty-six. Crystal left her sheltered world as a young woman to strike out in New York. Jacques used his marriage as a test for his morals, to improve one person's life, even if it didn't last forever.

And when prison wives find each other, the way I saw in Dallas and the way they do in digital and real communities every day, they make profound connections. What was once lonely and shameful, they rinse in the light of friendship. Yes, the men and prison were instrumental to their becoming. Yes, the wives love their husbands. But in many cases, they got something more than they bargained for, too. They got themselves.

As ever, Jo put it best. "I had a new girl cry to me the other day, 'My sister said my relationship isn't real!'" she told me. "I said, 'Oh, honey. You are going to hear that again and again. You are going to hear that so many times. But it doesn't matter. And you'll come to learn it doesn't matter. I'm seven years into this now, so I can say that,'" she laughed. Then she got serious. "What matters is your relationship, your sanity, your relationship with yourself," she said. "What matters is you."

THREE YEARS LATER

'VE WALKED DOWN to the Brooklyn waterfront with Jo on the phone more times than I can count. I've made this walk in every weather, in every season—the bite of February, the humidity of August. When I started taking these long walks to hear about her life, her marriage, her friendships, her struggles, I was living in a roach-infested apartment with a roommate. Now I have two kids, a house, a husband. The dog who used to pull the leash the whole way down to the pier is too old to hobble more than a few blocks. Then, Jo's twins were in first grade. In a few months they'll be starting high school. Today, it's early March. The wind blows an edge of winter, but the sun is warm. We've lived through a pandemic. We've all come to the other side of . . . a lot.

"Deciding to end the marriage was the hardest thing I've ever done in my adult life," she tells me. For a long time, she was consumed by grief, anger, and shame. "I asked God to let me die," she says, through tears. "I'm glad he didn't listen, because I'm better now."

BACK IN THE summer of 2020, we were all reeling at the height of the pandemic. On top of that, Benny and Jo were adjusting to his release and figuring out how to be married, while living in different states. I was fact-checking my manuscript, circling back with each couple for updates. Benny had done a long stretch in the hole so we hadn't talked much during the last part of his sentence. When I spoke with him a few weeks after he got out, on the cell phone Jo helped him arrange, it was the first time we were able to catch up unmediated by prison. I asked him to walk me through the last months of his time inside. He mentioned the dating site he posted on when he was in prison and that he and Jo weren't speaking. She'd learned about it when she read the galley of this book. It was the first she'd heard of it. I felt guilty, having brought this fact to light.

But the dominos continued to tip. Jo had already walked back one ultimatum she'd given Benny: Use drugs again and I'm gone. He did, in his final months in prison before release, and she stayed with him. When he got out of prison, he sent her home with a bag of his possessions. She found letters and pictures from other women. He hadn't even attempted to hide them, she said. By the fall he was dating someone else and posting about it on Facebook. She stopped communicating with him.

And then, on December 26, 2020, he was charged with burglary, criminal mischief, and theft. On December 29, 2020, he was charged with criminal driving with a suspended license, unlawful possession of methamphetamine, and attempting to elude a police officer. Jo served him divorce papers by proxy when he was in county jail. He was released pending trial, but—as of this writing—he has missed court dates, and there is currently a bench warrant out for his arrest. Because Benny is wanted by the state, I did not attempt to reach out to him after the book was published. And it's Jo's story more than his that lingers with me all these years later.

When her marriage fell apart, even Jo's closest friends didn't know how to support her. She was marooned in her grief. "I felt very isolated because no one understood. There were two camps," she explains. "The first was, *You married a guy in prison, so you can't be too surprised it didn't work.* And then the camp of: *He's an asshole, you're better off, let's pretend it never happened.*" Neither side offered much comfort. Only a few friends knew how to hold space for her—the friends she'd made in Strong Prison Wives & Families.

I ask her what she says to the I-told-you-sos, the people who say, "A marriage with a person you met when he was in prison didn't work out? Shocking."

Jo, passionate as ever, tells me, "First of all, not every prison marriage ends like that. Ro and Adam, they got their happy ending." The couple married on Valentine's Day 2022 with CJ, their one-year-old boy, snuggled between them. (They were supposed to marry on February 13—2/13, to commemorate Adam's 213-year sentence—but Ro had a bad case of food poisoning and had to postpone.) Indeed, Sheila and Joe are still married, as are Crystal and Fernando. Ivié is single and still working toward her appeal, which was featured in the *New York Times Magazine*. Sherry and Damon got to spend some time together on the outside, going out to eat, taking walks, taking pictures, before circumstances separated them to different parts of the state. "Take prison out of the equation," Jo says. "If Benny had stayed well, I think we would've been one of those happy couples. But when you have a spouse who is in active addiction, they choose their addiction over their blessings."

When she went public with the divorce to her friends, family, and prison wife community, she felt ashamed. "I had thought of us as this power couple," she says. "We had written books, we had been in documentaries, we were working together on all these projects. It was really embarrassing to have been the voice of a movement and then to have it work out this way. I'd been telling women how to do this for years and now my marriage is ending."

At this point, I have to interject: "From my point of view," I say, "after seeing how you've counseled women, what you've been telling them is to choose themselves. To choose what makes them happy, to choose a relationship that is worthy of them. And that's exactly what you did!" Most in SPWF agreed. She broke the news in a candid post on the group's Facebook page. She asked the members to allow her to stay on and help out when and where she can. Immediately, the response was, "Girl, you aren't going anywhere. Because you have taught us how to be strong," Jo reports. "They said, *You're doing what you've always told us to do*. I was so blessed by that response."

That's not to say navigating her new Benny-free identity has been easy. The past six years were built around supporting Benny, thinking about Benny, waiting for Benny's calls, waiting for Benny's release, helping Benny reintegrate into society. The past six years were about being the model prison wife. That organizing principle has come undone. So who is Jo now? She began a new job recently, as an administrative assistant at Augusta University Health. For the first time in a long time she walked into a room of new people where she wasn't Jo the Prison Wife. "But again, take prison out of the equation," she tells me. "Who are we when we have done the best we can and it fails?"

Today, her identity is one of autonomy: She is working full-time outside of the house for the first time since her twins were born. She is able to because Kyle, her ex who she still lives and co-parents with, has retired from the military and works from home. Her kids are older and her fibromyalgia is under control—she hasn't had a flare-up in a long time. She is a homeowner and a landlord—she bought a house she rents out to tenants. She is back in school full-time and has shifted her major from psychology to communications. She is on track to graduate in August 2023. She is single.

"I don't currently have anyone where being with that person is a part of my existence," she says. "I think that's probably the biggest thing to come out of the past couple of years." The trauma of her marriage ending shook loose some long-buried pain. "The divorce ripped me open," she says. "I had to really examine a lot of my abandonment issues, a lot of deep, deep wounds. The blessing that came out of it is I have been very intentional about doing deep personal work. I'm a much stronger and more centered person." That work has resulted in a sense of contentment: "I'm really good with where I am," she tells me. "But more importantly, I'm really good with *who* I am."

She has been through so much: judgment, sacrifice, pain. And also passion, elation. Love. It sounds like a great deal of healing has come out of it, after her shame and hurt abated. I think about the tattoo across her shoulders, the one we discussed on the eve of her wedding, in a motel room in Oregon, nearly seven years ago: *For the sake of love alone would I walk through fire again.* So. Would she?

"Girl, don't do it!" She laughs. "I don't regret it," she says. "There is nothing I would change about my decision to believe in him and marry him because of who he was at that point in his life," she continues with a sigh. "I did come out of the fire refined, but it was so incredibly painful. I don't know if I would have been brave enough to invite the suffering. The marriage didn't work out, but the future is fine."

I've reached the waterfront by now. She has to let me go. She has things to do to get ready for work, for school, for her boys. She says one last thing before getting off the phone, and it's in response to no particular question I asked her. It's her own lesson, distilled. "I now know there's a difference between an ultimatum and a boundary," she says. "An ultimatum is *if you do this, then I will do this.*" I think back to the ultimatum she gave Benny about using drugs, that she would break up with him. How he did, and he went to the hole, and she gave him another ultimatum around his sobriety, working a program, having a sponsor. He did, until he didn't.

"But a boundary," she continues, "is *this is what my life is. This is what I choose to allow for myself. I am in charge of me, my actions, and my decisions.* I'm responsible for my choices. I'm in charge of determining what is good for me. And if you fit into that, then great. And if not, I'll be over here, living my life in honesty and truth, in peace and power." I know this is not the love story Jo imagined on her wedding day. But right now, the present, with its beautiful boundaries, makes a lot of sense. Relationships end. Love evolves. Her story is still a love story.

ACKNOWLEDGMENTS

F ROM THE BOTTOM of my heart, I would like to thank:

The people who shared their stories with me, including the many that did not make it into these pages.

Jonathan Karp, Karyn Marcus, Jennifer Bergstrom, Aimee Bell, Megan Hogan, and Rebecca Strobel at Simon & Schuster, and Dan Kirschen, Andrianna Yeatts, and Estie Berkowitz at ICM, for making this book possible.

Will Palmer, copy editor extraordinaire.

The Virginia Center for Creative Arts, Hedgebrook, the Constance Saltonstall Foundation for the Arts, the Brooklyn Writers Space, and the Center for Fiction, where I wrote.

Heather and James, Helen Credle and Tony Irving, Regina and Manuel Sisneros, Marta Oller and Robert Rosso, whose thoughts and insights were invaluable in shaping the way I think about prison relationships.

Brooke Dawson, for occasional legal consulting and a friendship supreme.

Jean Murley, for introducing me to Crystal and Fernando, and for conversations that pushed me further.

Toni Armstrong, Tara Kun, Katherine Neville, Katie Walsh, and Mitchell Zhang, for research and transcription assistance.

Ruth Curry, Frances Dodds, and Jean Hannah Edelstein, my stalwart writing group, who saw these pages from beginning to end.

Elizabeth Blickle, Phil Eil, Janette Greenwood, Sarah Lageson, Benjamin Lorr, Sarah Perry, and Namwali Serpell for reading early drafts.

Dr. Abigail Merin, for blowing my mind forty-five minutes at a time.

Sindy Grappy, for taking such good care of my son while I worked.

Janette Greenwood (Gramono) and Jan Thomas (Grandma), who often stepped in to help so I could go on reporting trips.

Susannah Greenwood, my best little sister.

My family and friends.

Scott, Theo, and Baby TK, the loves of my life.

RESOURCES

Black & Pink
https://www.blackandpink.org/

Ella Baker Center for Human Rights
https://www.ellabakercenter.org/

The Innocence Project
https://www.innocenceproject.org/

The InterNational Prisoners Family Conference
https://prisonersfamilyconference.org/

The Justice Project, Ackerman Institute for the Family
https://www.ackerman.org/research/the-justice-project/

The Marshall Project
https://www.themarshallproject.org/

Represent Justice
https://www.representjustice.org/

Strong Prison Wives & Families
https://www.strongprisonwivesandfamilies.com/

Sylvia Rivera Law Project
https://www.srlp.org/

Women's Prison Association
http://www.wpaonline.org/

RECOMMENDED READING AND VIEWING

Alexander, Michelle. *The New Jim Crow: Mass Incarceration in the Age of Color Blindness*. New York: The New Press, 2012.

Bandele, Asha. *The Prisoner's Wife: A Memoir*. New York: Scribner, 1999.

Betts, Reginald Dwayne. *Felon: Poems*. New York: W. W. Norton, 2019.

Burton, Susan and Cari Lynn. *Becoming Ms. Burton: From Prison to Recovery to Leading the Fight for Incarcerated Women*. New York: The New Press, 2019.

Comfort, Megan. *Doing Time Together: Love and Family in the Shadow of the Prison*. Chicago: University of Chicago Press, 2008.

DuVernay, Ava, dir. *13th*. Sherman Oaks, CA: Kandoo Films, 2016.

Hart-Johnson, Avon. *The Symbolic Imprisonment of African American Women: A Legacy of Mass Incarceration*. Lanham, MD: DC Project Connect with Extant-One, 2015.

Jones, Tayari. *An American Marriage*. Chapel Hill, NC: Algonquin, 2018.

Legge, Catherine, dir. *Met While Incarcerated*. Toronto: Play Nice Productions, 2019.

Monroe, Rachel. *Savage Appetites: Four True Stories of Women, Crime, and Obsession*. New York: Scribner, 2019.

Peterson, Liza Jessie. *The Peculiar Patriot* (stage play). Premiered at the National Black Theater, Harlem, 2017.

Reed, Benjamin, VI, and Journey Reed. *Strength from Struggle, Volume One: A Relationship Guide for Couples Dealing with Incarceration.* Independently published, 2017.

Rule, Sheila R. *Love Lives Here, Too: Real-Life Stories About Prison Marriages and Relationships.* New York: Resilience Multimedia, 2011.

Senghor, Shaka. *Writing My Wrongs: Life, Death, and Redemption in an American Prison.* New York: Convergent Books, 2016.

Wilson, Ruth Gilmore. *Golden Gulag: Prisons, Surplus, Crisis, and Opposition in Globalizing California.* Berkeley and Los Angeles: University of California Press, 2007.

NOTES

AUTHOR'S NOTE

xvii **The words we use:** Two great articles and surveys from the Marshall Project capture the variety and ethos behind the descriptors people elect to use: Bill Keller, "Inmate. Parolee. Felon. Discuss," Marshall Project, April 1, 2015, and the response, Blair Hickman, "Inmate. Prisoner. Other. Discussed," Marshall Project, April 3, 2015.

INTRODUCTION

5 **2.3 million people:** The United States has the world's largest prison population despite not having the biggest population.

5 **African-American and Latinx people:** "Criminal Justice Fact Sheet," NAACP, https://www.naacp.org/criminal-justice-fact-sheet/.

CHAPTER ONE

15 **highest-paying job:** According to the Prison Policy Initiative, the average hourly wage for people in state prisons ranges from $0.14 to $1.41 per hour. These wages do not include deductions for restitution, child support, court costs, and other mandated fines. Curiously, prisons are paying less per hour today than they

were in 2001. As PPI reported, "The average of the minimum daily wages paid to incarcerated workers for non-industry prison jobs is now 86 cents, down from 93 cents reported in 2001."

CHAPTER TWO

42 ***Atlanta Constitution:*** "Found Guilty: Ladies in the Courtroom Wept When the Verdict Was Read," *Atlanta Constitution*, November 17, 1894, 5.

42 **She demonstrated so much emotion:** Katie Dowd, "The Tale of the 'Demon of the Belfry,' San Francisco's Forgotten Jack the Ripper," SFGate.com, October 31, 2016.

42 **"books, flowers and sweetmeats":** "The Sweet-Pea Girl: Durrant's Female Admirer Is Identified," *Los Angeles Times*, September 15, 1895.

51 **stigma of the sex offender registry:** Problems with the sex offender registry have been widely documented. According to Dara Lind, "the registry was designed for 'sexual predators' who repeatedly preyed on children . . . [but] it hasn't worked as a preventative tool. Instead, it's caught up thousands of people in a tightly woven net of legal sanctions and social stigma." Dara Lind, "Why the Sex Offender Registry Isn't the Right Way to Punish Rapists," *Vox*, July 5, 2016.

CHAPTER THREE

63 **"offender-on-offender":** *AHCC EBC Offender Orientation Workbook,* August 28, 2013, accessed via the University of Michigan Law School Policy Clearinghouse.

64 **cruel and unusual punishment:** According to the bioethics newsletter *BioEdge*, there are approximately 80,000 Americans held in isolation on any given day. Michael Cook, "Is Solitary Confinement 'Cruel and Unusual?,'" *BioEdge*, November 17, 2018. On October 18, 2011, UN Special Rapporteur Juan E.

Méndez told the General Assembly's Social, Humanitarian and Cultural Affairs Committee that "solitary confinement should be banned by States as a punishment or extortion technique." United Nations Human Rights Office of the High Commissioner, "UN Special Rapporteur on torture calls for the prohibition of solitary confinement," October 18, 2011, https://newsarchive.ohchr.org/EN/NewsEvents/Pages/DisplayNews.aspx?NewsID=11506&LangID=E.

64 **most vulnerable populations:** From the Prison Rape Elimination Act, 34 U.S.C. § 30301: "(3) Inmates with mental illness are at increased risk of sexual victimization . . . (4) Young first-time offenders are at increased risk of sexual victimization."

80 **the Justice Department issued its first set:** Alysia Santo, "Prison Rape Allegations Are on the Rise," Marshall Project, July 25, 2018.

81 **"Even if it truly is consensual":** I asked Dr. Mastrorilli about the unintended consequences of the LGBTQ+ prison population being unfairly punished. She introduced me to the concept of "street-level bureaucrats": "Policy makers put a policy in place like PREA. And that's a very progressive policy. But then you go to a state like Alabama, Arkansas, Mississippi, where the thinking around the incarceration of the individual is not progressive. So what a street-level bureaucrat will do is undermine the policy. They don't understand the policy, or gay or trans people, and they basically do their own thing."

82 **PREA sets up impossible paradoxes:** Though it is rare, prisoners can also marry one another. The 1987 Supreme Court decision *Turner v. Safley* upheld the right: "Although prison officials may regulate the time and circumstances under which a marriage takes place, and may require prior approval by the warden, the almost complete ban on marriages here is not, on the record, reasonably related to legitimate penological objectives." *Turner*

v. Safley, 482 U.S. 78 (1987). Yet this right has been challenged. Nebraska prisoners Paul Gillpatrick and Niccole Wetherell are being represented by the ACLU in order to wed. The couple met through a mutual friend before going to prison and have maintained their relationship through letters. Both have lengthy sentences for violent crimes. Prison officials refused their request, stating a provision denying prisoners transportation for weddings, then later denied them the opportunity to exchange vows over videoconference, saying a minister needed to be present. In 2014, then-Governor Dave Heineman declared spending taxpayer dollars to accommodate a prisoner wedding would be "an outrage." In 2019, they won their case before a federal judge, though the Nebraska Attorney General's Office is reviewing the decision.

83 **Studies back up this assertion:** Matthew Clark, "Contraband Smuggling a Problem at Prisons and Jails Nationwide," *Prison Legal News*, January 2013, 24; "Prison Corruption: The Problem and Some Potential Solutions," Center for the Advancement of Public Integrity, Columbia Law School, September 2016; Sandy Banks, "Allowing Phones in the Cells Might Be a Sound Call," *Los Angeles Times*, March 26, 2011.

CHAPTER FOUR

95 **The latest official figures:** Margaret E. Noonan, "Mortality in State Prisons, 2001–2014—Statistical Tables," Bureau of Justice Statistics, U.S. Department of Justice, December 2016.

105 **As she writes in her book:** Avon Hart-Johnson, *The Symbolic Imprisonment of African American Women: A Legacy of Mass Incarceration* (Lanham, MD: DC Project Connect with Extant-One, 2015), 20, 27. Dr. Hart-Johnson's book focuses on the specific plight of how the mass incarceration of Black men has impacted African-American communities and family structures, but many

prison wives I spoke with, from a variety of backgrounds, emphasized her work as a touchstone for them.

CHAPTER FIVE

107 **7 percent of the total U.S. prison population:** Jennifer Bronson
and E. Ann Carson, "Prisoners in 2017," Bureau of Justice Statistics, U.S. Department of Justice, April 2019.

116 **The challenges facing female prisoners are distinct:** Joseph
Shaprio, "In Iowa, a Commitment to Make Prison Work Bet-
ter for Women," *All Things Considered,* NPR, October 17, 2018;
Julie Moreau, "'Overwhelming' Number of Lesbians, Bisexual
Women Incarcerated," NBCNews.com, March 3, 2017; Aleks
Kajstura, "Women's Mass Incarceration: The Whole Pie 2019,"
Prison Policy Initiative, October 29, 2019; Melanie Deziel,
"Women Inmates: Why the Male Model Doesn't Work," *New
York Times,* https://www.nytimes.com/paidpost/netflix/women
-inmates-separate-but-not-equal.html; Keri Blakinger, "Can We
Build a Better Women's Prison?," *Washington Post Magazine,*
October 28, 2019.

123 **definitive history of Parchman:** Columbus B. Hopper, "The
Conjugal Visit at Mississippi State Penitentiary," *Journal of Criminal Law and Criminology* 53, no. 3 (September 1962).

124 ***Lyons v. Gilligan* decision:** *Lyons v. Gilligan,* 382 F. Supp. 198
(N.D. Ohio 1974).

125 **Conjugal visits today:** Dana Goldstein, "Conjugal Visits," Marshall Project, February 11, 2015.

125 **92,000 people locked up:** "New York Profile," Prison Policy Initiative, https://www.prisonpolicy.org.

125 **lowering sexual violence:** "Research Finds That Conjugal Visits
Correlate with Fewer Sexual Assaults," *Prison Legal News,* May
19, 2014.

125 **25 percent drop in technical violations:** Minnesota Depart-

ment of Corrections, *The Effects of Prison Visitation on Offender Recidivism* (St. Paul, MN: Minnesota Department of Corrections, November 2011), 27.

132 **The only exception:** "§ N.13 U.S. Citizens and Permanent Residents Cannot Petition for a Relative If Convicted of Certain Offenses Against Minors—The Adam Walsh Act," Immigrant Legal Resource Center, January 2013.

CHAPTER SEVEN

155 **selected Fernando's face:** Paul von Zielbauer, "Accusers Recant, but Hopes Still Fade in Sing Sing," *New York Times*, April 13, 2007.

156 **False identifications:** Sarah Lucy Cooper, ed., *Controversies in Innocence Cases in America* (New York: Routledge, 2014), 96. Researchers have found that not only is eyewitness error the leading contributor to wrongful convictions, present in more than three-quarters of the DNA exonerations, but also that the methods police use to collect identification evidence can and do contribute significantly to the rate of error.

156 **"just tell the truth":** Innocence Project Faces New York: Innocence Project, 2013, https://www.youtube.com/watch?v=ex9Z KCMYfKc.

162 **He taught English:** Julie Straus, "A Spirit of Thanksgiving Despite Wrongful Conviction and 18 Years in Jail," ABCNews.com, November 23, 2010.

164 **"I find no credible evidence":** John Eligon, "Man Jailed for '91 Murder Charge Is Cleared by Judge," *New York Times*, November 12, 2009.

164 **case history in New York:** John Eligon, "Hope for the Wrongfully Convicted," *New York Times*, November 22, 2009.

164 **The officer who questioned Fernando:** Benjamin Lester and Barry Paddock, " 'I'm the Bad Guy, Cause I'm a Cop,' Says NYPD Detective in DWI Crash," *New York Daily News*, March 7, 2010.

167 **an insidious beast:** Amaya Mandal, "What Is Post-Traumatic Stress Disorder (PTSD)?" *Medical Life Sciences News*, February 27, 2019.

167 **higher rate of PTSD:** Ashley Goff, Emmeline Rose, Suzanna Rose, and David Purves, "Does PTSD Occur in Sentenced Prison Populations? A Systematic Literature Review," *Criminal Behavior and Mental* Health 17, no. 3 (June 27, 2007).

167 **A 2013 study:** Marieke Liem and Maarten Kunst, "Is There a Recognizable Post-Incarceration Syndrome Among Released 'Lifers'?" *International Journal on Law and Psychiatry* 36, no. 3–4 (2013): 333–37.

170 **exonerations in the United States:** Emily Barone, "The Wrongly Convicted: Why More Falsely Accused People Are Being Exonerated Today Than Ever Before," *Time,* September 17, 2017.

170 **Not all exonerees:** "Compensating the Wrongfully Convicted," Innocence Project, https://www.innocenceproject.org/compensating -wrongly-convicted/.

170 **a paltry $5,000:** "Compensation for People Who Have Been Wrongfully Imprisoned," January 15, 2018, https://www.grgblaw .com/wisconsin-trial-lawyers/compensation-for-people-who -have-been-wrongfully-imprisoned. Wisconsin Innocence Project, University of Wisconsin Law School.

EPILOGUE

240 **report fewer sexual assaults:** "Research Finds That Conjugal Visits Correlate with Fewer Sexual Assaults," *Prison Legal News,* May 19, 2014.

240 **reduce rates of recidivism:** Alex Mierjeski, "Reasons Prisoners Should Be Having More Sex," Attn.com, September 22, 2015.

ABOUT THE AUTHOR

ELIZABETH GREENWOOD IS the author of *Playing Dead: A Journey Through the World of Death Fraud*. Her work has appeared in the *New York Times*; *Vice*; *O, the Oprah Magazine*; *Longreads*; *GQ*; and others. She lives in Brooklyn with her husband, son, and an elderly Jack Russell-chihuahua.